D1236668

HAITI

# ▣▣▣ HAITI

*Its Stagnant Society and*
*Shackled Economy*

*A Survey by*

## O. Ernest Moore

*An Exposition-University Book*
EXPOSITION PRESS    NEW YORK

EXPOSITION   PRESS   INC.

50 Jericho Turnpike                    Jericho, New York 11753

FIRST   EDITION

LIBRARY OF CONGRESS CATALOG CARD NUMBER: 78-187036

0-682-47425-8

In Memory Of

EMMANUEL GABRIEL JEAN-FRANÇOIS

and

MASSILLON COICOU

who fell by the wayside as they

worked for a better Haiti

# ◨◧◨ Contents

vii

# ⬚⬚⬚ Preface

Throughout its 167 years of existence as an independent republic, Haiti has persistently lagged behind most countries in its economic and social development. However, when the United Nations sent me to Haiti in April 1951 as monetary and fiscal adviser to the Haitian government, it seemed that at long last the country was ready to emerge from its long period of stagnation and to enter the modern world of progress. When I left Haiti in October 1956 for consultative work elsewhere, there was indeed clear evidence that the country had set foot on the road to economic and social development, in an atmosphere of political stability.

But in December 1956, with the fall of the Magloire government, there was a reversion to political chaos and economic stagnation, even retrogression. Up to the present time, despite some faint signs of improvement in the past couple of years, it is difficult to see how the rate of progress that was interrupted in 1956 can be regained. In two recent surveys of comparative economic-growth trends in underdeveloped countries, the Agency for International Development placed Haiti at the very bottom of the list of Latin American republics in practically every phase of economic growth. Haiti had by far the lowest GNP per capita ($65), the lowest life expectancy (45 years), the highest infant mortality (170 per 1,000 live births), the lowest ratio of hospital beds (70 per 100,000 population), the lowest ratio of medical doctors (1 per 14,000 inhabitants), the lowest per capita caloric intake (1,780 calories), the lowest ratio of students to the school-age population (24 per cent), the lowest literacy rate (11 per cent), the lowest index of agricultural productivity (73 per cent of the 1957-59 base period), and the smallest per capita output of electric power (16 kwh per annum).

The pages that follow are an attempt to get at the fundamental reasons for Haiti's development lag and to suggest possible remedies, based partly on my own observations and experiences during the Magloire era (1951-56), partly on impressions formed during several months' service as an economic adviser to the Duvalier government in 1958-59, and partly on analysis of the available data regarding political, economic, and social trends in Haiti since I left there in 1959.

My profound thanks go to a number of Haitian friends, now living in the United States, who took the trouble to review the manuscript, to correct certain errors of fact, and to suggest improvements. I am likewise greatly indebted to several American friends who have had long experience with Haiti's problems and who have made helpful suggestions. Both Haitian and American reviewers have preferred to remain anonymous. I alone am responsible for the conclusions reached and the recommendations made in the present work.

O. E. M.

# ◨◨◨ PART I
# Background

# Introduction

The diminutive Caribbean Republic of Haiti, with an area hardly larger than that of Vermont but with a population density more than nine times that of Vermont, ordinarily attracts little or no attention from the rest of the world. In modern times it has been exposed to the international limelight for only brief and infrequent intervals. One such interval was in 1915 when United States marines landed in Haiti to restore order following a rapid succession of sanguinary *coups d'état.* Another was in 1937 when thousands of Haitian peasants who had been peacefully working in the cane fields of the neighboring Dominican Republic were brutally slaughtered by natives of that republic, apparently at official Dominican instigation, or at least without official hindrance.

Since 1956, when a six-year period of Haitian political stability and incipient economic progress under President Paul E. Magloire ended, occasional news dispatches have given the outside world fleeting glimpses of the little country's ever-increasing economic and political difficulties, but there has been no serious discussion in the United States or elsewhere of the Haitian problem or of what, if anything, should be done about it.

The time has come to drag Haiti out of its obscurity and to ask whether it is not one of the key countries in the problem we face of helping to build a world that makes economic and political sense. Here is a nation which has been governing itself for 167 years but which remains one of the most poverty-stricken on the globe. Having won its freedom from France in 1804 by defeating the powerful army of picked troops sent by Napoleon, Haiti (until then known as the colony of Saint-Domingue) became the first Negro republic in the world. Now that so many new black republics have come into existence since World War II, we ought to take a good look at what happened to the first independent Negro country. It is all the more important to do so if one keeps in mind that Haiti's freedom was achieved by years of determined fighting, whereas the new Negro republics in Africa and the Caribbean went through no comparable birth trauma. If Haiti has failed to progress economically, it is not because its inhabitants were lacking in unity, enthusiasm, or will-power at the start of their national career. Unless the new Negro republics display an ever stronger morale and sense of cohesion, the question arises whether their chances of economic progress over the next few generations can be much better than Haiti's have been during the past 167 years. True, they have one great advantage that Haiti did not initially have: assistance from friendly foreign powers, from a United Nations, and from economic and financial institutions eager to help them. But from 1915 to 1934 Haiti did receive important United States assistance, and for the past 20 years or more substantial technical and financial aid has been given it by the United States and a variety of international organizations.

Haiti assumes special importance in the struggle of the democracies against the spread of communism because of its proximity to Cuba, its strategic location, and the fact that for much more than a generation it has been one of our most constant friends. The northern peninsula of Haiti reaches to within 50 miles of the Cuban shoreline, the two countries being separated by the Windward Passage, which is the channel for maritime traffic from the north and east to the Panama Canal and points beyond. Port-au-Prince, the Haitian capital, is little more than an hour from Florida by air. If this staunchest of friends of the United States should be won over to communism, hopes would be dimmed that the more distant (and in some instances less friendly) countries of the hemisphere would continue to side with the democracies.

Since 1957, when the dictatorial régime of President François Duvalier came into power, the United States and other democracies have been repelled by the many reports of that régime's brutality and corruption. As a result the United States in August 1962 terminated its technical-assistance program in Haiti, except for a malaria-eradication project under the Pan American Health Organization and a program of food distribution through private charity agencies. Diplomatic recognition, however, has not been withdrawn by the United States or any of the Latin American republics. Apparently it has been their hope that the régime of François Duvalier—who for years was reported in bad health and who died in April 1971—would be followed by one more deserving of aid. Now that the dictator's 19-year-old son has taken over the title of "President-for-Life," the situation remains unclear, but perhaps this is the time to think the Haitian problem through, to decide upon the scope and general lines of the assistance we must give when the proper moment arrives. For one thing is certain: we would be foolish to leave next-door Haiti to wallow indefinitely in extreme poverty and misery and thus constitute a standing invitation to communist infiltration and control. But if effective assistance is to be given to Haiti, we must first have a clear understanding of the country's unique history, and of its human and natural resources. One of the aims of this volume is to supply a basis for such an understanding. Apart from that, however, the story of Haiti is so fascinating that it can hardly fail to interest the intelligent American layman.

# ▣▣▣ 2
# The Republic of Haiti

Haiti occupies the western third of the island of Hispaniola, which is also known as Santo Domingo. Hispaniola lies immediately to the east of Cuba and is the second largest island in the Caribbean Sea. The eastern section of the island is occupied by the Dominican Republic. Haiti's area of 10,700 square miles slightly exceeds that of Vermont. Mountains ranging in height up to 8,800 feet occupy two-thirds or more of the area. The population density is the third highest among the self-governing countries of the Western Hemisphere, being exceeded only in the less mountainous countries of Trinidad-Tobago and Jamaica. A 1950 census—none has been taken since—showed 3,100,000 inhabitants, but taking account of errors and omissions, the actual number was probably somewhat higher. Today's population is estimated to be in the neighborhood of 4,850,000. The climate is tropical on the coast and in the valleys, but moderate, or even cool, in the upper altitudes. In the lower regions the heat and humidity are usually tempered by a gentle breeze.

The only large city is Port-au-Prince, the capital and principal port, which with its suburbs has a population probably in excess of 250,000. It is located on the west coast, in the hollow of the marvelously picturesque Gulf of Gonave. The second largest city is Cap-Haitien, which has a population of something over 30,000 and is the principal seaport on the north coast. Under its former name of Cap Français, it was the capital of the French colony of Saint-Domingue until 1749, when Port-au-Prince was founded.

During the eighteenth century Saint-Domingue was the richest of France's colonies and the source of a third or more of the mother country's trade. Haiti was the first country in Latin America (and the second in the Western Hemisphere) to win its independence.

The long years of fighting which preceded independence and the final ejection of the French left a completely illiterate population in possession of a country in ruins, more or less isolated from a hostile outside world, and deprived of the technical assistance which the former French inhabitants (had they remained) could have given. From 1806 to 1820 the country was divided between two régimes, one in the north and the other in the south. From 1823 to 1844 the reunited government ruled also over the Dominican part of the island. In 1915, following several years of political confusion, Haiti was occupied by American marines. The American occupation lasted until 1934. Thereafter political conditions were generally peaceful, and financial and economic conditions stable or gradually improving, until December 1956.

During the six years 1951-56, Haiti was governed democratically under the Constitution of 1950. The executive power was exercised by the President of the Republic, elected for a six-year period by popular vote. On December 6, 1950, Colonel (later General) Paul E. Magloire took office as President, having been elected by an overwhelming popular vote. He was assisted by a cabinet (the Council of Secretaries of State) of his own choice. The legislative power was vested in a Senate and a Chamber of Deputies, both elected by the people. The judicial power consisted of various courts whose judges were appointed by the President. The 1950 Constitution guaranteed basic human rights, including property rights and freedom of assembly, of expression, and of religion. The right of foreigners to own property was restricted to residential properties occupied by themselves.

Nominally, nearly all Haitians are Catholics, but in practice the vodou religion is widespread, particularly in the rural areas. The Catholic influence is pronounced in education, in the form of Church-administered schools. In recent years, however, various Protestant sects have been gaining ground; members of such sects now may number as high as one-tenth of the population.

In December 1956, as new presidential elections were about to take place, President Magloire was forced into exile when the army failed to support him against charges of corruption and plotting to remain in office. The government was at first taken over by the president of the Supreme Court, Joseph Pierre-Louis, as provided by the Constitution. Pierre-Louis, however, was ousted before elections could be held. Political and economic chaos prevailed for the next eight or nine months, during which two provisional Presidents, an Executive Council, and a military government held power for brief intervals. Finally, by popular vote, Dr. François Duvalier was elected President for a six-year term.

Although elected under a democratic Constitution, Duvalier gradually took over all power: first, by organizing and arming squads of roughnecks—known as Tontons Macoutes (bogeymen) —who busied themselves with the jailing, torturing, or killing of anti-Duvalier citizens; and second, by continuous dismissals of army officers found or thought to be hostile to him. A more detailed account of political developments since 1956 is given in Chapter 8.

Haiti has a unitary form of government, the whole country being ruled from Port-au-Prince. There are, however, five *départements* (provinces), subdivided into *arrondissements* (districts), municipalities, and "rural sections."[1] These political divisions are empowered to decide only minor administrative matters. The *arrondissements* are headed by prefects appointed by the President of the Rebublic; the municipalities are headed by locally elected councils, and each rural section by a *Chef de Section*. Unfortunately, these section chiefs have in the past often been despotic and corrupt, in the absence of effective checks on their power. Local taxes, formerly collected by the municipalities, are now collected by the central government but are in large part redistributed among the municipalities.

While some nine-tenths (mostly peasants) of the population are still illiterate, many of the remaining inhabitants are highly cultured and well traveled. This element of the population, often referred to as the "élite," speaks flawless French. The illiterate classes speak Creole, the vocabulary of which is derived almost entirely from French and the grammar in large part from African tongues.

Haiti has always been an agricultural country. In colonial times its prosperity was founded on the exportation of sugar, coffee, cotton, indigo, and dyewoods. Since independence, coffee has been the leading export. Other important exports in recent years have included sugar, sisal, bauxite, bananas, cacao, copper, essential oils, and handicraft articles, with year-to-year changes in their relative order.

For domestic consumption, Haiti produces substantial quantities of grain (corn, millet, and rice), beans, manioc, plantains, yams, fruits, etc. Animals raised domestically for food consist mainly of cows, goats, pigs, and fowl.

Agricultural holdings are extremely small, averaging only about six acres; the great majority of peasant plots are even smaller.

Most of the peasants own their own land, but many are squatters on government land. There are only a few plantations, the largest of which is an American-leased sisal plantation. Subsistence farming, carried on with primitive tools (machete, hoe, and dibble), is the rule, supplemented usually by the cultivation of minute quantities of commercial crops.

The principal highways are those which connect Port-au-Prince with the seaports of Cap-Haitien in the north and Cayes in the extreme southwest. Only the first of these two roads has ever been paved, and its maintenance has been entirely inadequate. Secondary roads are for the most part usable only during the dry season.

Mineral resources are few; bauxite, lignite, and copper are the principal ones. Apart from one small plant, there is at present no hydroelectric energy. During the Magloire administration Haiti's principal river, the Artibonite, was dammed for purposes of irrigation and flood control, and plans were drawn for developing electric power at the new dam. However, it was not until 1969 that the construction of power facilities at the Artibonite dam was begun; these facilities are approaching completion.

During the Magloire years intensive efforts were made to improve the quality and variety of crops, to induce a modicum of industrialization, and to stimulate tourism. By 1956 these efforts had begun to show concrete results. At the end of World War II the only important industries in Haiti had been a sugar refinery and a sisal-processing plant, both American-owned. Thereafter a number of new industries got under way, including two new sugar refineries, two textile mills, a cement plant, and a number of miscellaneous small undertakings for the processing of domestic produce. The greatest progress took place in tourism. The number of foreign tourists visiting Haiti increased sixfold between 1949 and 1960. In addition, many thousands of American sailors visited Haiti every year during the calls made at Haitian ports by United States Navy vessels. Most of the better-class hotels were enlarged to take care of the increased tourist traffic, and many new hotels were built. After 1960, Haiti's tourist traffic sharply declined.

Before and after World War I, Haiti's principal trade partner was France. From 1918 to 1936, France customarily took from one-half to two-thirds of Haiti's total exports, although supplying less than 10 per cent of total imports. Following a disagreement between the two countries regarding the terms of repayment of a 1910 loan, Franco-Haitian trade dwindled to insignificant proportions and Haiti was obliged to seek new markets, particularly for coffee. In this it was eminently successful; in the decade ending with the fiscal year 1945-46, 61 per cent of Haiti's total exports went to the United States. By fiscal 1965-66, however, exports taken by the United States had dropped back to 39 per cent. In the same year 49 per cent of total imports came from the United States.

The monetary unit of Haiti is the gourde, but U.S. dollar currency is also legal tender and circulates freely. Since 1919 the ratio between the two currencies has remained fixed at precisely five gourdes to one dollar. Haiti is one of the few countries which have not practiced currency devaluation or exchange control. Capital movements into and out of Haiti are entirely free.

# ▣▣▣ 3
# The Colony of Saint- Domingue

Before the coming of the white man, Hispaniola was inhabited by the Arawak Indians, a much less warlike tribe than the Caribs who dominated other parts of the Caribbean area. When Christopher Columbus anchored his ships in a bay of the northern peninsula on December 6, 1492, he met no resistance, perhaps because the natives thought he would help defend them against their Carib enemies. Columbus named the bay St. Nicholas, in honor of the saint whose day it was. The island, he called

Isla Española (Spanish Island), which has been anglicized into Hispaniola. The Arawak name was Quisqueya.

On Christmas Eve one of the ships, the *Santa María,* was wrecked on the northern coast of what is now Haiti. Its timbers were used for the construction of a fort, La Navidad (the term means "Christmas"), the first structure erected by Europeans in the Western Hemisphere. In it Columbus left 30 of his crew while he sailed back to Spain to report on his discoveries. Upon his return to Hispaniola in November 1493, Columbus could find no trace of the fort or of the men who had occupied it. He learned later that, disobeying his orders, the men had harassed and stolen from the Indians, who finally reacted by killing them off and burning the fort.

Proceeding further east, Columbus disembarked at a point on the north coast of what is now the Dominican Republic, where he founded the town of Isabela and, nearby, the fortress of St. Thomas. An attempt by some of the Indians to dislodge the Spaniards failed, and the offending chief, Caonabo, was shipped off to Spain (but lost his life in a shipwreck en route). Other Indian chiefs made a combined effort to oust the Spaniards, but they were overpowered by the latter's use of guns, horses, and hounds.

Columbus was now plagued by the grumbling of his followers, who had hoped to find plentiful gold on the island but so far had found only minute quantities. In an effort to appease his men, Columbus agreed to the unwise suggestion that the Indians be used as slaves, in both mining and plantation work. As complaints continued and inspectors from Spain made critical reports on his administration of the settlement, Columbus was finally returned to Spain in chains.[1] Those who succeeded him as leaders of the colony completed the task of conquering the island.[2] Unaccustomed to hard labor, the gentle Arawaks were quickly decimated by the harsh treatment to which they were subjected. An epidemic of smallpox was a contributing factor. According to one estimate (that of H. P. Davis in his book *Black Democracy: The Story of Haiti*), out of something like a million Arawaks who were living on the island in 1492, only a few hundred remained by the middle of the sixteenth century. According to another source, which seems more credible, there were about 300,000 Arawaks in 1492, and the number had been reduced to 60,000 in 1508 and less than 500 in 1548.[3]

Faced by a growing shortage of laborers, the Spaniards decided to bring Negro slaves into the island from Africa. The first Negro slaves arrived as early as 1503. They proved far more resistant to the hardships of mine and plantation labor than the Arawaks had. Thus the importation of Negro slaves became a steady and lucrative business.

Spanish settlements were confined to the eastern part of Hispaniola. The more mountainous western areas remained without white inhabitants throughout the sixteenth century. In 1625 a number of French and British adventurers established themselves on the tiny island of Tortuga (Turtle Island), just off the northern peninsula of what is now Haiti. Some of these were buccaneers, who built themselves rude huts and lived primarily as hunters of game and wild animals. The buccaneers gradually extended their activities, and finally their homes, into the empty western stretches of Hispaniola. Other adventurers who made Tortuga their headquarters were freebooters who preyed on Spanish and other passing vessels. In 1641 the French government sent a small expeditionary force to expel the British adventurers from Tortuga. Once this had been done, the chief of this expedition (Le Vasseur) engaged in more or less contant fighting with the Spanish settlers of Hispaniola. As a result the French obtained de facto control of Tortuga and parts of western Hispaniola, which were administered, beginning in 1664, by governors appointed by the Compagnie des Indes Occidentales (West Indian Company). Finally, in 1697, as part of the Treaty of Ryswick (which ended the war of the Augsburg League), Spain ceded to France the western third of Hispaniola. This became the French colony of Saint-Domingue.[4]

It was not long after western Hispaniola became a French colony that a rapid acceleration of progress and prosperity became evident. New immigrants in the 1720's established plantations for the cultivation of indigo, sugar, coffee, dyewoods, and cacao. They imported large numbers of African slaves and exported their produce on an extensive scale. Rum distilleries, lime kilns, tanneries, pottery works, and brick factories abounded. Good roads were built. The prosperity achieved by many settlers during the first half of the century was so great that the expression "wealthy as a Creole" became current.[5] The result was to attract more and more French immigrants, eager to make a fortune.

According to practically all accounts, there was a great deal of mistreatment of the slaves, who were subject to brutal punishment for the slightest infraction of rules or slackening of work. On the other hand, slaves were sometimes liberated, usually because they were concubines or the children of concubines. The widespread miscegenation between plantation owners and female slaves gave rise to a substantial and increasing number of so-called *gens de couleur*. Although the literal translation of this term is "colored people," the actual meaning is "mulattoes." Under the *Code Noir* (Black Code) which had been promulgated by King Louis XIV in 1685 for the regulation of slavery in all French colonies, an *affranchi* (freed slave) acquired all the rights of full French citizenship, including voting rights, choice of occupation, and the ownership of property and even of slaves. Thanks to this liberal attitude, the mulattoes of Saint-Domingue at first participated in the general prosperity, carried on various kinds of business, served in the colonial militia, acquired plantations, and bought slaves to do the menial work. As the number and wealth of the *affranchis* increased, however, the white Creoles—particularly the *petis blancs* (little white men), who did not own plantations—began to resent their success and finally tried to place restraints upon them.

The first legal discrimination against the mulattoes was enacted by the Saint-Domingue colonial council in 1758. It merely prohibited them from carrying swords or similar weapons, considered the marks of a gentleman. Four years after this opening wedge, the prohibition was extended to the bearing of firearms. In 1767 the council prohibited the sale of munitions to mulattoes except when ordered by a white officer. Although these measures evidently ran counter to the Black Code, Louis XV did nothing to invalidate them; indeed, he seemed to favor them. From then on, the road ran downhill for the *gens de couleur,* and they were successively prohibited from holding any responsible office in the courts or the militia, and from carrying on the occupation of goldsmith, medical doctor, apothecary, lawyer, or minister of religion. Mulatto women were forbidden to marry whites. Finally, in 1779, mulattoes were compelled to wear distinctive clothing, to retire by 9 P.M., and to sit in a separate section at church or theater.

How much longer the *gens de couleur* would have put up with such discrimination and humiliation in the absence of a French Revolution, it is of course impossible to say. By now they were two-thirds as numerous as the white population. According to the 1791 census, there were in Saint-Domingue some 500,000 black slaves, as against 40,000 whites and 28,000 mulattoes. At any rate, in 1789 the beginning of the French Revolution, with its emphasis on "Liberty, Equality, Fraternity," changed the whole aspect of the class struggle in Saint-Domingue. To make matters worse (for themselves), the whites of the colony, completely misreading the signs of the times, sent a delegation to Paris to ask that they be authorized to govern the colony without direction from France. Heretofore the colony had been governed by two officials appointed by the King and usually selected from the nobility. One of them was Governor, the other was called *Intendant* (a sort of administrative officer or comptroller).

The white planters' delegation in Paris found itself fighting a humanitarian group called the Amis des Noirs (Friends of the Blacks) which was seeking to achieve not only the abolition of slavery throughout the French Empire but even more urgently the restoration of the rights which had been lost by colonial *gens de couleur.* A resolution adopted by the French National Assembly ·called for the restoration of the mulattoes' lost rights, but the implementation of this measure was left to the colonial authorities. Later (in May 1791) the National Assembly decreed that colonial mulattoes must be allowed representation in the colonial assemblies. The pot was now boiling over in Saint-Domingue. The Governor-General suspended execution of the Paris decree, thus making it clear to the mulattoes that only by force could they regain their lost rights. Intermittent skirmishes between mulattoes and whites resulted in much bloodshed and cruelty. Then, suddenly, in August 1791 a violent change in the whole nature of the racial problem occurred: the slaves of Saint-Domingue revolted.

The revolt started in the north, where a few of the more cunning Negroes, in the course of a pretended vodou ceremony in the woods, made plans for a general uprising to take place on August 22 and communicated these plans by drum signals to the surrounding plantations. The uprising entailed the ghastly slaughter of whites—men, women, and children—wherever they could be reached, the burning of plantations, and various forms of torture. Whenever possible, whites who escaped death fled from the colony. It was the de facto end of French rule, although complete freedom for Saint-Domingue was not achieved until thirteen years later.

The *gens de couleur,* who were not molested by the rebellious blacks, tried unsuccessfully to turn events to their own advantage by becoming the rulers of Saint-Domingue. Commissioners sent by France for the purpose of restoring order also had no success. Meanwhile, two European enemies of the French Revolution— England and Spain—sent troops to Saint-Domingue, allegedly for the purpose of putting down the slave insurrection so that it would not spread to their own colonies. They were opposed by a French general, Laveaux, but his chances of defeating the invaders appeared at first slim. The British occupied Port-au-Prince and a number of other ports on the western and southern coasts, while Spanish troops seized control of extensive eastern and northern regions of Saint-Domingue. Fortunately, Laveaux received help from two powerful sources. One of these was General Rigaud, a cultured mulatto; the other was Toussaint L'Ouverture,[6] a full-blooded Negro of outstanding ability.

Rigaud was the idol of the south, where he had been born, and of the whole mulatto population. Toussaint had been a slave for 50 years, right up to the time of the rebellion, but he had played no active role in the uprising. He was devoted to his master, who appears to have been an extremely liberal-minded man; he had, for instance, allowed the slave Toussaint much leisure time for reading. Toussaint had taken full advantage of this opportunity to educate himself. He helped his master escape during the rebellion and is said even to have sent him money thereafter. While some students of Haitian history have felt that Toussaint was interested only in his own advancement, there is no doubt that he was a brilliant military and political strategist, a highly competent administrator, and the most remarkable man that Haiti has ever produced.

After the rebellion Toussaint went to the eastern part of the island, where he joined the Spanish army and quickly achieved a reputation for military ability. General Laveaux then offered him high rank in the French army if he would return to Saint-Domingue and help fight off the foreign invaders. Meanwhile the French Republic had proclaimed the end of slavery in the colonies, and Toussaint had become convinced that the British had no intention of abolishing slavery. He therefore accepted Laveaux's offer, bringing with him the black troops who had fought under his command in the Spanish cause. He now had little trouble in wresting from the Spaniards the territory they had (thanks to him) taken from Saint-Domingue. A surprising outcome of the Spanish defeat was that in the Treaty of Basle of July 24, 1795, Spain ceded to France the whole *eastern* part of Hispaniola.

After reorganizing and training his army, Toussaint turned to the British invaders and forced their withdrawal from Saint-Domingue. In the process he freed General Laveaux, whom the British had captured and imprisoned. Toussaint had become a national hero, except in the eyes of the *gens de couleur*, who still worshipped General Rigaud.

Appointed as a general and then as Lieutenant Governor, Toussaint now demonstrated great administrative ability, and calm was gradually restored throughout Saint-Domingue. As described by a Haitian historian,

> In whatever part of the countryside he appears, tranquillity returns as by magic; the settlers, reassured, return to their homes; the peasants, formerly slaves, work on the plantations. . . . Everywhere, blacks and whites sing the praises of the man who brought about the rebirth of prosperity, along with order.[7]

In one part of Saint-Domingue, however, conditions remained unsettled. In the southern peninsula General Rigaud was still supreme and was governing the area more or less independently of the rest of the colony. Persecution and oppression of the Negroes by the *gens de couleur* there continued in disregard of French law and the policies of Toussaint. In 1799 open warfare broke out between the forces commanded by Toussaint and those under Rigaud. A year later, after much bitter fighting, Toussaint occupied the whole southern peninsula. Rigaud and his principal aide, General Pétion, fled to France.

By this time, for one reason or another, Toussaint had caused the departure from Saint-Domingue of just about every man who could have disputed control of the island with him. General Laveaux and several others had been sent to France as deputies to the French Parliament. A prominent general—Hédouville— who had been dispatched to Saint-Domingue by the French government in 1798 to act as a check on the growing power of Toussaint seriously underestimated Toussaint, and after a number of *faux pas,* was shipped back to France within six months.

Early in 1801, Toussaint with a sizable army proceeded to occupy the eastern part of Hispaniola, which was still being ruled by Spanish officials despite its cession to France by the Treaty of Basle. His first act was to proclaim freedom for all inhabitants of the area. Next he reorganized the administrative system and gave the former slaves an option between military service and agriculture. Severe penalties were imposed for idleness and vagabondage.

Returning to Saint-Domingue, Toussaint decided that French laws were not adequate for the needs of the colony and he therefore held elections for a Constituent Assembly. Oddly, seven whites and three mulattoes, but no Negroes, were elected as deputies to the Assembly. Under the Constitution that was promulgated on July 8, 1801, Toussaint assumed the title and duties of Governor-General for Life, with the right to name his own successor. Many new laws were voted, and they are said to have been rigidly enforced through Toussaint's benign autocracy. If Toussaint asked much of his people, he asked even more of himself. He was an extremely hard worker, temperate in his habits, and forever on the move throughout the country, checking on the observance of the laws. As a self-educated man, he appreciated the need for a literate nation; he founded several schools and awarded scholarships to a number of young Negroes for study in France.

Naturally, the French government could not be expected to take a favorable view of Toussaint's self-propelled ascendency, especially after what had happened to General Hédouville. While Toussaint had been achieving his dominance in Saint-Domingue, another man—Napoleon—had risen to power in France, and this made it even less probable that France would accept the situation. A military genius like Napoleon, however, was unlikely to underrate the military capabilities of Toussaint. A powerful French fleet of no less than 86 warships was built. Manned by 22,000 soldiers, it proceeded to Saint-Domingue under the command of Napoleon's brother-in-law, General Leclerc. Leclerc was accompanied by a number of prominent Haitian mulatto exiles, including Generals Rigaud and Pétion. His secret instructions were to deport to France the principal native officers, to disband the native troops, to disarm the peasants and finally to re-establish slavery.

The French attacked at all the ports simultaneously. Following Toussaint's plan of defense, the native armies burned most of these ports, including Cap-Haitien, and withdrew into the interior. Ultimate and heroic resistance was offered at a fort in the valley of the Artibonite River, in central Saint-Domingue, but it was finally overcome. Some of Toussaint's generals surrendered to the French, and in the end Toussaint himself offered to negotiate. On May 6, 1802, he was received with honors at Cap-Haitien and agreed to an armistice under which he was allowed to retire to one of his plantations, while his principal generals were to cooperate with the French forces. The native army was not disbanded.

Shortly afterward two developments changed the whole trend of events. First, an epidemic of yellow fever began to decimate the ranks of the French armies. Second, armed bands of Negroes began to ravage the countryside, and the French suspected that

Toussaint was behind this activity. On the pretext of asking his advice, they summoned him to meet one of their generals at another plantation, where he was taken prisoner. He was then shipped off to France, with his family. After a winter in a cold, damp cell at a mountain fortress in eastern France, Toussaint died on April 7, 1803.

Following the capture of Toussaint, Leclerc ordered the disarming of the native population. This measure merely resulted in augmenting the number of insurgents in the countryside. When Leclerc resorted to terror tactics, the native generals who had been cooperating with the French decided that the time had come to defect. Thus the war was now resumed, under conditions less favorable to the French than during the first phase of their operations. Just at this point, Leclerc himself died of yellow fever. His successor, General Rochambeau, was a man of monstrous cruelty, a fact which prevented any weakening by the natives. General Dessalines, who had been Toussaint's right-hand assistant, was chosen as commander-in-chief of the native forces.

The French withdrew from the interior in order to concentrate their diminished strength in the port towns. One after another, these places were attacked by Dessalines's forces. The latter were helped by two circumstances: first, France had become engaged in a new war in Europe, and second, the British fleet had blockaded the ports of Saint-Domingue. By November 1803, Dessalines had cleared the French from all of the ports, and Rochambeau surrendered himself and his fleet to the British in nearby Jamaica.

On January 1, 1804, at the western port city of Gonaives, the assembled generals and officers of the army proclaimed Jean-Jacques Dessalines Governor-General for Life of Haiti. The name Haiti, meaning "mountainous land," was taken from the Arawak language.

The collapse of Napoleon's grandoise plan for the recapture of Saint-Domingue was a momentous event in world history. Napoleon's aims had gone far beyond Saint-Domingue. That colony was to be only a steppingstone to the exploitation of the vast Louisiana Territory, which France had recently reacquired from Spain. The failure of the Saint-Domingue expedition made it necessary to renounce the plan for exploiting the Louisiana Territory. Thus it was that the United States was able to buy for a mere $16 million the whole area from the Mississippi to the Rocky Mountains. By this purchase the United States was not only doubled in size but freed from the prospect of a powerful and possibly troublesome neighbor on the west.

# ▣▣▣ PART II
# Efforts at Economic And Social Development

◻️◻️◻️ **4**

# From Dessalines to
# Dartiguenave (1804-1915)

While the major effort to develop Haiti economically
and socially did not come until President Magloire took office in
December 1950, it is by no means true, as some have thought,
that nothing was done to develop the country during the first
century and a half of its existence. In the first few decades of
independence, however, development efforts were weakened, almost stifled, by the fear that the French would come back and by
the extreme precautions which the Haitians felt they must take
against such an eventuality. A large army was kept in being,
thus reducing the productive labor supply. Numerous strong for-
tresses, including the famous Citadelle near Cap-Haitien, were
built on mountaintops in order to ensure the islanders' ability to
resist indefinitely any new French attack. The vast numbers of
men used for these unproductive tasks were of course unavailable
for economic reconstruction and development.

Haiti had been left in ruins by the thirteen years of fighting
which culminated in independence. Plantations, irrigation systems,
sugar mills, all the capital assets of the country, had been
destroyed or badly damaged. Moreover, the ex-slaves had no
knowledge whatsoever of any economic system other than the
master-slave system of which they had been a part. The master
was he who never worked with his hands and who did as he
pleased, because he was a free man. Now that the slaves had
become free men, it was difficult for them to see why they still
had to do hard work or to obey orders from anyone else.

The ignorance and illiteracy of the former slaves were of

course almost total, and there were practically no schools in Haiti. The French colonials had either sent their children to France to be educated or brought private tutors from France.

The initial act of the first Haitian government was to order a vengeful slaughtering of most of the remaining French inhabitants—the only people who could have given the ex-slaves any technical assistance. So far as economic development is concerned, however, this factor should perhaps not be overrated, since it appears that most of the French citizens still in Haiti were not 'in a mood to offer advice or help of any kind but rather were trying to hold onto their properties and hoping for precisely what the Haitians feared—the arrival of a new French army. At any rate, priests, doctors, pharmacists, and artists were excepted from the massacre.

As though all this were not enough to prevent economic development, the first Constitution of independent Haiti (1805) proclaimed that no white man, of whatever nationality, could set foot on Haitian soil in the capacity of master or property owner or could even acquire property in Haiti.

Even after the first few decades of freedom, efforts at economic development were much less vigorous than they are today and were usually foredoomed to failure by an absence of scientific knowledge and skills, or by the difficulties of financing. Also, such efforts were mostly sporadic as a result of frequent political upsets, not to mention the numerous rebellions which not only hampered steady progress but even tended to undo whatever had been accomplished. Finally, considerable hostility existed abroad toward the struggling nation of ex-slaves which had destroyed so much of French colonial wealth and which stood as an obnoxious reminder to American and other slaveowners that slaves could become free men. It was more than 20 years after the surrender of Rochambeau before any foreign government recognized Haiti's independence. And it was not until the Civil War that our own government gave diplomatic recognition to Haiti. During the following half-century we extended no helping hand to Haiti and on more than one occasion we allowed the little republic to be insulted and penalized by European governments. Admittedly, the anti-white racialism of successive Haitian constitutions was hardly conducive to a sympathetic attitude in other governments.

Although a brilliant military strategist, Dessalines was anything but a political or administrative genius. Upon learning that Napoleon had been crowned as Emperor, Dessalines in September 1804 adopted the same title, but he refused to create a nobility, stating that he alone was noble in Haiti. "You are wrong," he replied to those who urged providing the people with moral and religious education so that they would not fall into evil ways. "The laborers can be controlled only by fear of punishment and even death; I shall lead them only by these means; my 'morale' shall be the bayonet."[1]

While some of Dessalines' acts must be recorded on the negative side of the economic balance sheet, others had constructive aspects. Thus he attempted to overcome the chaotic state of property titles resulting from French colonials' efforts to hold onto properties through simulated transfers, gifts, and leases; from inheritance claims by Haitian-born mulattoes; from squatters' claims; etc. A general verification of all titles was ordered, but its execution gave rise to considerable corruption.

The state took over all domains which had been actually French-owned at the time of liberation. Some of these estates were awarded to army officers. The rest were leased to the highest bidders. A "territorial tax" of one-fourth of all produce was payable to the state. A quarter each went to the owner, the manager or supervisor, and the laborers.

The 1805 Constitution required that every Haitian residing in a town know a trade. Those who were not in the army and who possessed no skill, if they were found in a town, were sent to a government plantation to do forced labor. Townspeople were prohibited from sheltering runaway peasant laborers. Every agricultural worker was thus bound to the land. Since artisans were few and far between, the overwhelming majority of the population was either in the army or on the land. Under this system of forced labor, agriculture again became productive, and the Artibonite Plain was soon covered with cotton fields, while many of the burned sugar mills were revived.

The Dessalinean Constitution provided that there should be six public schools in Haiti, one in each military district. A beginning was made in the field of foreign trade, but mainly for the purpose of ensuring a plentiful supply of arms and munitions against the feared return of the French.

Dessalines' harshness created great discontent and, before long, rebellion. He died in an ambush carried out by unknown assassins in 1806. His political accomplishments appear well summed up by Leyburn's statement that "Dessalines had restored order to his country and had founded a state. Both achievements rested upon a display of force which inspired cringing fear and denied normal human aspirations. His entire social and economic order was based upon the subservience of the many to the few."[2]

During the 13 years following the death of Dessalines, Haiti was split into a northern kingdom and a southern republic, ruled by two men of diametrically opposed types and temperaments. In the north Dessalines' mantle fell on another full-blooded Negro general, Henry Christophe, who refused the offer to rule Haiti as a President subject to severe constitutional curbs which were set up in order to prevent another Dessalinean dictatorship. Failing to impose his will on the south by military means, Christophe proclaimed himself king in the northern area. In the south Alexandre Pétion, a French-educated mulatto who was also a general, was then elected President under the Constitution which Christophe had rejected. Like Dessalines, Christophe believed in compulsion and enforced discipline, but he had what Dessalines lacked— administrative ability and a clear understanding of Haiti's needs. Pétion also understood the need for developing his people and his economy, but he used the totally different method of incentives, persuasion, patience, and tolerance. Historians are agreed that Christophe's method succeeded where Pétion's failed. But one ultimate consequence was that Christophe died a widely hated man while Pétion's passing was a matter of almost universal regret. Another and more important consequence was that at Christophe's death the people of the north were glad to come under the mild rule of Boyer, who two years earlier had peacefully succeded Pétion as President.

Christophe, who had been born a slave on the British island of Grenada, admired British discipline and organization and was undoubtedly influenced by British models in some of his attempts to raise his people to a higher level. He created a nobility and endowed it with land. He kept a very close watch on all administrative matters. Every morning he received reports on the condition of the Treasury, the customs, and the state warehouses. He founded a Royal Academy and tried to set up a school in each *arrondissement,* in addition to the central school which Dessalines had created in each military district. He brought to Haiti Anglican pastors to teach at these institutions and two American ladies to tutor his own daughters. However, only the children of aristocrats attended the schools, since other children were kept busy on the plantations. The social differences between classes thus increased. Christophe had a factory erected for the manufacture of cotton cloth and produced arms and munitions in his own foundry. He concerned himself with the construction and maintenance of roads. He built the Citadelle, an impressive mountaintop fortress which has been aptly described as the "eighth wonder of the world." In addition, he constructed a number of palaces, including the beautiful Sans Souci palace whose ruins amaze the modern tourist.

Christophe's agricultural policy was essentially the same as Dessalines's. Unskilled workers continued to be bound to the land and to work under compulsion in the production of money crops, such as sugar, coffee, and cotton. "It was clearly stipulated that if a worker shirked his job he was to be put in prison and made to do forced labor there. Laziness in the fields was to be punished by strokes from the overseer's liane . . . but only rarely was there complaint, as there had been constantly under Dessalines, of cruelty on the part of overseers."[3] As wages the workers received the proceeds of one-fourth of the output. They also had family plots for the cultivation of their own food crops. Christophe tried to introduce the plow in Haiti, where only the hoe had been known, but he had no success in this, evidently because the workers preferred to work in groups and because there was a shortage of horses and mules.

In 1812, Christophe promulgated a code of laws (the *Code*

*Henri*). It was in seven parts: civil, commercial, shipping and maritime, civil procedure, criminal and police procedure, military, and agricultural. All but the agricultural part followed French models. In the agricultural part Christophe regulated in detail the reciprocal duties of proprietors and cultivators, the policing of plantations, and the growing and processing of the major crops. The Code set forth industry as the parent of virtue, and idleness as the source of vice.[4] This section of the Code clearly revealed Christophe's interest in Haiti's primary source of income, as well as his "skill in devising an integrated functioning of a social order of nobility and serfs with a plantation economy based on money crops."[5]

Christophe's policies produced what for the times was a flourishing agricultural and commercial economy. The state's annual revenues of about $3.5 million were greater than they had been since 1791, and at Christophe's death several million dollars in the northern treasury could be taken over by the southern government. Christophe shot himself in 1820 when, having become a paralytic, he saw himself helpless in the face of a military revolt against his iron rule.

Meanwhile economic conditions in the easygoing southern republic had remained unsatisfactory, despite earnest efforts at improvement. President Pétion returned to mulatto aristocrats the lands of which they had been despoiled by Dessalines. He made no effort, however, to restore the plantation system. Indeed, he seemed to follow a policy of encouraging small-scale family farming. The one-quarter tax, which was less suited to small farms than to big plantations, was replaced by a tax on the exportation and domestic sale of coffee. This should have stimulated sugarcane growing, which thus was exempted from taxation, but in fact it was only a partial offset to the disadvantages of sugar cultivation under the prevailing conditions. Sugar cane required laborers, machinery, and careful attention, whereas coffee grew wild throughout Haiti at elevations up to 3,000 feet. Pétion believed that by permitting greater certainty as to the amount of annual taxes to be paid, the new fiscal system gave landlords an added inducement to increase their output.[6]

Next Pétion provided for subsidies to agriculture in years of low prices for coffee and sugar. In those years the government bought large quantities of coffee and sugar in order to raise the price of these commodities. The result, says Leyburn, was that the government debt was increased and people were made to feel that the state was responsible for individual economic success, rather than their own efforts.[7]

In 1807 an old law prohibiting the holding of plantations of less than 50 acres was amended so as to reduce the minimum holding to 30 acres. Two years later Pétion began the distribution of land in even smaller plots to the veterans of his army. Every soldier received 15 acres, while officers received more sizable tracts. This parceling out of the land continued for a decade. Moreover, much of the public domain was sold at such moderate prices that thousands of the humbler classes were able to become landholders. Other thousands became squatters on the public domain without being molested.

In Pétion's republic, corporal punishment was legally abolished and agricultural workers were guaranteed certain social security rights, such as medical care at the landowner's expense, generous time off for pregnant and nursing mothers, and the right of aged and infirm workers to keep their homes and garden plots on the employer's estate. District farm inspectors, who had held office under Toussaint and Dessalines and still functioned in Christophe's kingdom, were abolished, thus effecting a great economy for the state, but another immediate result was reduced crop yields.

The difficulties of managing large estates under the conditions which prevailed in the southern republic were such that few large planters could afford to operate. Many owners subdivided their land into plots which they leased to tenant farmers on a crop-sharing basis known as the *métayer* system. With the owner supplying the necessary capital and the tenant supplying the labor, each received one-half the eventual income. Such contracts were sanctified and regulated by law.

Pétion sought to stimulate the growth of foreign trade by loading "exposition ships" with Haitian agricultural products, manning them with Haitian crews, and sending them abroad to show what Haiti had to sell. These vessels were the subject of much favorable comment.

Education received special attention from Pétion, and in his Constitution he made public instruction gratuitous. He created a *lycée*, or secondary school (now named for him), at Port-au-Prince, as well as a girls' boarding school, with mixed staffs of Haitian and foreign teachers. From his personal finances he paid the rent for several private schools, bought classical books for distribution to army and government officials, and popularized a school reader. These efforts to improve and expand educational facilities were carried on in the face of opposition from some of the President's counselors.

Pétion's illness and death in 1818 brought grief to all Haitians, and it was said of him that he had never caused anyone to shed tears until he died.[8] But some historians have criticized him for consistently taking the easier course in an effort to please all elements of the population, and thus allowing the state to drift slowly downstream, instead of building a strong state through the enforcement of discipline.[9]

Jean Pierre Boyer, a mulatto who had been Pétion's private secretary and then chief of the presidential guard, succeeded Pétion as President and ruled over a reunited Haiti. Boyer's 25 years as President—the longest term in office of any Haitian chief executive—might have been the means of laying a permanent basis of strength for the Haitian economy had he not been headstrong and unwilling to listen to anyone else's advice. Thus he made several blunders which he could easily have avoided and which in the end led to his overthrow and set Haiti on the path of political chaos.

First, Boyer extended the southern republic's system of exaggerated *laissez faire* to the northern part of the country. Thus the habits of discipline and hard work which Christophe had inculcated in the north were soon lost. No attempt was made to achieve a compromise between northern discipline and southern laxness.

Second, against the advice of some of his best counselors,

Boyer decided on invasion and annexation of the eastern part of Hispaniola, which had just revolted from Spain. Owing to the differing racial, historical, and economic backgrounds of the eastern and western parts of the island, this action raised profound problems with which Boyer failed to cope successfully, with the result that later efforts to maintain the political union proved costly and undoubtedly accentuated Haiti's political and economic weakness. The union collapsed shortly after the end of Boyer's rule.

Third, long after the whole of Haiti had grown accustomed to the delights of individual freedom, Boyer suddenly revised his policy and attempted, through an ingenious new Rural Code resembling Christophe's, to regiment Haitian laborers. The attempt was an adject failure.

Fourth, in 1825 Boyer took it upon himself to pay an indemnity of 150 million francs to France in return for official French recognition of Haiti's independence. The indemnity was payable in five equal annual installments. In order to meet even the first installment of such a heavy debt, a loan had to be contracted in the Paris market; the remaining installments were defaulted. Boyer's rash action was criticized not so much on the ground that Haiti could not afford to make such payments—which it obviously could not—as because it involved the mistaken principle of paying for a sovereignty which in fact Haiti already had. Additional causes of criticism were the form which this transaction took, namely, an order-in-council of the King of France in lieu of a treaty, and the salary cuts and other economies which Boyer ordered in 1825 in an effort to raise funds for paying the indemnity.

Why did Boyer's Rural Code not work? First of all, too much time had elapsed since Haitians were subjected to such severe discipline; having tasted personal freedom, they had no intention of giving it up again. Second, the soldiers of the independence armies to whom land had been distributed were profoundly displeased with a measure which regulated in detail the exploitation of their holdings. In the third place, too much land had been given away and there were not enough large plantations left to make it feasible to apply the Code, the provisions of which were hardly applicable to small farms. The Code was not enforced as it was supposed to be by the soldiers assigned to individual plantations, nor by the local courts. It was, in fact, universally ignored. Since fear of a return of the French had been ended by the formal recognition of independence, there was a letdown in the morale of the army. Even if the military and the courts had cooperated to enforce the Code, they lacked the trained and literate officials for doing so.[10]

Boyer also introduced other new legal codes (civil, civil procedure, penal, criminal, commercial) which had a measure of success and which, with minor changes, remained in effect until modern times.

Although Boyer showed no interest in education, his administration saw the passage of the first law regulating the organization of public instruction and the creation of an "Academy of Haiti" offering courses in medicine, law, literature, astronomy, etc.[11]

Boyer's efforts failed to bring real prosperity to Haiti, and in the end he had to give way to the numerous enemies he had made through his autocratic methods. In 1843 he sailed away into exile; and thus began for Haiti a period of ephemeral regimes, with occasional interludes of dictatorship and serious statesmanship, which was not to end until 1915. During this long period, efforts at economic development were infrequent and often without practical result. Nevertheless there were some important achievements.

The Constitution written in 1843 after Boyer had gone into exile provided that a free public school should be maintained in each town, and a secondary school in each principal town, and that a new ministry should be put in charge of education, justice, and religious matters. Under President Guerrier (1844-45), who was the first Negro ruler since Christophe, secondary schools were established at Cap-Haitien and Cayes, the first public primary school for girls was organized, and encouragement was given to the 24 schools existing at Port-au-Prince.

Under President Geffrard (1859-67), who was more black than white, progressive reforms were undertaken in the fields of education, agriculture, trade and industry, and municipal improvement. As for education, Geffrard made attendance at primary schools compulsory (at least in theory), sent many young Haitians abroad to study at government expense, reorganized the School of Medicine, set up schools of law, music, and painting, founded secondary schools at Jacmel and Gonaives, reorganized both primary and secondary instruction to include the teaching of certain practical skills, and signed a concordat with the Holy See under which Catholic priests came to Haiti and organized schools which have endured until the present day and have left a deep imprint on Haiti's intellectual and economic life. By October 1861, Haiti had 242 public schools, including 8 secondary schools, 89 elementary schools for boys, 50 elementary schools for girls, 90 rural schools, 2 "state-subsidized girls' schools," and 3 "state-subsidized boys' schools."[12]

In the agricultural sector, Geffrard had irrigation facilities repaired, arranged for certain machines (gins?) to be made available to cotton planters, and in an effort to stimulate production, brought 2,000 immigrants from the southern part of the United States and settled them on the land.[13] An amendment to the existing Rural Code made landowners responsible for the upkeep of roads in their respective areas. Trade and industry were encouraged by the construction of new roads, the creation of a coastwise shipping service, and the setting up of a National Foundry which was to turn out mechanics and metalworkers. Municipal improvement under Geffrard took primarily the form of providing water supplies and gas lighting.

The administration of President Nissage Saget (1870-74), who was light of skin, was marked by a monetary reform, which withdrew from circulation the greatly depreciated state-issued notes and substituted silver coins equivalent in value to U.S. dollars (see pp. 229-30).

Michel Domingue, a Negro, who was President from 1874 to 1876, had ambitious development plans which included the building of railways from Port-au-Prince to St. Marc in the north and Miragoane in the south, of five metallic river bridges, of public markets in six towns, and of three lighthouses; the dredging of the harbors at Port-au-Prince and Cayes; and the creation of a national bank. These plans, however, could be realized only by further government borrowing, and the terms on which this borrowing was done, in Haiti and in France, were such that only a fraction of the needed cash was ever received, the rest remaining unsubscribed or being absorbed by commissions and by the redemption of old debts. The government then abandoned its public-work plans and concentrated on the one idea of setting up a national bank. But even this effort proved unsuccessful (see p. 230), and shortly afterward Domingue was swept out of power by a military revolution.

A state bank was finally established during the administration of President Salomon (1879-88), a Negro (see 230). Salomon also established many new rural schools, reorganized the National Law School, generously equipped the secondary schools, and arranged with the Alliance Française for two groups of visiting French professors, one for the Port-au-Prince *lycée* and another for the army. He sought increased agricultural production through a law of 1833 authorizing the free but conditional grant of 9 to 16 acres of land to anyone who would undertake to cultivate one or more money crops (coffee, sugar cane, cotton, cacao, tobacco). If three-fourths of the land was planted to these crops within a period ranging from two to five years, the grant became final. This measure aroused considerable enthusiasm, and many applications for grants were made. It proved abortive, however, because of inadequate supervision of the new landholders, the latter's lack of capital, and the absence of agricultural credit facilities.

Another Negro President, Hippolyte (1889-96), took active steps—indeed, in a pecuniary sense, they were too active—to develop the Haitian economy. "No government," says Dorsainvil, "has signed more contracts; information is available about more than 50, some of them relating to water supply, telegraph services, the telephone, the extension of a submarine cable along Haiti's coast; others relating to wharfs, slaughterhouses, public markets (Port-au-Prince, Cap Haitien), bridges (Momance River), etc." Some of these contracts were badly placed, either through errors of judgment or through collusion or friendship. In any event, the total expenditures involved were beyond the government's means. Issues of coin, government paper money, and loans only made matters worse.[14]

Further loans were issued by Hippolyte's black successor, Simon Sam (1896-1902), for various public projects, including work on the Cul-de-Sac railway and the initiation of reconstruction of the Lycée Pétion and of work on a railway from Cap-Haitien to Grande-Rivière-du-Nord.

President Nord-Alexis (1902-8), another black, completed the rebuilding of the Lycée Pétion, built the Port-au-Prince cathedral, created the Elie-Dubois professional school, and bestowed public-utility rights on the Free School of Applied Science, which was organized at that time as a private institution. To finance these and other projects he issued, not loans but large sums of paper money, which depreciated rapidly to as low as ten gourdes to the dollar, but the exchange rate was subject to wild gyrations. This was a serious handicap to trade, and the cost of living soared. The financial impasse led indirectly to rebellion.

The next President, Antoine Simon (1908-11), who was likewise a Negro, set up a new state bank, the Banque Nationale de la République d'Haiti (BNRH), to replace the Banque Nationale d'Haiti, whose concession was withdrawn as a result of various scandals (see pp. 230-31). The new bank was owned by a group of European and American banks. In connection with the concession granted to it, the Haitian government floated on the Paris market a 65-million-franc loan, part of the proceeds being earmarked for a monetary reform. The monetary reform, however, did not take place until 1919 (see pp. 56-57 and 232).

Under Antoine Simon, Port-au-Prince acquired a modern wharf, electric lights, and a number of paved streets, and the government signed contracts with American interests for the construction of a railway linking Port-au-Prince and Cap-Haitien and for the development of banana exports.[15]

President Leconte (1911-12), who was not a full-blooded Negro, revised the Rural Code, reorganized the Elie-Dubois professional school, and drew up plans for the creation of normal schools, for teachers' pensions, and for the enforcement of school attendance.

Michael Oreste (1913-14), also less than a full-blooded Negro, put through a law on public administration, set up two normal schools, and signed an agreement with the Catholic clergy in Haiti under which they were to operate rural schools on three-acre plots donated by the government.[16]

After Oreste the presidency was held successively by three men for only a few months each. Following the mob killing of President Guillaume Sam in July 1915, Haiti was occupied by American marines, who brought about the election of Sudre Dartiguenave, a mulatto, as President.

The above recital of Haiti's economic development efforts before 1915 cannot be taken entirely at face value. Some of the measures adopted were not fully executed; others failed of their purpose. We have omitted mention of the numerous administrations under which no progress whatsoever was achieved or, worse yet, under which the country actually slid backwards. If the achievements between 1804 and 1915 were not greater, the causes lay at least partly in the basic difficulties discussed at the beginning of this chapter. To overcome such difficulties could be nothing less than a herculean task.

□ □ □ 5
# The U.S. Occupation (1915-34)

After more than a century of independence, Haiti appeared to the outside world as a retrograde nation, incapable of progress and rent by corruption and strife, both political and military. As indicated in the following passage, the once highly productive economy had deteriorated into a shambles:

In 1915, there was not a single plantation in the country, and in spite of relatively prosperous periods agriculture and peasant life in general had remained on a primitive level. Extensive areas, once cultivated and highly productive, had been entirely abandoned and were overgrown with brush. There was little cultivation of tobacco, and exports of cacao had declined—two products which manifestly called for skill in raising and harvesting. Sugar, although still produced for local consumption, was no longer shipped abroad. . . . Generally speaking, there was no tilling of the soil, fencing, breeding of livestock or use of farm implements. The only cultivation deserving the name was of garden vegetables. Coffee, cotton, bananas and other products grew in a semi-wild state. The rural homes were thatch-roofed shacks. Sanitation was practically nonexistent. . . .[1]

In the great majority of cases, the chief executive had been an army general who was chosen (or who imposed himself) because of his strong personal following. There was little or no party philosophy or organization. Of the 19 men who had headed the state as emperor, king, or president during the years 1804-1911, only four had been able to complete their term of office or to die peacefully while in office. The others had been removed by revolution, assassination, or suicide, or had resigned because of personal disgust or despair. Beginning in 1911, the turnover of chief executives became more rapid. In a four-year period, six men held the office of President for fleeting intervals. The first of these died in a palace explosion, the second suffered a death which some attribute to poisoning, the next three were forcibly ousted, and the sixth (Guillaume Sam) was hacked to pieces by a mob. The political and economic chaos had done serious harm to the country's financial condition. The value of the Haitian currency (the gourde) had fallen from 24 cents early in 1914 to 10.5 cents in July 1915.[2] By 1914 the national debt service was absorbing some 80 per cent of total budget revenues.[3] The American-owned National Railway Company had defaulted on the service of its dollar bonds, and the Haitian government in August 1914 had been unable to make good on its guarantee of those bonds.[4]

It was the events surrounding the demise of President Guillaume Sam that finally precipitated the oft-contemplated American intervention. On July 27, 1915, besieged by *cacos*[5] and other partisans of Dr. Rosalvo Bobo, Guillaume Sam had taken refuge in the French legation. On the same day, the officer in charge of the Port-au-Prince prison (Gen. Oscar Etienne) proceeded to slaughter the 167 followers of Bobo who were imprisoned there; only five of them escaped. The next day, July 28, as American warships were sighted in the harbor, grieving relatives and friends of the slaughtered men abandoned the funeral processions, rushed to the French legation, hauled out Guillaume Sam and cut him to pieces, which they then paraded around town. Another mob invaded the Dominican government's legation, seized and shot Etienne, then tore down his home.

While the purposes of the American occupation were primarily political, they were apparently tinged with economic motives. Before World War I, German and French intervention in Haitian affairs had taken place more than once, and there was considerable fear in Washington that Haiti, strategically located in our Caribbean backyard, might cede naval or coaling stations to a European power. Nervousness on this score increased with the outbreak of war in Europe in 1914. On the economic side, American bankers had a stake in Haiti's national bank and its railway system, and a substantial part of Haiti's trade was with the United States. Whatever the basic aims of the occupation may have been, the convention which the American-dominated government of Haiti was compelled to sign shortly after the start of the occupation laid the major emphasis on the solution of Haiti's economic problems.

Within a few days of disembarkation, the American forces under Admiral Caperton became convinced that the restoration of order and the creation of conditions in which peaceful progress would be possible for Haiti would take much longer than originally estimated. The situation has been summarized in the following paragraph by a Marine Corps historian:

> Realizing the impossibility of ever establishing lasting order in Haiti so long as the cacos retained their power to terrorize the country, Admiral Caperton so advised the American Government, stressing the necessity for completely breaking the power

of these bandits. The United States Government then resolved to settle once and for all the troublesome Haitian situation, which had necessitated the sending of United States naval vessels to protect the lives of Americans and foreigners frequently since 1857. Admiral Caperton was directed to inform the Haitian people that the United States was going to establish a firm and stable government for, of, and by the Haitian people, and would remain in Haiti only so long as necessary to effect this aim.[6]

As a first step, the occupying forces pressed for the election by the Haitian legislature of a new President, making it clear that they preferred the mulatto Senator Sudre Dartiguenave. Unlike Dr. Bobo, Dartiguenave expressed his willingness to consider with the Americans the terms of a treaty under which internal order and financial reform could be ensured. As soon as Dartiguenave was elected, the Americans presented him with the text of a proposed convention and asked him to request legislative authorization to sign it. After several political resignations and some minor changes in the text, the convention was approved and signed.

The convention provided that the President of Haiti would appoint, upon nomination by the President of the United States, a General Receiver of Customs and a Financial Adviser. The former was to collect and administer all customs revenues (constituting at that time almost the whole of the government revenues), while the latter was charged with "setting up an adequate system of public accounting, helping to increase revenues and to adjust them to expenditures, inquiring into the validity of the Republic's debts, advising the two governments with respect to any future indebtedness, recommending improved methods of collecting and disbursing revenues, and making such other recommendations to the Secretary of State for Finance as may be judged necessary for the well-being and prosperity of Haiti." The payment of interest and amortization of the public debt was to be a first charge on the customs revenues (after a deduction of 5 per cent to cover salaries and office expenses of the two American officials). The convention further stipulated: (1) that the Republic would not incur new indebtedness without prior approval by the President of the United States, unless revenues were sufficient to cover, in addition to current expenses, interest and complete amortization; (2) that it would not alter customs duties in such a way as to reduce the total yield; and (3) that it would cooperate with the Financial Adviser in the improvement of tax collection and disbursement methods and in creating any necessary new sources of revenue. The Haitian government also undertook to carry out such measures as "in the opinion of the contracting parties may be considered essential to public health and to the progress of the Republic." This was to be done under the supervision of engineers appointed by the President of Haiti upon nomination by the President of the United States. The small Haitian army was disbanded and replaced by a constabulary of 2,000 men under American officers.

For its part, the United States undertook to assist the economic development of Haiti and to help in the preservation of Haitian independence and the maintenance of a government capable of protecting lives, property, and individual freedom.

The extent to which the Americans actually assisted the economic development of Haiti appears to vary according to whether one consults American or Haitian sources. If one is to believe a scholarly American account,

> The Marines did much that was of indisputable benefit to Haiti. This was acknowledged even by the most vocal patriots who soon began to campaign for an end of the Occupation. Where there had been no real work in public health, Americans now built hospitals, established clinics, cleaned up the sources of many diseases, laid down sewage systems, gave the towns pure water. In 1915 there were only three automobiles in the country, and no roads for them to travel; the Americans built many miles of paved roads. In 1915 there had been only one wharf, two short stretches of railroad, two lighthouses, one electric plant; the Americans undertook electrification, telephone systems, the construction of administration buildings, and other public conveniences. Whether in such visible matters or in the obscurer realms of currency, banking, and budgets hardly a phase of daily life was left untouched.[7]

If, on the other hand, one is to be guided by an equally scholarly Haitian account, it would appear that the American officers in Haiti were primarily intent on ensuring the rapid amortization and regular interest service of Haiti's foreign debt and had little interest in, and often opposed, projects of economic development which the Haitian authorities considered essential.[8] Both versions are nearer the truth than their apparent contradiction would lead one to believe. To reach a well-rounded judgment, one must take a detailed look at the record.

It is certainly true that the Americans did the first important work in building hospitals, clinics, and sewage systems, and in supplying Haitian towns with pure water. But the élite did not have too much use for hospitals and clinics, since they received most of their medical aid from family doctors or during their frequent trips to Europe. There was no large middle class such as American hospitals and clinics serve. As for the illiterate, poverty-stricken, and disease-ridden non-élite, making up over 90 per cent of the population, what hope was there of building enough hospitals and clinics to meet their needs? Whatever the Americans built along these lines could not be much more than a trickle. This is not a criticism; it is simply another way of saying that building hospitals and clinics could not be a solution of Haiti's economic problems. Indeed, some might argue that by reducing the mortality rate and thus increasing the rate of population growth, it tended to make some of the problems (such as employment and nourishment) more acute.

Another basic need of Haiti was primary education. In this field the Haitian and American authorities were completely at loggerheads, due to some extent to conflicting views as to the type of instruction that should be offered, but due even more to distrust and misunderstanding. The American view was that the literary type of education which prevailed in the Haitian schools was worse than useless. As stated by Millspaugh,

> The stigma which slavery had cast on manual labor was perpetuated by a system of literary education which, apart from its inefficiency and its almost complete failure to reach the mass of the people, was unsuited to the primary needs of the country, accentuated class distinctions and was viewed mainly as a ticket of admission into the white-collar class.[9]

The occupying authorities consequently endeavored to hold back funds for the development of education of the traditional Haitian type, and to promote actively a utilitarian type of instruction. They proposed to the Haitian government the formation of a mixed commission to study the problem and the employment by the government of an educational adviser, but these suggestions were rejected. Later, in 1924, the Americans established what was called the Service Technique de l'Agriculture et de l'Enseignement Professionnel for the direction of both agricultural development and vocational education. They explained this action as follows:

> "To students of Haitian affairs," wrote the high commissioner in January, 1925, "it is manifest that government stabilization must come from the development of Haiti's economic resources through agricultural and industrial education. . . . It is therefore essential that the educational system of Haiti should, at the present time, be designed to furnish agricultural education to the rural classes, and industrial education to the urban population." It is among the white-collar class, he added, that "revolutions are bred."
>
> "In accord with this policy," the high commissioner reported three years later, "there are being developed in the rural districts agricultural schools and in the urban communities industrial schools. Of course, this does not mean that the rural schools teach only agriculture or that the urban schools teach only a trade. They teach, besides, all that is necessary for the development of an intelligent and efficient citizenship and for the student to become a productive unit of his country."[10]

By April 1930 the Service Technique had set up 70 rural and 10 urban schools, with a total enrollment in the 80 schools of 9,349. In 1929 evening instruction was being given to 635 adult students in 16 rural schools. As against these American-controlled schools, the Haitian Ministry of Education in 1929 reported 1,087 Haitian-directed schools, with a total enrollment of 85,359 pupils.

> American policy was to eliminate or "absorb" these Haitian-directed schools, and the latter were denied any material increase in appropriations. For some time the minister of public instruction was permitted to increase salaries and other current expenditures

by means of savings effected when his schools were reorganized, consolidated or abolished; but early in 1929 this permission was withdrawn.[11]

The rebuffs which the American occupying authorities administered to most of the Haitian plans for enlarging and improving the educational system were usually justified on the ground that funds were not available, but a more important reason appears to have been a desire to discredit Haiti's French-type educational system and then take it over and refashion it on American principles.

The American view with respect to Haiti's educational needs was firmly combated by the Haitian government, notably by Dantès Bellegarde, as Minister of Education. Writing in 1937, Bellegarde had this to say:

> Haiti had no need of any foreign expert for the organization of its system of public education. The system which it has adopted . . . is based on the French school system, and whatever criticism one may make of that system . . . the Americans are hardly qualified to express contempt for it. The needs of Haitian education can be summed up as: (1) the training of teachers and equitable remuneration for their services; (2) the construction of school buildings and their equipment . . . (3) the development of an agricultural and industrial education answering the economic needs of the country and the social conditions of the Haitian environment; (4) reorganization of the system of inspection and supervision of the schools from the viewpoints of hygiene as well as physical culture.
>
> Methodically, untiringly, I tried . . . to satisfy these different needs. The struggle between my firm determination to execute this program of national education and the resistance of the American authorities to any progressive undertaking for the intellectual or professional instruction of the Haitian people constitutes one of the most painful episodes in the history of the Dartiguenave government. . . .[12]

With respect to the Americans' creation of a separate school system under the Service Technique, Bellegarde remarked that

> . . . they set up a costly administration which, because it had no national foundation, threatened to collapse when they departed in 1932. To save it from ruin, the government had to give it a

new organization; and in order to save it from anarchy, it was obliged to put in charge of it a Belgian agronomist, Mr. Marcel Montfils. And the latter soon declared . . . that after 18 years of American occupation "the Haitian peasant has remained stationary." Is it not permissible to suppose that the outcome would have been different if the Americans had not opposed my 1918 program?[13]

That Bellegarde's view was not without substance is demonstrated by the following statement attributed by McCrocklin to Dana G. Munro:

> It was not so easy to find Americans who combined technical training in agriculture or industrial education with the peculiar qualifications needed for work in Haiti, and the fact that many of the Americans who were selected did not speak French greatly handicapped their teaching work. The development of an adequate Haitian personnel was still more difficult. Since it was impracticable for financial reasons, as well as inadvisable for reasons of policy to employ a large number of American teachers, no considerable part of the population could possibly be reached by educational work until Haitian teachers could be trained . . . the required Haitian personnel could be obtained only from among the élite who, as a class, had never had any interest in agriculture and who were greatly handicapped in dealing with the peasants by barriers of caste prejudice and suspicion. The work of the rural farm schools was therefore carried on under great difficulties. . . .[14]

McCrocklin's own conclusion is that the question of how to secure the proper material for the educational program which the Americans were pursuing was never fully answered. Under the circumstances, it would appear that the American occupation authorities might have achieved more in the educational field by a policy of close collaboration with the Haitians, inducing them to supplement and broaden their system, rather than by attempting the complete displacement of their traditional system by a new and radically different one for which the basic ingredients were lacking. Their impetuous overriding of Haitian tradition was all the more open to criticism because the Haitian-American convention contained not one word authorizing American control of the educational system.

With over 90 per cent of its population living in rural areas, Haiti in 1915 was (as it still is) dependent on agriculture for its well-being. Indeed, it was a bountiful agricultural production that made Saint-Domingue France's most prosperous colony. But with the disappearance of plantations, sugar mills, irrigation systems, and roads, the decline of agriculture doomed free Haiti to poverty. The decline was accentuated by the inability of the former slaves and their descendants to grasp the true meaning of freedom. There was little or no understanding of the fact that discipline in *some* form is an essential ingredient in the lives of human beings—imposed from above in the case of slaves, self-adopted in the case of free men. To the Haitian masses, liberation from slavery meant primarily the freedom to live as they pleased, without dictation or imposed discipline. This attitude, combined with the breaking up of land into tiny parcels and a profound ignorance of modern agricultural techniques, entailed a progressive deterioration of the soil and its produce and made impossible a return to the prosperity of two centuries before.

Article I of the Haitian-American treaty of September 16, 1915, read in part as follows:

> The Government of the United States will, by its good offices, aid the Haitian Government in the proper and efficient development of its agricultural, mineral and commercial resources. . . .

Actually, it was not until 1922 that the occupying forces got around to giving direct aid to agriculture. Indirect and incidental aid may be said to have been given in the form of pacification of the rural areas, administrative and currency reform, road-building, etc. In 1922 an agricultural survey of Haiti was carried out by an American farm expert, and in 1923 a protocol was signed with the Haitian government covering the creation of the Service Technique and its direction by an American agricultural engineer.

One of the aims of the American-directed agricultural program was diversification of crops so as to relieve Haiti of its excessive dependence on the production and export of coffee and cotton. Sisal and tobacco culture was encouraged for export, corn-growing for domestic consumption. Experiments in rubber-growing were made. Despite these efforts, non-coffee exports showed little growth, and coffee as a percentage of total exports actually increased. Ten coffee demonstration farms and a coffee experiment station were established, and bonuses were given for new coffee-planting. Coffee grades were standardized, and the President was authorized to regulate methods of cultivation, harvesting, inspecting, and packing. From 13 to 16 agricultural agents annually made thousands of visits and rendered thousands of services to Haitian peasants, according to the American High Commissioner's reports. An agricultural extension department with 34 Haitian supervisors and demonstration agents was organized. The cooperative method was tried for corn-growers.[15]

An American veterinary staff gave instruction in the care and treatment of animal diseases. Animal clinics were held at various stations throughout the country, and stockbreeding stations were established.[16]

As indicated in the above discussion of education, the Service Technique devoted much attention to the establishment and direction of agricultural schools in the rural areas. It also set up in Port-au-Prince a Central School of Agriculture where some 400 agriculturists and teachers were given training.

The occupying authorities aimed at diversification not only of crops but of the sizes of landholdings. They felt that Haiti with its tiny family plots was at a disadvantage in competition with plantation economies. Since Haitians were hardly in a position to supply the capital for plantation investment, this meant bringing in American or other foreign investors. The Constitution of 1918, which had been voted under American pressure,[17] had abolished the traditional Haitian prohibition of real-estate ownership by foreigners, but it was difficult for foreigners to acquire enough land from private Haitian owners for plantation purposes. Although the Haitian government owned almost one-half of the country's total area, this land could not legally be sold. Moreover, much of it was mountainous or otherwise unsuitable for agricultural use, while other portions had been leased or were occupied by squatters. Nevertheless, it was found possible to arrange for the lease of sizable tracts to American companies:

> In 1927 contracts were entered into with the Haitian-American Development Corporation and the Haitian Agricultural Corporation, by which these American-controlled interests were given a preferential right over all except Haitian tenants and occupants, to lease limited areas of public land in northern Haiti. Each corporation was guaranteed against an increase of export duties and against discriminatory and confiscatory legislation. At the end of 1929 four American companies were leasing state lands: the Haitian-American Sugar Company about 630 acres, the Haitian Pineapple Company with about 40 acres, the Haitian-American Development Corporation about 14,000 acres, and the Haitian Agricultural Corporation about 2,200 acres. There were also about 1,000 acres leased by a Haitian in association with an American.[18]

However, as Millspaugh points out, one of the above-mentioned companies, the Haitian-American Sugar Company, had entered Haiti before the American occupation. In 1930 seven American companies occupied not quite 50,000 acres in all, of which the Haitian-American Sugar Company alone held 24,000 acres. Four of the American companies were engaged in the production of sisal, one in growing castor beans and cotton, and one each in the cultivation of sugar and pineapples. Of the 50,000 acres, only about 13,000 had been acquired by purchase. Over 1,000 Haitians were employed by the Haitian-American Sugar Company.

The Haitian-American Development Corporation had taken over land which had lain unproductive for a century, cleared it and planted it to sisal. This enterprise also employed more than 1,000 Haitians.[19]

Haiti's agricultural possibilities could not be fully realized without overcoming two important obstacles: the lack of irrigation and the extremely confused state of land titles. The occupying authorities made at least a start at tackling these two problems. As to irrigation, Millspaugh states:

> A project of rebuilding and extending irrigation works in the Cul-de-Sac Plain[20] was started by the Public Works Service

in 1924 and completed in 1925. In this and other districts, about 50,000 acres were under irrigation in 1929, and since the intervention 100 miles of canals serving 8,000 farms and over 60,000 people had been constructed. But the total irrigable area in Haiti was over 300,000 acres.[21]

In 1924 the Haitian government appropriated funds for soil and topographic surveys of the Artibonite Plain in central Haiti, and in 1927 a two-year option for its irrigation was given to an American group. When this group was unsuccessful in raising the necessary capital, the American occupation officials, who had at first been enthusiastic about the project, advised against any extension of the contract. Although the Haitian government granted a one-year extension, it appears from Millspaugh's account that the project was never executed.[22]

Some $600,000 of the proceeds of the Haitian government's dollar bond issue in 1922 was originally intended to finance irrigation of the Gonaives Plain, in northwestern Haiti, but the funds were diverted in 1929 to the construction of school buildings.[23]

The American officials found it difficult to agree among themselves on the importance of the land-title problem and the best way of solving it:

> Land title legislation was actively considered in 1927 and 1928. Finally, an American lawyer was employed in 1929 to draft a bill; but "these well-thought-out plans did not meet with the entire approbation of the Haitian government. . . ." On the other hand, the financial adviser-general receiver pointed out in 1929 that "land property in Haiti is in fact currently conveyed, mortgaged and leased." While there is every good reason for working toward a modern titles system, the present land situation in Haiti, as such, presents no more difficulties toward securing a title than obtain generally in many Latin American countries.[24]

Because of their doubts about the land-title situation, the occupying authorities did not pursue two projects which they would otherwise have favored, namely, the creation of an agricultural bank and a system of land taxation. In 1929 they proposed measures to deal with squatters and to permit homesteading, but both proposals were turned down by the Haitian government.

With respect to assisting in the development of Haiti's mineral and commercial resources, as provided for in the 1915 convention, the occupation authorities' principal effort was in the establishment of vocational schools in the towns, under the aforementioned Service Technique. The encouragement of industry and commerce was one of the aims of a 1926 tariff revision (see p. 55). According to Millspaugh,

> A preliminary investigation by members of the United States Geological Survey in 1922 showed that the commercially exploitable mineral resources of Haiti were not sufficient to contribute materially to an increase of production. Nevertheless, some progress occurred in this field. An American company holding a copper concession at Terre Neuve, near St. Marc, which had ceased operations before the intervention, now obtained additional capital and a modification of its contract, and resumed operations. Exportation of salt was encouraged.[25]

From start to finish, the occupying forces concerned themselves with a variety of public works:

> By 1922 Americans were credited with building 385 miles of new roads and repairing 200 miles of old construction. Very little, if any, work was done on the [mountain] trails, but streets were paved in Port au Prince. . . . Under American supervision, telegraph and telephone lines were repaired and extended. . . .[26]

Apart from the building of hospitals and clinics, as mentioned above,

> Streets were kept clean, incinerators built and garbage was burned; sewers were opened, sanitary toilets built and drainage was installed; mosquito control was begun, water systems were repaired and markets cleaned.[27]

It was in the fields of finance and administration that the American occupiers exerted the greatest efforts, and the emphasis on these aspects was clearly evident in the 1915 convention. Most Haitian critics of the occupation felt that this emphasis was due to a desire to protect American financial interests, or even to obtain a stranglehold on the Haitian economy, rather than to any altruistic motive. However that may be, the measures taken in this field did entail many improvements in the functioning of the economy.

The reason for so much emphasis on financial controls lay in the deplorable state of the Haitian government's finances at and before the time of the intervention. As one analyst has described the pre-occupation situation,

> The Haitian Government had been shamelessly incompetent and corrupt. Three of the Presidents to hold office during the six years that preceded the American intervention had been convicted of embezzlement. Public works, sanitation, and public welfare were neglected. During the period of ephemeral government, public works, although paid for, were rarely completed. The customs service was so notoriously riddled with graft that the immensely greater amount of coffee that was received in France compared with the record of exports from Haitian custom houses had ceased to cause comment.[28]

Millspaugh was equally severe in his condemnation of Haiti's pre-occupation financial mess:

> Incompetence, demoralization and corruption in finance had brought the Government to virtual bankruptcy. Political and personal plundering of the treasury had been so flagrant, so customary and so shameless that it may best be characterized as unmoral rather than immoral. . . . Loans were floated on onerous terms to meet recurring deficits and to satisfy the rapacity of successful revolutionists and their followers. . . . In 1913-14 about 80% of the Government revenue was required for debt service. In 1912-13 there was a deficit, amounting to almost one-quarter of the receipts, which was partly covered by an internal loan and partly by borrowing from the National Bank of Haiti. In the following year the deficit amounted to about 60% of the receipts and was covered by an issue of paper money. In June, 1914, another internal loan was floated. In the meantime Haitian currency, ordinarily subject to violent fluctuations, responded to the issuance of paper money by further depreciation.
>
> In expenditure from ordinary receipts or from loans the budget was commonly ignored; and Government funds were rarely applied to constructive and productive undertakings.[29]

Actually, the U.S. government appears to have worried about the financial chaos in Haiti, not so much because American interests were directly involved as because French and other European interests were primarily affected and might therefore be tempted themselves to intervene in Haiti. Under the Monroe Doctrine, the United States conceived that it had a duty to forestall such a possibility by helping Haiti restore financial order. Haiti's public debt was owed mainly to French creditors, and French banks had a majority ownership of the National Bank and controlled the cable monopoly, while the bonds of the National Railway were also owned in France. German and British interests held certain concessions. Americans held two railway concessions, as well as the wharf, electric-light, and tramway concessions, and a substantial interest in the BNRH was held by the National City Bank of New York and other American banks.[30]

Since Haiti's foreign indebtedness was secured by its customs receipts, the United States had for some time contemplated offering its help in maintaining and improving that revenue. In February 1914, following the seizure of the Haitian customs by revolutionaries, it offered to give such help "in any practical way," if the Haitian government desired. In July 1914 it sent to Port-au-Prince a draft convention which provided for customs control under an American General Receiver and for an American Financial Adviser to act as a comptroller of accounts. In November, when one ephemeral President (Zamor) had been overthrown by another (Théodore), the U.S. government took the position that it would recognize Théodore as provisional President only when the Haitian government agreed to negotiate conventions providing: (1) American fiscal control; (2) settlement of certain railway and bank controversies; (3) full protection to all foreign interests; (4) an undertaking never to lease any Haitian territory to any European government as a naval or coaling station; and (5) settlement by arbitration of American claims against Haiti. During the proposed negotiations, the U.S. government was to cover the Haitian government's current expenses. The Haitian authorities agreed to all of these points except the first, fiscal control. In addition, they offered certain economic privileges to American citizens, if the United States would assist Haiti in obtaining a loan; but fiscal control by Americans was adamantly refused. On this point the Haitian Senate accused the Minister of Foreign Affairs of trying to sell his country to the United States. The U.S. Secretary of State (William Jennings Bryan) refused the Haitian offer, stating that the United States preferred to encourage investment in Haiti rather "by contributing to stability and order than by favoring special concessions to Americans."[31]

In March 1915, Guillaume Sam became President, and the U.S. and Haitian governments resumed negotiations, as described by Millspaugh:

> About two months later Paul Fuller, accredited as special agent and minister plenipotentiary . . . presented to the Haitian minister for foreign relations a draft treaty which proposed the armed intervention of the United States whenever necessary "to protect the Republic of Haiti from outside attack and from the aggression of any foreign power" and "to aid the Government of Haiti to suppress insurrection from within." The Government of Haiti would obligate itself in return not to grant in any manner whatsoever any rights, privileges or facilities concerning the occupation or use of Môle St. Nicholas "to any foreign government or to a national or the nationals of any foreign government," and to enter into an arbitration agreement to provide for the equal treatment of all foreigners. . . .
>
> . . . the Haitian Government offered a counter-project, accepting the armed intervention of the United States to prevent "intrusion of any foreign power in the affairs of Haiti and to repulse any act of aggression attempted" against Haiti. It also accepted the American proposal regarding Môle St. Nicholas. It was further proposed that the United States "shall facilitate the entrance into Haiti of sufficient capital to assure the full economic development" of the country, to improve its financial situation, to unify the debt and to reform the currency. The Haitian Government was willing to agree to employ in the customs houses "only Haitian officials whose morality and capability" were "well known," and the "lenders" might be "consulted regarding the choice of the higher customs officials." The Haitian Government further agreed to organize a rural horse guard, and in the meantime resort might be had to the aid of the American Government "to check disorders and serious troubles." In such case, however, the American forces "must be withdrawn from Haitian territory at the first demand of the constitutional authorities."[32]

In essence, the Guillaume Sam proposals were very similar to the provisions of the convention which was signed following the American intervention, the main difference being the degree of control to be exercised over Haiti's finances. The September 16 convention contained clauses relating to the Môle St. Nicholas and commercial arbitration, but the prohibition of ceding territory to a foreign country was now broadened to include the whole of Haiti. The convention provided for the creation of an American-trained gendarmerie. It omitted one important point that had been stressed by the Guillaume Sam government: the agreement to withdraw American forces "at the first demand of the constitutional authorities." The provision that the United States should facilitate the entrance of foreign capital for Haiti's economic development was replaced by a United States undertaking to "aid the Haitian Government in the proper and efficient development of its agricultural, mineral and commercial resources and in the establishment of the finances of Haiti on a firm and solid basis."

Signature and ratification of the September 16 convention were not achieved without much passive resistance on the part of the Haitian cabinet and legislature. Two resigning ministers had to be replaced, and one of the new ministers (Louis Borno, a mulatto who later became President) agreed only after some of the language had been modified to assuage native susceptibilities and to eliminate features which he considered to be in conflict with the Haitian Constitution. Despite cajoling and threats, the legislature took two months to ratify the document. As a result of the changes insisted upon by Borno, parts of the convention became subject to more than one interpretation, and these differing interpretations were a cause of much of the friction which developed, almost from the start.

In the realm of finance, the American authorities intervened actively in such matters as the public debt, preparation and control of the budget, collection of customs duties, nature and effects of the taxation system, and stabilization of the currency.

As a Haitian writer describes the situation at the beginning of the American financial hegemony:

> The General Receiver claimed, on the one hand, the right to appoint and dismiss, without any interference by the Haitian Government, the staff of the customs administration, as well as

the right to "receive and apply" the public revenues other than the customs duties.

The Financial Adviser, on the other hand, claimed the right to exercise general control of the execution of the budget, with all public expenditure being submitted to his prior authorization. Moreover, he considered it indispensable to the accomplishment of the purposes of the treaty that his recommendations, whether or not approved by the Haitian Government, should be sanctioned and applied by the latter, and that his right should be recognized to prevent if need be the execution of any governmental initiatives contrary to his directives or to his conception of the purposes of the treaty.[33]

The Haitian government energetically opposed these claims as an invasion of national sovereignty. Even when the U.S. State Department intervened to support the views of the two financial experts, the Haitian government gave in on only one point: the General Receiver's right to appoint his own staff. The Marine Corps commander thereupon blocked the government's account at the National Bank until the demands of the two experts should be met. A month later the government capitulated.

A similar confrontation took place less than two years later, when the General Receiver withheld the salaries of the President of the Republic, the ministers, and the members of the Council of State pending the repeal of certain laws and the adoption of four new laws proposed by the General Receiver.[34] After a three-month trial of strength, this struggle ended in a compromise, but the occupying authorities' right of veto over further legislation received de facto recognition.

On October 3, 1919, a Haitian-American protocol was signed providing for the settlement by a mixed claims commission of most of the foreign claims against Haiti (the three French bond issues were the principal exceptions). Partly for the purpose of financing the payment of the adjusted claims and the government's outstanding debts, the protocol provided for the issuance of a 30-year Haitian government dollar loan up to an amount of $40 million, redeemable in 15 years. Any balance remaining from this loan after the debt settlements was to be applied, subject to the agreement of the Financial Adviser, either to public works or to the service of the loan. Interest and amortization of the loan was to be a first charge on all internal revenues of Haiti and a second charge (after the expenses of the General Receiver and the Financial Adviser) on all customs revenues. Since the loan was to be for a longer period than the 1915 convention, it was agreed that "the control by an officer or officers duly appointed by the President of Haiti, upon nomination by the President of the United States, of the collection and allocation of the hypothecated revenues, will be provided for during the life of the loan after the expiration of the aforesaid treaty. . . ."

The contemplated loan was not actually issued until 1922, after Borno had become President. Not surprisingly, the National City Bank of New York, which in the meantime had acquired all the shares of the National Bank, was the highest bidder for the first *tranche*, which was for $16 million, at a 6 per cent interest rate. The proceeds of this Series A *tranche* were used to pay off the government debts to the French bondholders, the National Railway, and the BNRH. Owing to the depreciation of the French franc, only a little over $6 million was needed for refunding the three French loans, which in 1915 had had a value equivalent to $21.5 million.[35] Of the remaining proceeds of the Series A bonds, $2.4 million was used for public works (including school buildings) and $300,000 for amortization.

Subsequently, two further *tranches* of the Haitian government loan were issued in a total amount of $7,660,000. The proceeds were used for redeeming certain internal loans and National Railway bonds, as well as for funding those awards of the claims commission which were payable in the form of bonds.[36]

The policy of most of the Americans who acted successively as General Receiver or Financial Adviser[37] was to build up a large cash reserve, while at the same time amortizing the government loan more rapidly than required by its terms. At the end of the 1923-24 fiscal year there was a government cash balance of $1,399,800. By the end of fiscal 1929 this reserve had risen to $4,072,200, the largest in the modern history of Haiti. The public debt of Haiti was reduced from $24.2 million on September 30, 1924, to $16.5 million six years later.[38]

According to McCrocklin, it was not until three years after the American intervention that the full authority of the two American financial officials over the Haitian budget and expenditures was established:

> In spite of the handicap under which these officials labored improvements were gradually accomplished . . . the budgetary requirements [were] closely analyzed, and expenditures coordinated in logical relation to the revenues and the needs of the people.
>
> There was such a mass of necessary reconstruction in every department of the government, and such a small revenue available, that the estimates of expenditures were generally in excess of estimated revenues. From the beginning the Financial Adviser maintained a policy of careful examination and scrutiny of the estimates of the spending department of the government, and excluded from such estimates all items not deemed of urgent necessity. A large proportion of the revenue was devoted to expenditures for public works, public health, and public safety.
>
> . . . The increase in revenue was accomplished primarily by increased honesty and efficiency in collection under American influence and not materially by any additional legislation.[39]

According to Millspaugh,

> Technical details of fiscal control were perfected after 1923; budgetary procedure was improved, a modern accounting system was introduced and preauditing of expenditures established.[40]

The American officials concluded early in the intervention that the Haitian tariff was one of the worst in the world and that its burden rested much too heavily on the peasantry. In the fiscal year 1911-12, for example, export duties produced more revenue than came from import duties.[41] Moreover, the tariff offered no incentive to the creation of native industries. Luxuries were taxed lightly and necessities heavily. The Americans favored the elimination or reduction of export duties, and the levying instead of internal taxes, until then almost nonexistent. Since, however, the customs revenue was pledged as security for the government's foreign indebtedness, tariff and tax reform had to await the refunding of the foreign debt. Meanwhile attention was concentrated on the elimination of abuses in the customs service and the voting of legislation to reduce smuggling.

The 1915 convention did not specifically authorize American control or intervention in the matter of internal taxes, but the Americans felt that this problem was inextricably intertwined with the other financial responsibilities they had undertaken. In April 1922 the American High Commissioner urged the government to enact an internal-revenue project. As related by Millspaugh,

> This project experienced delay, objections and prolonged discussion in the Council of State, but was passed on June 6, 1924, shortly after the financial adviser-general receiver had agreed to an increase in the salaries of the councillors. The law created a Bureau of Internal Revenue under an American director responsible to the general receiver; but no new internal taxes were imposed until 1928. Nevertheless, administrative improvement resulted in a gradual increase of revenue from existing sources.[42]

In 1926 a new tariff was enacted which placed higher duties on luxuries and protective duties on a number of articles which it was thought could be produced in Haiti, for example tobacco. In 1928 and 1929 various items (agricultural implements and machines, books, printing equipment, etc.) were put on the free list in order to encourage agriculture and education. Despite the conviction that the export duties were an oppressive burden on the peasantry, the Financial Adviser-General Receiver stated in 1925 that they could not be reduced until equal revenue could be gotten from other sources.

In 1928 a moderate excise tax was placed on alcoholic beverages and manufactured tobacco. In the same year, export duties on bananas were abolished and export duties on crude salt were reduced. The new excise tax produced nearly half a million dollars in its first year, thus tripling the total of internal revenue. Thereupon the export duty on the better grades of coffee was reduced.

The Financial Adviser-General Receiver felt that Haiti's greatest fiscal need was a land tax, which he thought would discourage the holding of uncultivated land for speculative purposes. He drafted a law providing for a small tax on real estate, with a doubling of the rate in the case of unimproved or uncultivated land. This project, however, was opposed by the High Commissioner because of the ignorance of the peasants and the absence of proper land laws, land surveys, registration offices, and means of settling titles.[43] However, the administration of public lands was transferred from the Department of the Interior to the American-controlled Bureau of Internal Revenue, and all lessees or squatters on state lands were required to pay a rental equal to 6 per cent of the sales value of the property.

As already noted, the Haitian gourde before the American intervention was a fluctuating and depreciating currency. It was a paper currency issued by the government. Various projects of monetary reform had been debated before the American occupation, but there was never any full agreement on the best type of reform, and there was constant bickering between the government and the National Bank. The latter was the government's fiscal agent and as such the custodian of government revenues and of a 10-million-franc monetary reform fund which the government had set aside from the proceeds of a 1910 bond issue in France.

In July 1915, with American encouragement, the government and the bank signed in Washington an agreement settling their pre-occupation dispute:

> The Bank was made the depository of revenues collected by the Receiver General, the portion of the monetary reform fund which had been shipped to New York was returned to Port-au-Prince, and the unused balance of the fund was made freely available for use by the Government in carrying out a monetary reform.
> . . . Three years later (on April 12, 1919) the Government and the Bank signed a Convention laying down the details of the reform. A currency Retirement Fund of $1,735,664.89 was set up. . . . Holders of the Government-issued gourde notes, amounting to G. 8,877,972, were to receive in exchange, at their option, dollar notes at a ratio of 1 dollar to 5 gourdes, or new Bank-issued gourde notes on a 1-to-1 basis. On the back of each new gourde note was the Bank's printed promise to exchange it on demand for dollar currency, at a 5-to-1 ratio. The Bank was

obligated to keep a cash reserve of at least 33-⅓% in dollar notes and dollar sight deposits against its own note liabilities. To the extent that its note liabilities exceeded the cash reserve, they had to be fully backed by short-term commercial paper. . . .

The Convention . . . was sanctioned by a law . . . which stipulated that ". . . the Bank's notes shall be accepted in transactions at the rate of 5 gourdes for one dollar and vice versa." A communiqué issued by the Finance Ministry . . . made it clear that this was intended to make the dollar, as well as the gourde, acceptable as legal tender at the 5-to-1 ratio and that anyone engaging in transactions at a different ratio would be subject to sanctions under the Penal Code.[44]

In the initial months of this reform, there were some slight deviations from the 5-to-1 ratio, and some speculative attempts to profit from this situation. Actually, because the new gourde notes of the BNRH were not yet available in sufficient quantities while there was a redundancy of dollars, there was a premium on the bank's notes. It was partly because of a suspicion that the bank was deliberately slowing down the issuance of its notes in order to maintain a premium on them that the government published the above-mentioned communiqué.

The government communiqué purporting to make the dollar legal tender led to the paradoxical result that the Financial Adviser demanded repeal of the government action and the affirmation of the gourde as the sole legal currency. The government, however, refused to back down, and the Financial Adviser went to the extreme of stopping payment of the salaries of the President of the Republic, the ministers, the members of the Council of State, and the palace interpreter, in order to enforce his decision. The occupation authorities seized the opportunity to demand the repeal of various other laws that had been voted against their advice. In the end, however, the Americans gave way, and Haiti ever since has had a dual currency.[45]

The American occupiers apparently worked hard to achieve an orderly and prosperous country. It is clear, however, that they found the task much more arduous than they had anticipated. They were convinced the greater part of the time that they had gained the understanding and goodwill of most Haitians, but by 1929 they found themselves surrounded by feverish agitation for their departure. In the United States, too, politicians and newspapers had taken up the Haitian cause and demanded our withdrawal from the island. On October 31, 1929, the students at the Central School of Agriculture near Port-au-Prince went on strike, and strikes followed at the customhouse and the Service Technique. Martial law was declared, and U.S. marine reinforcements were brought in, but the disorders spread to the provinces. Confronted by a peasant mob near Cayes, a marine patrol had to use its guns, killing six and wounding 28, four of whom later died. In Washington, President Hoover requested Congress to authorize the immediate dispatch of a commission of inquiry to Haiti. Arriving in Haiti at the end of February 1930, the Forbes Commission, composed of distinguished liberals, spent the first half of March making its investigation.

In its report the commission noted that Haiti had made great material progress during the American intervention, and it praised the "whole-hearted and single-minded devotion" as well as the unremitting labor and painstaking efforts of the American High Commissioner, General Russell. There was abundant evidence, it said, that great improvement had taken place in the health of the people. It was under no delusions as to what might happen in Haiti after the restoration of constitutional government and the withdrawal of the United States forces, since it was not convinced that the foundations for democratic and representative government were broad enough in Haiti. "Until the basis of political structure is broadened by education—a matter of years—the Government must necessarily be more or less unstable and in constant danger of political upheavals." Nevertheless, the "failure of the occupation to understand the social problems of Haiti, its brusque attempt to plant democracy there by drill and harrow, its determination to set up a middle class—however wise and necessary it may seem to Americans—all these explain why, in part, the high hopes of our good works in this land have not been realized." Unfortunately, the American officials' plans and projects did not seem to have taken into account that their work should be completed by 1936, and the commission was disappointed to find that the preparation for the political and administrative training of Haitians for the responsibilities of government had been inadequate.

The commission questioned whether it had been wise to pay off Haiti's public debt in excess of amortization requirements. "It might have been better to have reduced the taxation, especially the export tax, and left the debt to work itself out during its normal term." Although no undue advantage had been taken of the enforced right of foreigners to own property in Haiti, this provision had been a source of Haitian irritation and suspicion, and it should be dropped from the Constitution.

The commission worked out a plan under which a temporary President acceptable to all parties should succeed President Borno on May 15 and remain in office until the election of a constitutional legislature and the election by the legislature, in turn, of a regular President. Upon the regular President's inauguration, General Russell should be succeeded by a non-military minister. The marines should be gradually withdrawn thereafter by agreement of the two governments. American intervention should be limited "to those activities for which provision is made for American assistance by treaty or by specific agreement between the two governments." It should be suggested to the Haitian government that it employ one American adviser in each administrative department, and the U.S. government should assist in the payment of such advisers. There should be "increasingly rapid Haitianization of the services, with the object of having Haitians in every department of the government ready to take over full responsibility at the expiration of the existing treaty." Only those Americans should see service in Haiti who were free from strong racial antipathies.

A special commission under Dr. R. R. Moton, president of Tuskegee Institute, investigated the education problem in Haiti. It concluded that "the setting up of a distinct and separate system of schools for primary children in city and country under a different and distinct state department, the Department of Agriculture, was a mistake"; that a "limited program of demonstration of a desirable type of school for town and country is all that can be justified under temporary American occupation," and to attempt more was "to incur the serious risk of having the whole superstructure collapse at the close of the occupation"; and that competent Haitians should be enabled to acquire practice in educational administration, "Americans standing in the background to advise and counsel with them." From a financial point of view, the commission said, education in Haiti was worse off under American occupation than it had been under exclusive Haitian control. Haiti was spending twice as much on elementary pupils in city schools as on approximately the same number in rural schools. The commission recommended, among other things, restoration of a unified educational program under the Minister of Education; an immediate cessation of capital outlay for farm schools until those already built could be adequately staffed and efficiently operated; that opportunity be given advanced students to study abroad; that the U.S. government assist in financing, or in obtaining financing for, completion of the Haitian educational program within a prescribed period; that private philanthropy be enlisted; and that a permanent joint commission on education be established by the two governments.

The reports of both commissions were approved as a basis for action. Eugène Roy, a Haitian businessman unconnected with politics, served as temporary President. On October 14, 1930, the legislature was elected, mostly from among opponents of the pro-American Borno government, and on November 19, Sténio Vincent was elected President for a six-year term. Prior to the American intervention Vincent had been an educator, Minister of Justice and of the Interior, Minister to the Netherlands, and President of the Senate. He had been a constant opponent of the Borno régime and of the occupation. Meanwhile General Russell had resigned, and a new American minister, Dr. Dana G. Munro, had arrived and was charged with supervision and control of the treaty officials and marine forces as long as they remained in Haiti. He was also made responsible for negotiating progressive measures of American withdrawal and Haitianization of the public services, and the degree of American assistance to be rendered to Haiti after 1936.

On August 5, 1931, a Haitianization agreement was signed by our minister and the Haitian Minister of Foreign Affairs, under which most of the functions directed by Americans reverted to Haitian direction on or before October 1, 1931. The Financial Adviser–General Receiver was temporarily continued, but without any power over orders of payment or the land-title registry. The Garde d'Haiti was maintained without change, pending a final solution.[46]

On August 7, 1933, a Haitian-American executive agreement provided for the withdrawal by October 1934 of all U.S. military forces, complete Haitianization of the Garde d'Haiti, and limitation of the financial functions performed by American officials. The actual withdrawal of our military forces took place in August 1934.

# ▣▣▣ 6
# Democracy or Dictatorship? (1934-39)

Under Sténio Vincent a number of measures of economic or social import were carried out by the Haitian government.

In 1934 a contract was signed for the purchase of the BNRH from its American owners, the National City Bank of New York. The actual transfer of ownership took place in 1935.

Early in 1935 a concession was granted to an American company, the Standard Fruit and Steamship Company, under which for a period of 20 years that company was to enjoy the exclusive privilege of buying all bananas produced in Haiti. This contract resulted in a very substantial increase in the production and exportation of the fruit.

A trade treaty was signed with the United States in March

1935. Under its terms United States duties on imports of Haitian rum, pineapples, and mango and guava jellies were reduced; these were, however, insignificant items in Haiti's exports. The United States also undertook to leave Haiti's principal exports (coffee, cacao, sisal, logwood, bananas, and ginger) on the free list. Similar concessions were made by Haiti in favor of certain United States products.

During the Vincent administration, three new secondary schools were organized, a number of rural dispensaries were built, encouragement was given to private charities, public libraries were established in the principal towns, and certain slum improvements were effected.

The economic and social progress made under Sténio Vincent contrasted with the course of political events. One by one, conflicts of authority arose between the President and the legislature, and Vincent was accused of dictatorial tendencies. In July 1933, when the President asked the Chamber of Deputies to grant him "exceptional powers required by circumstances," his request was refused. The Senate refused to approve the J. G. White contract (see p. 63) and the contract for the purchase of the National Bank. Vincent had recourse to a popular referendum, which voted him the authorization to carry out "any measures of an economic character aimed at improving the general situation of the country." He then ejected from the Senate 11 senators who had refused to be bound by the results of the referendum, which they claimed was unconstitutional.

In 1935 the President submitted for popular ratification a new Constitution under which the legislative and judicial branches of the government were made clearly subordinate to the executive. The President was given the right to dissolve the legislature and to pass "decree-laws" between legislative sessions with the aid of a committee of six deputies and five senators approved by himself. He also acquired the right to appoint 10 of the 21 senators and to submit to the Chamber of Deputies a list of candidates from which the chamber was to elect the remaining 11 senators. The new Constitution, after lauding the accomplishments of Sténio Vincent, proclaimed him President for a new term of five years, while laying down a general prohibition of any third presidential term. The new Constitution was duly ratified by the compliant masses.

In July 1938 the J. G. White Engineering Corporation, an American company, was awarded a Haitian government contract for $5 million worth of public works, for which financing was supplied by the Export-Import Bank of Washington. This three-year program included drainage works, irrigation, agricultural extension, and road construction.

Relations between Haiti and the neighboring Dominican Republic were usually friendly during Vincent's first years as President, and the Dominican dictator, Trujillo, paid a cordial visit to Port-au-Prince. What, however, was the surprise of all Haitians a year and a half later to hear that thousands of Haitian workers in the cane fields of the Dominican Republic had been slaughtered, under circumstances clearly pointing to Dominican government instigation. There was considerable dissatisfaction in Haiti with the lack of vigor shown by their President in forcing the Dominicans to make honorable amends for this crime. It was only four months later that the Trujillo government expressed its regret and offered an indemnity of $750,000. Of this sum, only about two-thirds was ever paid. The first installment, of $250,000, was used for the creation of agricultural settlements for the refugee families who had escaped from the neighboring republic.

It was commonly believed that Vincent wished to have a third term as President, despite his denial and the constitutional prohibition. His followers campaigned in favor of a third term, and the legislature passed a joint resolution urging that he accept a third term after submitting the matter to a popular referendum. On the other hand, it was also believed that Washington had intimated its displeasure to Vincent. In the end the President designated as his successor a mulatto friend, Elie Lescot, whom in April 1941 the legislature elected by 56 out of 58 votes, for a five-year term. Elie Lescot had been a judge, a Minister of the Interior, and Minister Plenipotentiary in the Dominican Republic and the United States.

In September 1941 a Haitian-American agreement terminated the services of the Fiscal Representative and assigned his duties to the Fiscal Department of the BNRH. It was also provided that three of the six directors of the bank should be Americans.

At about the same time, agreement was reached on the creation of a Haitian-American Company for Agricultural Development, or Société Haitiano-Américaine de Développement Agricole (SHADA). The Export-Import Bank of Washington opened a credit of $5 million for this enterprise, which it was hoped would soon be in position to supply rubber and other products in the event that the United States was cut off from its Far Eastern sources of supply.

SHADA had as its object the development and exploitation of the agricultural and other resources of the republic by: (1) planting and promoting the cultivation of rubber, oil plants, spices, fibers, medicinal and food plants, forest products, and other agricultural resources; (2) experiments with a view to improving existing crops, combating or preventing plant diseases and determining the possibilities of adapting certain growths to Haiti; (3) the development of methods of preparing and processing commodities and likewise the development of industries and agricultural artisans; (4) the purchase and marketing (domestic and foreign) of the agricultural and manufactured products of Haiti.

In exchange for the issue by SHADA of 10,000 shares of $100 par-value common stock in favor of the state, the Haitian government awarded the company, for a period of 50 years, the exclusive privilege of buying and exporting all the natural rubber cultivated and produced in the Republic. It also leased to the company for 50 years 150,000 acres of land planted with trees capable of producing construction timber, with the exclusive privilege of cutting such timber and otherwise exploiting the leased lands. Both the President and the General Manager of SHADA were Americans appointed by the Export-Import Bank, to whom the common stock was pledged as collateral for the $5-million loan.

SHADA undertook as its principal aim the production of rubber from an indigenous latex plant, the cryptostegia. By September 30, 1943, it had spent $4.2 million in this undertaking. The program had looked like madness to those who knew agricultural conditions in Haiti. They had recommended instead an intensive development of food plants. Nevertheless, the government had ostentatiously endorsed the costly program, permitting SHADA to expropriate peasants, to destroy their homes, to devastate their fields, and to chop down their fruit trees, wherever it established itself. The report of a Haitian agronomist on these expropriations and depredations circulated secretly and made a painful impression on the public, especially since, after all the fuss made about the program in the American press, not a single ton of rubber was exported. Millions of dollars had simply gone down the drain. When SHADA was finally forced to abandon its rubber project, the government tried to obtain compensation for the damages done to the rural properties, but without success.[1]

As the J. G. White Engineering Corporation had used up most of its $5-million credit, a new contract was signed with the Export-Import Bank in September 1941 under which an additional $500,000 became available. In June 1942 completion of the public-works program was entrusted to SHADA.

The Lescot government established a minimum wage; created a Social Security Fund; made some provision for workers' housing; created the University of Haiti; tried to alleviate the shortage of rural doctors by requiring graduates of the Faculty of Medicine to serve two years in the rural districts at the beginning of their careers; set up an Ethnological Institute, an Art Center, and a Superior Normal School; arranged with the Congregation of Oblat Missionaries of Canada to carry out educational work in Haiti; and signed an agreement with the Interamerican Education Foundation of Washington for a program of intellectual and professional cooperation in Haiti.

But, as in the case of Vincent, Lescot's contributions to economic and social progress were more than offset by the harmful effects of political dissension. Lescot was extremely sensitive to any criticism:

> For every measure adopted . . . Elie Lescot claimed the full responsibility, considering as an infringement of his authority the slightest criticism of a ministerial or administrative act, whatever its nature. He fired officials who had dared, even in matters

unrelated to politics, to express an opinion considered not in conformity with the views of the government. He deprived of the legislative mandate a deputy who had read from the tribune a draft Resolution which he claimed to be "an infringement of the national sovereignty" and replaced him by another person of his own choice. He sent journalists to jail and allowed them to languish there for long months without trial, as "prisoners of the State," and he turned over to courts-martial, at his own discretion, people who were simply suspected of plotting against public safety, or common law prisoners, who thus saw themselves deprived of the protection of impartial justice.[2]

Upon hearing the news of Pearl Harbor, Lescot immediately sought and obtained from the legislature authorization to declare war on Japan and Germany and their allies. Haiti thus declared war on December 8, the day after Pearl Harbor. At the same time, a state of siege was declared and all the nation's activities were declared subject to the control of the military authorities, "under the supreme direction of the President of the Republic." Enemy property was taken over, and business establishments owned by enemy subjects were liquidated. Shortly afterward the President obtained power to decree whatever measures the circumstances might require, and constitutional guaranties were suspended for the duration of the war. Other similar measures followed, until Lescot had in his hands absolute power to act by himself in every field. Finally, the rubber-stamp legislature presented Lescot with a new Constitution, in which he was granted a new term of office of seven years, and all elections were postponed until one year after the signing of peace treaties following the end of the war.

The end of the Lescot dictatorship came when the President ordered the incarceration of two young journalists who had simply written of their hatred of despotism (without naming Lescot) and asked that the Atlantic Charter be made applicable to Haiti. A strike by the pupils of a private school spread like wildfire to other schools and then to the community in general.[3] The cabinet resigned, and the next day (January 11, 1946) Lescot was taken into protective custody by an Executive Military Committee of three army officers, which temporarily assumed power.

Following the election of a new legislature with the powers

of a constituent assembly, Dumarsais Estimé, a full-blooded Negro, was voted into the presidency on the basis of the democratic Constitution of 1932. Shortly afterward a new Constitution was drafted and approved. Estimé had been a member of the Chamber of Deputies and had served as Minister of Education and of Agriculture. As President he was granted a term of office of five years, and was ineligible for immediate re-election.

Early in the Estimé administration, a "Goodwill Mission" was sent to the United States in the hope of eliciting prompt financial assistance for a program of economic development. As the desired assistance was not forthcoming, it was decided to issue an internal loan. Bonds of the 1922-23 loans still outstanding amounted to only about $5 million, and it was felt that the time had come to liberate Haiti from its financial bondage to foreigners by paying off these bonds out of the proceeds of the new internal loan, which was labeled the Loan of Financial Liberation. The government and the BNRH both had ample cash reserves which could be used, in part, for subscriptions to the new loan. Thus, in July 1947, a law was voted authorizing a 10-year 5 per cent internal loan in an amount up to $10 million, with a first charge on all government revenue. By the end of the fiscal year 1948, $7.6 million of bonds had been issued, of which, however, nearly $5 million was in exchange for bonds of the 1922-23 loans. Net proceeds of only $2,642,000 became available for the financing of economic development. Most of this money appears to have been used for projects of dubious classification, such as the construction and equipment of an international exposition to celebrate the 200th anniversary of the founding of Port-au-Prince and the building of a model but needlessly expensive town (Belladère) on the Dominican border.

The law authorizing the Loan of Financial Liberation also changed the composition of the board of directors of the BNRH, which was henceforth to consist of five Haitian directors instead of three Haitians and three Americans. The function of the bank's Fiscal Department was no longer to control the government's finances, but to perform only administrative duties related thereto.

The Estimé administration took two important steps forward

in fields of critical significance to Haiti—education and health. In 1947 it invited UNESCO (the U.N. Educational, Scientific, and Cultural Organization) to set up a pilot project of fundamental education. After a preliminary six-month survey, a detailed plan was worked out, and the pilot project began operations in 1949. It was located in one of the most poverty-stricken areas of Haiti—the Marbial Valley, on the south coast. Its purpose was, in the words of UNESCO, "to raise the social and economic level of the community and to train up Haitian staff so that it may become self-supporting as rapidly as possible by the withdrawal of non-Haitian personnel."[4] The program comprised: (a) primary and adult schooling; (b) literacy teaching in the Creole language, followed by French; (c) health education and medical services; (d) agricultural and veterinary education and extension work; (e) community cultural activities; and (f) establishment of small rural crafts and industries, and of producer and consumer cooperatives. Begun as a joint UNESCO-Haitian government undertaking at an initial annual cost of less than $50,000, the project later became the exclusive responsibility of the government. While the project was unquestionably beneficial, its results fell far short of the ambitious objectives, for reasons which will be discussed in Chapter 11.

In the matter of health, the Estimé administration agreed early in 1950 with the World Health Organization (WHO) through its regional office, the Pan American Sanitary Bureau, and with UNICEF (the U.N. International Children's Emergency Fund) on a joint program for the complete eradication of yaws, the high incidence of which in Haiti was one of the causes of the people's low productive capacity. Execution of this program began several months later, when Estimé was no longer President. After careful advance indoctrination, penicillin injections were given to all rural victims of the disease by two-man field units moving from place to place. Checks were later made in order to catch cases of relapse or new infection, and peasants were taught what precautions to take to avoid further contagion. The program was received enthusiastically by the peasant population and was pronounced highly successful.

Another important development during the Estimé administration was an invitation to the United Nations to send a mission to Haiti for the purpose of surveying the economy and recommending measures for economic and social improvement. In October 1948 a mission headed by Ansgar Rosenborg arrived in Haiti. It included, in addition to six U.N. experts, three technicians from the FAO (Food and Agriculture Organization), and one technician each from the IMF (International Monetary Fund), UNESCO, and WHO. The mission's report, published in 1949, made numerous recommendations, of which the major ones may be briefly summarized as follows:

1. Establishment of an independent advisory development and planning board
2. Improvement of the civil service through reform of laws, regulations, practices, and administrative arrangements
3. Measures to encourage local initiative and self-help
4. Preparation of a master plan for road improvement and construction
5. Organization of a coastal small-boat transportation service
6. Study of possibility of encouraging emigration as a means of relieving population pressure
7. Collection, preparation, and publication by the government of complete and accurate statistics[5]

In addition to the above major recommendations, the mission submitted a great number of specific recommendations in the fields of agricultural development, fisheries, industrial development, education, public health, money and credit, and public finance.

This was a rather overwhelming set of recommendations for poor little Haiti, which obviously could not carry them into effect without foreign assistance. The report, however, called attention to the possibility of invoking U.N. technical assistance on a long-term basis. In due course the Estimé government did request such assistance, and the United Nations sent to Haiti a Resident Representative, A. J. Wakefield, for the purpose of organizing and administering a technical-assistance office, to which specialists from the United Nations and its economic and social affiliates were to be assigned. By the time of the Resident Representative's arrival Estimé was no longer President, but the succeeding (Magloire) administration agreed to the carrying out of the U.N. program.

In July 1949 the Estimé government signed an agreement with the Export-Import Bank of Washington for the partial financing of a program of irrigation, flood control, agricultural development, and road-building in the Artibonite Valley. The cost of the program was estimated at about $6 million, of which $4 million was to be supplied by the Export-Import Bank.

Also in 1949, a law was enacted granting partial tax exemptions for new industries established in Haiti. Any industry of a new type was granted exemption during its first year from all customs duties and from 50 per cent of the income and occupational taxes. Thereafter, for four more years, it would enjoy full customs exemption and a 20 per cent exemption from occupational taxes. Industries which were new, but not the first of their kind in Haiti, were granted more limited exemptions. A separate law granted certain tax exemptions as an encouragement to the construction or expansion of modern hotels.

Once more the progress in economic matters was overshadowed by the political developments. Just as the Artibonite Valley agreement was being signed in Washington, the Haitian legislature voted in favor of a constitutional amendment which would remove the time limitation on Estimé's mandate as President. When this action gave rise to popular disturbances, the President dissolved three political parties and shut down their newspapers. Following new elections, the Senate refused to approve the proposed amendment. A mob, apparently led by government employees, then invaded and sacked the Senate and threatened the senators with death. President Estimé published a message to the people in which he supported the action of the mob. At this point the army again intervened. Estimé was taken into protective custody, and the triumvirate which had temporarily assumed power after Lescot now again set up a provisional régime, called the Government Junta.

The Government Junta dissolved the legislature and called new popular elections for the two houses and, for the first time in Haitian history, for the office of President. The most popular member of the junta, Colonel Paul E. Magloire, resigned to become a candidate for the presidency and was elected by a well-nigh unanimous vote. Under a new Constitution the presidential mandate was fixed at six years, but in the case of Magloire, whose term of office began on December 6, 1950, the expiration of the mandate was fixed for May 15, 1957.

Since the departure of the U.S. marines in 1934, Haiti had been governed successively by three Presidents, two of them mulattoes, the other a full-blooded Negro. Only the first of these (Vincent) had completed the term of office for which he had been elected. All three had shown dictatorial tendencies. On the other hand, it was popular resistance to their dictatorial tendencies which prevented their indefinite continuance in office. In the absence of such popular resistance, it may be doubted that the army would have intervened to oust Lescot and Estimé. The election of Magloire appears to have been a genuinely democratic manifestation and therefore a good augury for Haiti's political future. Unfortunately, and despite obvious efforts by the Magloire administration to maintain racial and class harmony and teamwork, the favorable prospects of December 1950 were to dissolve six years later in chaos.

# □□□ 7
# Progress and Collapse (1950-57)

With the election of Paul E. Magloire, a full-blooded Negro, as President, Haiti entered its most active period of economic and social development, based on three main supports: (1) the technical and financial assistance given by the American Point Four program; (2) the technical assistance provided by the United

Nations and its specialized agencies; and (3) the projects planned and financed by the Haitian government itself, partly under what was called the Plan Quinquennal (Five-Year Plan).

The U.S. government had been giving Haiti technical and financial assistance on a limited scale since the early part of World War II, as part of the activities of the Office of Interamerican Affairs. After the war these activities were continued by the Institute of Interamerican Affairs, which later became an arm of the Point Four program. The IIAA operated on the basis of bilateral agreements with the various Latin American governments, upon their request. As described in an IIAA leaflet,

> A simple, easily directed type of organization is maintained by the Institute. In each cooperating country, the appropriate ministry sets up a special *servicio* or bureau within its department. The director of this bureau is generally a citizen of the United States, and serves as chief of the "field party" working in all the projects of that division. U.S. experts are assigned to him by the Institute. The local government supplies all other technicians, field men and workers.[1]

According to the same source, about two-thirds of the cost of this aid was borne by IIAA and the rest by the recipient country. If the salaries of the U.S. technicians are excluded, however, the recipient country's share of cost is several times the U.S. share.[2]

In Haiti the IIAA's assistance was given mainly through two *servicios,* known as SCIPA (Service Coopératif Interaméricain de Production d'Aliments) and SCISP (Service Coopératif Interaméricain de Santé Publique). SCIPA was concerned with such things as the development of a more adequate food supply, the introduction of better crops, improved livestock, soil and water conservation, farm-extension work, better tools and methods of cultivation, and the compilation of basic agricultural statistics. SCISP busied itself with the operation of health centers, dispensaries, clinics, and mobile units; campaigns against specific diseases (yaws, malaria); improvement of water-supply systems; etc. During 1944–47 the Inter-American Educational Foundation, a division of the Office of Interamerican Affairs, cooperated with the Haitian government in an educational *servicio* by supplying specialists, awarding training grants, developing visual and other teaching materials, etc. In 1954 a new *servicio,* SCHAER (Service Coopératif Haitiano-Américain d'Education Rurale), was launched. (Its activities are described on p. 139.)

United States help was also given to Haiti in the form of a geodetic survey. In 1953 a series of detailed topographic maps covering 65 per cent of the country was issued. In 1958 the first of a new series of more accurate maps was completed. Such maps are essential in the planning of land-use and irrigation projects, as well as for the accurate registration of property titles.

The United Nations aid program to Haiti operated through the office of a U.N. Resident Representative in Port-au-Prince and the assignment of experts, usually on one-year contracts (in many cases renewed) in special fields jointly agreed upon with the Haitian government. The number of these experts usually fluctuated between ten and twenty. Each expert was exclusively responsible for the quality and content of his work in Haiti. The Resident Representative, in addition to carrying on all necessary negotiations with the government and representing the United Nations in a diplomatic capacity, maintained liaison and, to the extent possible, coordination between the work of the various experts.

During the six years of the Magloire government, the United Nations supplied experts for periods of time varying from a few weeks to several years, in the following fields:

| | |
|---|---|
| Basic education | Salt-water fishing |
| Audio-visual work | Forestry |
| Statistics | Rural industries |
| Monetary and fiscal problems | Electric light and power |
| Economic problems | Vocational education |
| Community development | Hotel work |
| Crop surveys | Domestic economy |
| Agricultural extension | Nutrition |
| Agricultural credit | Civil aviation |
| Poultry raising | Eradication of disease |
| Livestock raising | (yaws, malaria) |
| Fish culture | Social welfare |

The experts under this program were sent in some cases by the United Nations itself; in other cases by its specialized agencies, such as ILO (International Labor Office), UNESCO, FAO, WHO, and UNICEF. They were of many nationalities, with French nationals usually predominating.

Both IIAA and the United Nations supplied annually a number of fellowships and scholarships which enabled promising young Haitians to study or get specialized training in the United States and other foreign countries.

At the beginning of his administration, President Magloire announced his Plan Quinquennal, entailing the expenditure of $40 million for basic investments, as follows:

| *Public health* | | *(millions of dollars)* |
|---|---|---|
| Urban organization | 3.6 | |
| Rural division | 0.4 | |
| Sanitary works | 1.0 | 5.0 |
| | | |
| *Public works* | | |
| Asphalting main road | 8.1 | |
| Secondary roads | 2.0 | |
| Urban improvements | 6.4 | 16.5 |
| | | |
| *National education* | | |
| Primary | 3.8 | |
| Secondary | 0.8 | |
| Other | 0.4 | 5.0 |
| | | |
| *Agriculture* | | |
| Promotion of coffee, sisal, cotton, and cacao production | 2.4 | |
| Soil conservation and reafforestation | 1.5 | |
| Irrigation | 1.4 | |
| Drainage and flood control | 1.0 | |
| Organization of rural centers, demonstration farms, etc. | 0.8 | |
| Other | 1.4 | 8.5 |
| | | |
| *Unspecified* | | 5.0 |
| | *Total:* | 40.0 |

This was not a plan in the scientific sense of a set of priorities, time limits, and sources of financing for individual items, although efforts were made to complete the road-improvement program during the first three years. An *exposé des motifs* showing the relative need or desirability of the various items and how the amount for each had been determined was not made public, nor was a detailed breakdown of each item revealed. Furthermore, the Plan Quinquennal was not comprehensive, in that it did not include the Artibonite undertaking and several other projects. Nevertheless, it was a milepost of progress on the part of a government which before the Magloire administration could make no pretense of a well-rounded program of development.

During the first two years of the Five-Year Plan, expenditures were financed mainly out of revenues collected in excess of current budget estimates. However, most of the road work was financed by installment-type contracts signed with a variety of foreign engineering firms. For example, two stretches of the highway between Port-au-Prince and Cap-Haitien were paved by an American firm in Havana, the Compañía de Industrias Marítimas, under a $3-million contract payable in one-year notes of the Haitian government maturing at the rate of $200,000 monthly. These notes, endorsed by the BNRH, were discounted with a New York bank as specified stages of the road work were completed. Similarly, a $7-million road contract with a French company, the Société des Grands Travaux de Marseille, was financed by a combination of notes and monthly cash payments. In general, the method of financing contracts under the Plan Quinquennal was unnecessarily complicated, entailed excessively short-term maturities and failed to provide appropriate guarantees against faulty work and corruption of government officials.

In fiscal 1953 the government's revenues fell as a result of a short coffee crop and a decline in sisal prices, making it necessary to slow down parts of the plan, despite some moderate borrowing from the BNRH.

An engineering survey of the Artibonite irrigation and flood-control project revealed that the original plans were impracticable, that an extensive reservoir dam would have to be built, and that watershed protection and an underground drainage system in the lower reaches of the valley were essential to success of the program. Instead of $6 million, the total cost of the program was now estimated at about $21 million. The Export-Import Bank agreed to increase its share of the financing from $4 million to $14 million, provided the Haitian government covered the remaining cost by means of annual appropriations of between $1.5 million and $2.5 million. The bank's advances were to be repaid over an 18-year period beginning in 1956. A new agreement was signed on this revised basis. An autonomous body, the Organisation de Développement de la Vallée de l'Artibonite (ODVA), had meanwhile been set up to administer the project, with technical assistance from the Point Four organization (then called the ICA).

In September 1951, in order to fill a vacuum in domestic credit facilities, legislation was approved creating IHCAI, the Haitian Institute of Agricultural and Industrial Credit, jointly owned by the government and the BNRH. The new bank opened for business in February 1952 with an authorized capital of $2 million, of which one-half was paid in. By way of supplementing this capital, the law required certain exporters to use a small percentage of their export proceeds for subscriptions to 4 per cent non-negotiable bonds which IHCAI was authorized to issue (up to a maximum of $10 million). In September 1952 the authorized capital was increased to $5 million. The institute operated under the supervision of the Board of Directors of the BNRH. Credits could be granted only after inspection of the borrower's property and subject to continuing guidance and supervision of the borrower's affairs by the technicians of IHCAI. In view of the diminutive size of Haitian farms and the lack of creditworthiness of most farmers, a special department was charged with stimulating the creation of agricultural cooperatives, for which preferential loan terms were made available. By the end of 1954, IHCAI had loans and investments outstanding in a total amount of $2.1 million.

In 1953 a comprehensive law governing the creation, functioning, and supervision of production and credit cooperatives was passed. By the end of 1954 the number of cooperatives in Haiti had grown from a mere handful to about 60.

To facilitate the planning and execution of economic development, the Haitian government set up in 1951 the Haitian Institute of Statistics, which began to collect, analyze and publish statistics covering the main features of the country's economic activity. The only statistics regularly available had been those relating to foreign trade and government finances.

Although Haiti had been one of the countries represented at the 1944 Bretton Woods Conference, where the International Monetary Fund and the International Bank for Reconstruction and Development were born, it had not exercised its right to be a charter member of these two institutions. The government reconsidered the situation in 1951 and applied for membership. Both institutions approved the application, with a subscription of $2 million to each.

At the request of President Magloire, the U.N. Monetary and Fiscal Expert drew up a plan of monetary and banking reform under which the BNRH could act as a central bank and the gourde would become the sole legal-tender currency in Haiti. Although since 1919 the BNRH had been issuing gourde notes redeemable in dollars, it had conducted its business like any commercial bank, with no conception of the role which central banks play in modern economies. However, despite the fact that the reform had been drawn up at his own request, President Magloire never got around to having it enacted into law.

In 1952, SHADA (see p. 64) was Haitianized by agreement with the Export-Import Bank. The latter's holding of shares was cancelled, and the American directors retired from the board. Since SHADA was unable to repay the outstanding $3,875,000 balance of the original $5-million loan, which matured in May 1952, a new schedule of low-interest payments was worked out, under which the debt would be amortized over a 15-year period. The Haitian government guaranteed the payment by SHADA, which was now placed under the control of the Board of Directors of the National Bank. In view of the slump in sisal prices, sisal production was temporarily suspended, while SHADA's rubber and forestry operations continued.

In June 1953 a new, temporary coffee export tax was enacted in order to stem the decline in revenues resulting from the drop in value of exports that had taken place, and to permit of additional development expenditures. The law provided that the proceeds of the new tax must be paid into a special earmarked account at the BNRH and could be used only for the following purposes and in the amounts specified:

|  | | *Gourdes* |
|---|---|---|
| 1. | Repayment of the bank's temporary advances to the government | 5,000,000 |
| 2. | Increase in capital of IHCAI | 1,500,000 |
| 3. | Financing of public works at Gonaives for the 150th Anniversary Celebration of National Independence | 3,000,000 |
| 4. | Aid to coffee plantations | 1,000,000 |
| 5. | Renewal of sisal plantations of SHADA | 1,000,000 |
| 6. | Development of banana farming | 1,000,000 |
|  | *Total* | 12,500,000 |

'The law further authorized the issuance of up to 12 million gourdes of 3½ per cent Treasury tax-anticipation notes, maturing in six or nine months, which made possible the financing of the above items before the proceeds of the tax were fully available. The notes in question were sold to two American banks and were paid off well in advance of maturity.

The proceeds of the new coffee tax totaled (in fiscal 1954) more than 23 million gourdes.

In the summer of 1953 the Haitian Finance Minister, Dr. Lucien Hibbert, discussed with a U.S. engineering firm, the Utah Construction Company, the possibility of a program of varied development projects in Haiti, to be financed by a dollar bond issue in the American market. Upon sounding out the banks which had bought the above-mentioned tax-anticipation notes, he found they would be interested, in principle, in floating such a loan. The banks sent representatives to Haiti to negotiate the terms for an issue of $24 million of dollar bonds, of which $4 million would be used to pay off the outstanding bonds of the 1947 internal loan and the remainder to finance the following projects:

1. Modernization and extension of the electric power and light plants at Port-au-Prince and Cap Haitien
2. Modernization of the telephone and telegraph service
3. Construction of a new and larger international airport at Port-au-Prince
4. New port facilities at Port-au-Prince
5. Paving and improvement of certain roads
6. Construction and equipment of a 200-bed hospital at Port-au-Prince
7. Construction of modern beach facilities for tourists
8. Preliminary plans for water-supply works in various towns
9. Preliminary plans for an electric-power network throughout the country

It will be noted that most of these projects differed in character and purpose from those put forth in the Plan Quinquennal. None of them dealt directly with agriculture. They were intended, in the main, to give Haiti the facilities and equipment of a modern country, partly with a view to stimulating the growth of tourism. The number of tourists visiting Haiti for the past three years had been growing rapidly, and receipts from tourism had exceeded the amount earned from any one export except coffee.[3] However, it was believed that Haiti could attract much greater numbers of tourists and that they would remain for longer periods of time if the country could offer the modern comfort and variety of such resorts as Puerto Rico, Cuba, and Mexico.

Tentative contracts were signed with both the Utah Construction Company and the bankers, and final arrangements were on the point of being concluded, when a surprising thing happened. The Minister of Labor, Clément Jumelle, had been opposed to the program, arguing that tourism brought few if any benefits to Haiti and that what was needed was greater help to agriculture. As the most influential member of the cabinet, Jumelle was able to persuade the President that the Hibbert program was a mistake. Thus there was a cabinet shakeup, and in the new cabinet Jumelle emerged as Minister of Finance and of Economic Affairs. Shortly afterward a law was approved authorizing the issuance of a $13-million internal loan, $3 million of which would be offered in exchange for outstanding bonds of the 1947 loan, $5 million would be bought by the BNRH, and $5 million would be used as collateral for a loan from a large American bank. The projects to be financed under the new program, as well as their priority, were to be determined by a committee of technicians after consultation with the BNRH. However, a preliminary list submitted to the President by Minister Jumelle included, in addition to all the projects contained in the Hibbert program, some eight or ten irrigation projects, a low-cost housing project, a military hospital, a University City, a "Military City," and a police headquarters building.

Meanwhile, a "get-acquainted" mission of the International Bank had visited Haiti and begun to survey existing possibilities for creditworthy projects. The Haitian government submitted to this and subsequent missions of the International Bank four projects for which financing would be welcome. The bank finally agreed in principle to a gradual program of road financing, with the admonition that Haiti should refrain from further short- and medium-term contracts with suppliers. An Italian engineering firm, Techint, was employed at the bank's suggestion to make a detailed road survey and recommend priorities. Techint recommended as the first priority the expenditure of $3,980,000 for a road-maintenance department and the training of its personnel, following which the paving or reconditioning of about 700 miles of roads in various parts of the country should be undertaken. In May 1956 the International Bank made Haiti a 10-year 4½ per cent loan of $2,600,000 to cover the dollar portion of the initial cost of this program.

In 1954 the Magloire government spent substantial sums on what was called the Tricinquantenaire—a festival celebrating the 150th anniversary of Haitian independence. Although this festival may have been justified as a means of stimulating patriotism and the national desire for progress, it could hardly be classified as a "development project"—a term which was nevertheless applied to it. The project involved extensive rebuilding of the town of Gonaives (including a cathedral, housing facilities, beautification of public squares, etc., and the re-enactment of the last battle of the Haitian revolution.

As mentioned above (p. 76), the cost of the enlarged Artibonite project had been estimated by the engineers in 1951 at $21 million, of which the Export-Import Bank agreed to lend $14 million. By March 1955 it had become clear that the actual cost would be greatly in excess of $21 million. On the basis of a revised estimate of $30 million, the Export-Import Bank raised its loan to $21 million, at the same time extending the period of loan amortization from 18 years to 22. A year later, however, even the $30-million cost estimate was found to be too low. In order to help cover the excess cost, the ICA made a grant of $2 million to Haiti, and the Export-Import Bank opened a further credit of $6 million, reduced the interest rate on the whole operation to 3½ per cent[4] and extended the amortization period to 25 years. Since the beginning of work on the Artibonite project, the Haitian government had itself spent some $10 million.

After the great improvement which the government achieved in its finances following the slump of 1952, a severe setback occurred in October 1954 in the form of Hurricane Hazel, which caused hundreds of deaths, destroyed or damaged many thousands of homes, destroyed much of the current coffee harvest, reduced large segments of the population to near starvation and led to a sharp drop in exports, imports, and fiscal revenues. The silver lining to this frightfully dark cloud was that the U.S. government, which had been giving only token financial aid to Haiti, suddenly opened its wallet to show its concern for Haitian well-being (see p. 247).

Under the concession granted in 1935 to the Standard Fruit and Steamship Company (see p. 61) and concessions subsequently granted to two Haitian companies, Habanex and Hafrusco, exports of bananas had increased rapidly and steadily until the fiscal year 1946-47, when they totaled $6.1 million, making bananas the second most valuable export commodity. In 1947, however, the Estimé government passed a law under which the state assumed the monopoly of banana exploitation and the right to grant banana concessions to anyone it chose, as well as the right of rigid supervision and control of such concessions. At the same time, Habanex was shut down and its director jailed because of alleged monopolistic practices. Some of the new concessions were granted to Haitian businessmen and politicians, who made arrangements with various small traders in the United States to market their product. Meanwhile Standard Fruit began contracting its own operations, and finally it pulled out of Haiti altogether. The new system proved a total failure, and Haiti's exports of bananas declined as rapidly and steadily as they had risen, until in fiscal 1952 they amounted to only $500,000. Thereupon the Magloire government reconstituted the Habanex company, gave it a monopoly, and invested $550,000 of public funds in the enterprise. The production and exportation of bananas was gradually turning upward again, when Hurricane Hazel destroyed many of the banana groves and seriously disrupted the program. The Haitian Institute of Agricultural and Industrial Credit then took charge of the program, granting credits for rehabilitation and extension of producing areas. It was the aim of IHCAI to raise the annual volume of banana exports to 12 million stems by or before fiscal 1965, compared with the 7.3 million stems exported in fiscal 1947.

An essential part of the government's development efforts was the fostering of new private industries, both Haitian and foreign. In 1955, therefore, the tax privileges which had been granted by the Estimé government in 1949 were somewhat liberalized. By the end of the Magloire administration, a considerable variety of industrial enterprises had been set up. Among the larger ones were a French cement plant, a flour mill owned by the Murchison interests, and a bauxite-mining plant owned by the Reynolds Metals Company. Several dozen smaller enterprises were also set up during this period (see pp. 207-08). Hotel facilities were expanded through financing by the Agricultural and Industrial Credit Institute. By placing land and housing facilities at the disposal of an American philanthropist, Dr. Larimer

Mellon, the government encouraged him to build a modern hospital in the Artibonite Valley for the treatment, at little or no cost, of the countless illnesses of the peasant population of the valley.

Throughout the Magloire administration, successive Resident Representatives of the United Nations urged upon the government the desirability of a central planning bureau in order to avoid confusion, overlapping, and waste in the efforts toward economic and social development. In 1953 a small planning section was set up within the Ministry of Economics, but it was only meagerly staffed, with men who had no special qualifications for such work. It was not until the middle of 1956 that a serious effort was made to organize an efficient planning bureau. By that time it was generally expected by partisans of Magloire that he would be succeeded as President by Clément Jumelle, then Minister of Finance and Economic Affairs, and it was Jumelle who took the initiative of forming a Planning Commission made up of Haitian and foreign technicians borrowed from the various departments and agencies of the government and from the local offices of the United Nations and the ICA (see pp. 253-54). The Haitian members of the commission had just been appointed and two U.N. experts assigned as advisers to the commission, when political events caused the postponement of further action.

As so often happens in Haiti, the approaching end of the President's term of office was characterized by political tension and fears. The air was full of charges of corruption, and it was alleged that Magloire was planning to remain in office for at least a second term. The outs claimed that Magloire's term of office ended December 6 (despite the clear statement in the 1950 Constitution that "The President of the Republic, citizen Paul E. Magloire, elected on October 8, 1950, will begin his functions on December 6, 1950 and his term shall end on May 15, 1957"). On December 4 and 5 several bombs exploded in crowded areas of Port-au-Prince, causing a general panic and the closing of all shops. No one knew who had planted the bombs, but some persons now believe that followers of Dr. François Duvalier, a presidential aspirant, may have been the guilty parties.[5] The

Police Department ordered all civilians possessing firearms to turn them in and prohibited further electioneering, whether through groups or by radio. To appease his critics, Magloire resigned as President on December 6, but he was immediately asked by the army to remain as "Provisional Executive Head" and Commander-in-Chief. This was taken by the outs to be a clever ruse to stay in power, and a wave of street riots began, primarily on the initiative of adherents of Duvalier. Businesses remained closed, either because they favored the candidacy of Senator Louis Déjoie, a prominent businessman, or because they feared damage and looting. The strike of businessmen and their employees spread to the rest of the city, including some government offices. Finally, with elements of the army deserting him, Magloire flew into exile in nearby Jamaica.[6]

Under Paul Magloire, Haiti had made slow but sure progress in the difficult task of economic and social development—a task which most previous Presidents had been unwilling or unable to undertake, or which it had not even occurred to them to undertake. Corruption there had been in his administration, notably on the part of the Chief of Police. To hope for a Haitian government completely free from corruption is probably wishful thinking. If the Magloire administration shines by contrast with preceding and subsequent administrations, it is not by reason of an absence of corruption but because of its freedom from class and racial prejudice and its comprehension of the urgency of economic and social development. Indeed, the main mistake of Magloire may have been that development was pushed too hard, too fast, beyond the financial capacity of his country.[7] Mistakes were also made in the choice of projects and the determination of their priorities. Both types of mistakes could have been largely avoided had a competent planning bureau been set up at the outset, and it is to the credit of Clément Jumelle that even as he prepared himself to become Magloire's successor as President, he recognized the need for careful planning from the start. Unfortunately, as we shall now see, Jumelle was destined to be, not President but a tragic victim of fate.

The fall of Magloire was followed by ten months of political and economic chaos, during which the executive power was held successively by five individuals or groups, as follows:

| | |
|---|---|
| Joseph Pierre-Louis | Dec. 12, 1956-Feb. 4, 1957 |
| Franck Sylvain | Feb. 7, 1957-Apr. 1, 1957 |
| Executive Council | Apr. 6, 1957-May 25, 1957 |
| Pierre E. Fignolé | May 26, 1957-June 14, 1957 |
| Military Government Council | June 14, 1957-Oct. 22, 1957 |

This period was filled with dissension, sporadic strikes, riots, looting, arson, and occasional shooting. During much of the time business concerns, the banks, the customhouse and other government offices were unable to function. The following excerpt from a Port-au-Prince newspaper graphically describes the deterioration of political and economic conditions:

> What matters is the continued life of the country, the maintenance of family security, an end to this daily growing alarm which gives each of us the impression of living in a nightmare. This nightmare has lasted only too long. Fed by the chiromancers of politics, it seems that it will destroy common sense. . . . For more than five months we have been living a nightmare. The economic life of the nation has slowed down; exports are a haphazard affair; imports have declined dangerously. Import agents are becoming excessively cautious; ships no longer stop at our ports; arrivals are more and more infrequent; there is a shortage of essential products on the market; the customs administration has slowed down; the tax service is slower and slower; drafts are delayed in payment; sales have fallen off; personal credit is at its lowest point; bank credit does not exist; foodstuffs have had an exaggerated price increase; all consumer goods, such as soap, flour, must be paid for at high prices; this skyrocketing of the cost of living entails the threat of a black market.[8]

Matters were made even worse by an unusually small coffee crop and by the fact that most of the staff of the National Bank were on strike during the first three months of 1957, after accusing the top officers of the bank of violating professional ethics, if not the law, by lending large amounts on an unsecured basis to a sugar-mill company in which the bank's president was an important shareholder. This dispute ended by the government's forcing the resignation of not only the top officers but the whole Board of Directors of the bank.

On September 22, 1957, popular elections were finally held, with only two candidates still in the field: Senator Déjoie (a mulatto) and Dr. Duvalier (a black). On the eve of the election a third candidate, Clément Jumelle (also a black) withdrew, stating that he did not wish to give the election an appearance of legality when in fact the army, by intimidation and coercion, was ensuring victory for Duvalier. The army's partiality to Duvalier had previously and repeatedly been criticized by Senator Déjoie. The reason for that partiality appears to have been the mistaken belief that the apparently mild little country doctor could be more easily controlled than could either Déjoie or Jumelle. Whatever the reason for the army's misplaced favoritism, the election did result in a Duvalier victory. Moreover, in the legislative election Duvalier's adherents won all of the Senate seats and two-thirds of the Chamber of Deputies. Many business houses remained shut by way of protest. The military government declared martial law, a curfew, and press censorship, then used brute force to reopen closed shops. Some shooting occurred, in the course of which an American citizen was beaten up by the police and died. On October 22, Duvalier assumed office as President.

Not long afterward both Déjoie and Jumelle were condemned to death on suspicion of being responsible for a suburban bomb plot. Déjoie managed to slip out of the country, while Jumelle went into hiding in the countryside. Two brothers of Jumelle who had hidden in the home of a friend were discovered by Duvalier partisans and shot down in cold blood. The man who had given them shelter was tortured to death. Clément Jumelle himself, taken ill and unable to get prompt medical treatment at his place of concealment, died as he was finally taken to a hospital. A reign of terror now began, with the help of spies and squads of armed gangsters called Tontons Macoutes (bogeymen). Enemies and critics of the régime were rounded up, beaten, and otherwise tortured, or shot down in public.

# The Bitter Medicine of Papa Doc (1957-71)

If one were to be guided only by a reading of the speeches made by government officials and by the laws and decrees passed during the administration of President François Duvalier, one could hardly fail to be impressed by the firm expressions of a will to achieve progress and prosperity for Haiti, as well as by the allegations of progress actually being made. Unfortunately, that would be living in a dream world, to which the real world—the world of actual methods and results—is in stark contrast. Why this should be so is a complex question, for which a variety of answers have been offered, depending on the viewpoints and prejudices of the observers.

Duvalier had been a medical doctor, an ethnologist, and a writer. According to some accounts, he was also an *houngan* (vodou priest), a belief fostered by his writings in defense of the vodou religion and by rumors of secret rites carried out in the palace after he became President. As a medical doctor he had, among other things, worked for the American aid authorities in anti-yaws and anti-malaria programs in the late forties and early fifties. As an ethnologist and a writer he had been part of a group of intellectuals which in the thirties stressed Haiti's African origins and religion as reasons for pride, extolled Negro literature, condemned the American occupation and demanded social justice for the impoverished blacks. He had served as Minister of Labor and Public Health in the administration of Dumarsais Estimé, another full-blooded Negro. In 1954 he had gone into hiding in order to escape arrest by agents of the Magloire government. Shortly before the departure of Magloire in 1956, he emerged from hiding and announced his candidacy for the office of President.

The Haitian government's finances had been seriously disrupted by the ten months' political chaos, and the public debt, the budget, and the balance of payments all presented difficult problems. Fortunately, however, Haiti was now a member of several international institutions which could and did offer advice and help. The IMF, for instance, stationed a representative in Haiti and made available a standstill credit on which Haiti drew an initial $1 million to replenish its dollar reserves. Arrangements were made with various creditors to reschedule the payments due them, so that the excessively heavy early maturities could be spread over a long period.

The Planning Commission which Clément Jumelle had set up in 1956 was unable to function during the period of political confusion. However, the Agricultural and Industrial Credit Institute took it upon itself to organize an emergency planning group:

> Pending the revival of the commission by a permanent Government, the Director of the Haitian Institute of Agricultural and Industrial Credit has gathered a committee of 30 national and foreign experts, comprising government and private industry members and representing all major segments of the economy: Agriculture, Industry, Commerce, Banking, Transportation, Tourism, etc. For the study of specific questions several subcommittees were organized and a preliminary report has just been submitted to the administration, the IMF and the World Bank.[1]

The report in question pointed out that the Reynolds Mining Company had started exporting bauxite and was expected to produce 500,000 tons by the end of 1957; that the Société Haitienne de Minoterie (the Murchison flour mill) had begun operations in August, and that by importing wheat in bulk, in lieu of flour, Haiti should make a saving of over $700,000 in 1958; and that if new financing could be gotten for the banana-production program (which had had to be suspended), another $1 million of foreign exchange could be earned in 1958.[2]

One of the first acts of the Duvalier government was to have a new Constitution drafted and approved by the Legislative

Assembly. Promulgated on December 19, 1957, the new Constitution contained two articles reading as follows:

> Article 107.–There is created a Great Technical Council of National Resources and Economic Development. It is an independent organism the members of which shall be appointed by decree of the President of the Republic.
> Its manner of functioning shall be determined by law.
> Article 108.–The Office of the Budget, a direct dependency of the Head of the Executive Power, is charged with preparing, in direct touch with the Permanent Secretary of the Technical Council of National Resources and Economic Development, the Budget of Expenditures and Receipts of the State, and to supervise the execution thereof. It shall furthermore undertake to promote the National Economy by integrating the Public Expenditures and Receipts in the general plans of the country's economic development.

A law of February 28, 1958, specified that the Technical Council would have seven members and that its powers included the preparation of an overall plan and of annual plans, the determination of priorities and costs, supervising the execution of the plans, hiring of Haitian or foreign technicians, borrowing of technicians from Haitian government departments, examining all projects submitted by the government, making reports, etc.

In June 1958 the Technical Council submitted a report setting forth a development plan for the two years ending September 30, 1960. This plan called for an ambitious program, the cost of which it estimated at $52.9 million. Of this estimated cost, $29.5 million would come (it was hoped) from private investors; $22.9 million from the U.S. Development Loan Fund, the International Bank and its affiliates, or from the Inter-American Development Bank (then in process of formation); and the remaining $500,000 from the state budget. The program laid considerable stress on agricultural and social improvement, especially in the Artibonite Valley, on road construction, and on the negotiation of contracts for the construction of sugar mills. It also provided for a hydroelectric-power station at the Artibonite dam; a jet airport and a new wharf at Port-au-Prince;

a modern sewage system at Port-au-Prince; improved supplies of food, water, etc., through private enterprise; additional paved streets in Port-au-Prince; and some reforestation. There is no evidence that the government ever attempted to carry out the council's recommendations in toto (see p. 255). However, as will be seen, some of the recommended projects have since been launched.

In December 1958 the government signed an agreement with a private firm of management consultants—Klein and Saks of Washington, D.C.—and with a New York firm of investment bankers—Lehman Brothers—under which a Klein and Saks mission of about five economic and financial technicians was to be attached to the office of President Duvalier for the purpose of studying and giving advice on problems of public administration, taxation and revenues, banking, and agricultural and industrial development, while Lehman Brothers would cooperate with the mission and, "when necessary," send representatives to Haiti to help set up a development bank. The Klein and Saks mission was envisaged as extending over a period of several years, on the basis of a fee payable semiannually. Actually, it withdrew at the end of a year when the President voiced dissatisfaction at the "failure" to supply Haiti with a big loan, which he apparently thought had been promised. No such promise was contained in the written agreement.

As had been the case during the Magloire administration, there was during the early years of the Duvalier government a constant parade of foreign entrepreneurs, investors, and get-rich-quick adventurers seeking to get lucrative contracts of one sort or another. A Chicago firm, through a "Haitian Resources Development Corporation," offered to build a 550-room hotel and an airport at Cap-Haitien (the total of hotel rooms in Port-au-Prince was then 712, while the number in Cap-Haitien was only a small fraction of that figure). In addition, it undertook to restore various national monuments (including the Citadelle and the palace of Sans Souci) and, if it was found necessary, to build a radio broadcasting station, a hippodrome, a yacht basin, and a golf course. Financing was to be by means of an $18-million bond issue. Although a contract covering this proposition was signed and apparently received legislative approval, it never became effective. A contract was signed with the Starlite Construction Company of Miami to tear down the capital's waterfront slum, build on the site a shopping and residential center, and relocate the slum dwellers elsewhere; the cost, of which the government was to bear one-half, was estimated at $1 million. A 15-year concession was granted to the West India Fruit and Steamship Company, an American enterprise, for the production and purchase for export of bananas in the *départements* of the north, northwest, and Artibonite.

Meanwhile a $4-million loan for seven years at 5½ per cent interest had been obtained from the Banco de Colonos of Cuba. This loan was said to be based on $7 million of mostly unclaimed deposits of Haitian sugar workers in Cuba. The loan was not shown in the government's official debt statement, and no information was given out on the use made of the funds. According to one source, $1 million of the money went as a "kickback" to the followers of then President Batista of Cuba, while Duvalier himself received the other $3 million, "none of which was repaid."[3]

In March 1958 a contract was signed and approved for the construction and operation by a French company of a factory to make particle boards out of waste products from wood, sisal, coconut, etc.

In July 1958 the government contracted with a Haitian engineer, Adrien Roy, to rebuild the main business street of Port-au-Prince at a cost of $980,000. Several months later Roy was entrusted with certain electrical installations related to the street contract, at an additional cost of $475,000. Payments were to be made out of the state budget, with a one-month lag.

A contract was signed in 1958 with the Haitian-American Meat and Provision Company for the construction and operation of a modern slaughterhouse in the outskirts of Port-au-Prince. This company planned to fatten and slaughter cattle brought in from other parts of Haiti, to operate or supply local meat markets, and to export meat to other Caribbean islands and possibly to the

United States. The name of this company became familiar to many Americans in 1964 when it was reported that a U.S. Senate employee, Bobby Baker, had received a finding commission for sales of its meat in the United States.

In addition to the cooperation offered by international financial institutions, the aid and advice of U.S. agencies and of the United Nations continued to be at the disposal of the Haitian government. In the two years ended September 30, 1957, U.S. technical and economic aid, together with famine and disaster relief, had amounted to $18,688,000.[4]

One of the projects for which the government applied to the U.S. Development Loan Fund for financing was the paving of three important southern roads, namely, Port-au-Prince to Cayes, Grand Goâve to Jacmel, and Miragoâne to Jérémie. A preliminary survey and estimate of cost was made under contract by a Florida firm, Freeman H. Horton and Associates, and on this basis the government applied to DLF for a loan of $12.3 million. DLF was also looked to for the financing of new sewage and water-supply systems at Port-au-Prince, and of a new jet airport. The latter was becoming urgent, as propeller planes were disappearing from international traffic and being superseded by jets. The Port-au-Prince airport had been built to handle, at best, DC-4's, although it had for some time been accommodating DC-6's. In the absence of jet facilities, Haiti's tourist trade would be doomed.

Meanwhile, ICA was contributing substantial sums and technical aid to a program of small irrigation and drainage projects, farm-to-market roads, and land rehabilitation. In the Cayes-Torbeck Plain area alone, the cost of such work was estimated at more than $1 million. In the Jérémie area, road and bridge construction was undertaken by ICA at an estimated cost of $1.75 million.[5] In the Department of the North, ICA took an important participation in a Duvalierist regional development project called Poté Colé (Creole for "Hold tight" or "Stick with it"). This project aimed at increasing and diversifying agricultural production, as well as improving regional education, health, housing conditions, transportation, and communications. As an initial part of the Poté Colé program, ICA carried out at

Quartier Morin a pilot project of irrigation and secondary roads costing in the neighborhood of $1 million.[6] Apart from all this, AID made in 1959 an outright cash contribution of $7 million to the Haitian budget, despite the fact that the Haitian government had large "non-fiscal" (unbudgeted) receipts for which no public accounting was made.[7]

The financial and technical cooperation given the Duvalier régime in its early years by the United States took place despite disturbing reports that the régime was using violent and dictatorial methods. It was fairly clear, to begin with, that Duvalier had attained power through an election whose results had been manipulated by the army. The use of violence followed immediately in the forcible reopening of closed business houses, and soon afterward in the form of decreeing the death penalty for the two defeated presidential candidates, the coldblooded shooting of the Jumelle brothers, the imprisonment and beating up of many members of the opposition,[8] and the shutting down of several newspapers. Hundreds of persons who had opposed (or were suspected of having opposed) policies of the Duvalier government had fled into exile; many of these were technicians whose services were badly needed in Haiti. It had become clear, moreover, that the Duvalier régime was characterized by as much corruption—and possibly more—as had existed under the Magloire administration. At one point U.S. officials had to stage a brief suspension of aid in order to prevent the government from appointing an allegedly corrupt ex-minister to a key post in the Artibonite Valley project.

It might have been wiser for the United States to withhold all aid as soon as the dictatorial and violent nature of the Duvalier administration was made manifest. At any rate, it was definitely imprudent for the United States to supply Duvalier, as it did in January 1959, with a mission of some 60 marines, under Colonel Robert D. Heinl, Jr., for the purpose of training the Haitian army. This mission was described by both governments as "a further demonstration of the close bonds of friendship" between them.[9] The move must have been galling to Haitian businessmen and numerous others who had been partisans of Déjoie, Jumelle, Fignolé, and other defeated presidential candidates, especially in view of the oppression to which they were now subjected. It has been said that in supplying a military training mission, Washington was acting on the theory that "the Army has proved to be the only stable political force in the country," and that "Washington also hopes that it would act as a deterrent against a Cuban invasion."[10] The first point overlooks the fact that both Estimé and Magloire had been ousted by the army, as had two of the temporary Presidents (Sylvain and Fignolé) during the chaotic days of 1957. It also overlooks the fact that the army had shown poor judgment when it rigged the elections in favor of Duvalier, who promptly subordinated the army to his will, by frequent changes in its personnel and by having all weapons stored in the palace under his own control. As for the theory that a well-trained Haitian army would be a deterrent to a Cuban invasion, it may be doubted whether Castro would attempt openly to conquer Haiti by military means; much more likely would be a secret and gradual infiltration of Haitian political ranks.

At no time since François Duvalier became President, can it be said that Haiti was peaceful and relaxed. There were half a dozen invasions by small contingents of refugees—ex-soldiers or civilians—all of them successfully repulsed. There were anonymous bombings, and mysterious disappearances of citizens, many of them prominent. Hundreds were jailed and tortured, and quite a few of these were turned over to firing squads. The officers of the army were subjected to repeated mass purges, on suspicion or knowledge of plotting against the President. General Kébreau, who as head of the military government had "arranged" the presidential elections that brought Duvalier into power, was promptly sent to Italy as ambassador to the Vatican; his successors were simply dismissed. Duvalier even turned on his intimate friend and secretary, Ernest Barbot, who was said to have been the head of the Tontons Macoutes and who temporarily ran the country when Duvalier suffered a heart attack in 1959. Barbot was jailed for a year and a half, then released. After going into hiding, Barbot let it be known that he would assassinate Duvalier. Through helpers, he did attack and kill several of the bodyguards of Duvalier's young children (whom, according to some accounts, he had planned to abduct). In July 1963, Barbot was tracked to his hideout and killed.

Despite such goings-on, American financial and technical assistance to Haiti continued on its even and generous course until the summer of 1962.

In August 1960 the President had the legislature vote him full powers to decree any economic measures he felt necessary during the following six months. In April 1961 he again obtained a vote of full powers for six months and thereupon dissolved the bicameral legislature and announced that elections would be held for a unicameral parliament.[11]

In September 1960, following a strike by university students caused by the dismissal of certain professors, Duvalier exiled two Catholic priests accused of fostering the strike. Shortly afterward he ordered Archbishop François Poirier out of the country for issuing a mild statement of protest; this sentence was at first suspended, but was later carried out on the incredible charge that the Archbishop had given the striking students $7,000 to help overthrow the government.[12] At the same time, several other priests and the head of the Catholic secondary school were jailed and all copies of the Catholic newspaper *Phalange* were confiscated. Martial law and a curfew were imposed temporarily. Some weeks later, after the government had released from prison a score of arrested students, it received from the U.S. government a grant of $11.8 million for economic and technical assistance.[13]

When some students resumed the strike in January 1961, Duvalier ordered the expulsion from Haiti of Bishop Rémy Augustin (a native Haitian), together with four priests. Not long thereafter the Bishop of Gonaives, Jean-Marie Paul Robert, was required to move to Port-au-Prince, and in 1962 he also was expelled from the country.[14]

In the elections for a unicameral legislature, Duvalier personally chose the 58 candidates whose names appeared on a "yes or no" ticket, and, without any warning or announcement, had his own name and title as President printed on the ballots. When the results were disclosed, the Haitian people learned that they had unconsciously "re-elected" Duvalier for a second term as President, despite the fact that his first term was due to end only in May 1963.

Although the U.S. embassy—like other diplomatic representatives in Port-au-Prince—informed the President that his "re-election" for a second term could not be recognized, American aid was neither discontinued nor reduced at this point. Indeed, the United States withheld its veto from a $3.5-million loan to Haiti by the Inter-American Development Bank (IDB), for the purpose of merging the Haitian Institute of Agricultural and Industrial Credit and the Fonds Spécial d'Investissement (a Duvalier-created investment agency based on special tax revenues) and thus providing funds for a sugar mill in the southern peninsula, for "livestock raising, cotton, textile industry, coastwise shipping, fishing, etc."[15] The two merged institutions now became the Institut de Développement Agricole et Industriel (IDAI), with an authorized capital of $10 million.

Early in 1961 the government undertook a so-called development project consisting of the rebuilding of a small town (Cabaret) north of Port-au-Prince, which was renamed Duvalierville. To finance this project, the Tontons Macoutes pressured all sectors of the Haitian community—Haitian and foreign businessmen, government employees, members of the armed forces, etc.—for contributions. The project was never completed and was in any case of no value for economic and social development.[16]

In August 1961 the U.S. Development Loan Fund approved a loan of $250,000 to the Haitian Agricultural Corporation, S.A. (see p. 45), for the expansion of a sisal plantation and of a sisal mill.

Throughout its initial years the Duvalier administration had apparently done little or nothing in the way of settling various outstanding debts to U.S. firms.[17] In January 1962 the United States warned the Haitian government that until it settled these debts, it would be ineligible for further aid.[18] Two months later Haiti set up a Commission for the Verification and Settlement of Private American Claims.

In April 1962 the United States allotted $7.25 million for

further economic and technical aid to Haiti under its 1962 program. Six weeks later it was reported that a $3.4-million loan was being made available for construction of the Port-au-Prince to Cayes highway, and that a $2.6-million loan was under consideration for a jet airport.[19]

The summer of 1962 was a turning point in U.S.-Haitian relations. In May the United States sought to prevent any further occurrence like the one that had taken place in the fall of 1961, when the Haitian government had insisted (without success) on its right to appoint a reputedly corrupt ex-minister to a key position in the Artibonite project. Under a revised system, the United States required that Haitians working on an aid project either become employees of the United States (and thus subject to selection, control, and payment by it) or continue as employees of the Haitian government, which would then be responsible for their selection, control, and payment. The Haitian government rejected the new system, and as a result American aid was cut off on all except a malaria-eradication project and the distribution of relief goods supplied by certain private American charities.

During this interval (in June) the 12-year-old son of Colonel Heinl, head of the marine training mission, was arrested by the Tontons Macoutes when he was overheard commenting, during a bus ride, on the famished appearance of some poor Haitians who were passing by. Although the boy was soon released through the efforts of Duvalier's son, Colonel Heinl was reported to have said, before knowing of the release, "I'll take that palace myself." Also in June, Heinl wrote a note (with advance U.S. government approval) to the head of the Haitian armed forces, General Boucicault, complaining about the continuous growth of a new militia which the President had organized on a countrywide basis, now numbering some 8,000 as against the army's 5,000, and suggesting abolition of the militia. He also complained about neglect of the army and the closing of the military academy. "The practice on the part of individual *miliciens* or their leaders of establishing themselves as vagrant law officers exercising police authority has had a degrading effect on the regular armed forces," wrote Heinl. The colonel sent copies of this letter to the President and the

Minister of Defense. Other copies found their way into the hands of the general public. The immediate effect was that General Boucicault fled with his family to safety in the Venezuelan embassy. Some months later (in February 1963) Duvalier ordered the prompt withdrawal from Haiti of Colonel Heinl. At United States insistence, however, Heinl was allowed to finish his current assignment in Haiti, which in any event terminated shortly thereafter.

Undeterred by this trend of events, the AID in Washington announced late in November 1962 that a 40-year $2.8-million loan would be made to Haiti to help finance the jet airport. The airport, it said, would be built by an American contractor selected through public bidding, and Pan American World Airways would manage and operate it.[20]

In the meantime, despite continued help from international institutions, heavily increased taxation, and the negotiation of various contracts with private entrepreneurs, the government's financial and economic position had been going from bad to worse. The situation at the end of 1962 may be summed up by the following excerpts from a press dispatch:

> The Government is badly pressed for funds and faces an even tighter squeeze next year.
> Haiti's poverty, the cut-off of United States aid and what observers concur in describing as graft of overwhelming proportions has left the Government almost penniless.
> . . . The Government is behind in meeting its payrolls. A number of departments have failed to pay the Christmas bonus of one month's wages made mandatory this year.
> All of the projects that officials point to when asked what the Government is doing for the country have been stopped or slowed. The Poté Colé project . . . has collapsed. Work in the Artibonite . . . has tapered off.
> . . . Government indebtedness halted cement production for two days recently. . . .
> The tourist industry, declining for some time, has been all but killed by the scarcity of air service. . . .[21]

The United Nations meanwhile continued to give technical assistance to Haiti on a generous scale and in particular advised on industrialization and on the management of the Dessalines sugar mill in southern Haiti. The IMF continued to maintain a representative in Haiti to advise on fiscal and banking matters and maintained a standstill credit of up to $6 million at the disposal of the BNRH.[22] The International Bank also had a representative in Haiti during part of this period, and through its subsidiary, the International Development Association (IDA), it extended to Haiti in November 1962 a 50-year credit of $350,000 to finance the foreign-exchange costs of highway maintenance and rehabilitation for a one-year period; this credit was to be without interest until 1972, when an interest rate of 1 per cent per annum was to be charged. The U.N. Special Fund agreed in November 1961 to survey subterranean water possibilities for irrigation of the Gonaives Plain; to promote cooperatives and community development in the area; and to train staff to use the new water supply and to introduce and market new crops. A 12-man joint mission of technicians from the IDB, the OAS, and the U.N. Economic Commission for Latin America (ECLA) spent the winter of 1961-62 in Haiti in order to help draft short- and long-term development plans (see p. 255).

By the time Colonel Heinl was ousted, the U.S. government had apparently decided on a showdown with Duvalier on the ground that his term legally expired on May 15, 1962, the 1961 "re-election" having been invalid. U.S. Navy ships entered the Gulf of Gonave supplied with helicopters capable of landing marines at key points in and around Port-au-Prince.[23] At this juncture an acute crisis suddenly arose over the action of Haitian police in breaking into the Dominican embassy on April 26 in order to seize several Haitians who had taken refuge there. The Dominican government mobilized its armed forces, threatened to invade Haiti, and so informed the Organization of American States in Washington. The Haitian government was given a one-day ultimatum to make "reparation" and give assurances of no future repetition of its offense. In view of the inferiority of Haiti's armed forces, Duvalier had little choice but to withdraw his guards from the Dominican embassy and give the desired assurances. Meanwhile an OAS mission visited both Port-au-Prince and Santo Domingo in an effort to smooth out the relationship between the two countries, traditionally hostile to each other. The Dominican executive, President Bosch, was not easily appeased, however, and renewed the threat of invasion unless Haiti were subjected to sanctions.

Meanwhile Port-au-Prince had been put under martial law and an eight-to-five curfew, and the United States had ordered the evacuation of dependents of all government personnel and offered to evacuate other American residents. At Haiti's request the United States withdrew its 30-man naval training mission, its 10-man air-force training mission, and the remainder of its marine training mission. American helicopters staged practice flights over the bay to check on their landing capabilities. On the Dominican side of the border, ex-Senator Déjoie and ex-President Fignolé announced the formation of a Haitian government-in-exile.

Shortly before May 15 it was learned that plane reservations for eight unindentified Haitians had been made from Port-au-Prince to Curaçao and from there to New York and Paris—although the New York–Paris leg of the flight was reported to have been made in the name of Duvalier. At the last moment, however, these reservations were cancelled, and May 15 came and went with Duvalier still in his palace. On that date Washington "suspended" relations with the Duvalier government, thus marking its refusal to recognize the legality of the régime from that point on. The U.S. ambassador (Raymond L. Thurston) remained in Port-au-Prince in view of possibly critical developments within the next few days, but he refrained from contact with the government. Several Latin American governments (Dominican Republic, Venezuela, Costa Rica, Ecuador) took similar action.

As he previously announced that he would, Duvalier had himself inaugurated for a second term on May 22. On June 13 the OAS committee, after a second visit to Haiti and the Dominican Republic, asked Haiti to observe "the principle of respect for human rights" and implicitly blamed the Haitian government for the existing tensions. Meanwhile, on June 3, to the general surprise, the U.S. government resumed normal diplomatic contacts with the Duvalier government.

While the sudden reversal of U.S. policy toward Duvalier has never been adequately explained, an account which appeared in an American-owned Spanish-language review appears sufficiently plausible to warrant mention. According to this account, consultation between the U.S. State Department and the council of the OAS had resulted in a plan, drafted primarily by Gonzalo Facio, the Council's chairman, but approved by the United States, under which the council would assume the responsibility of asking the United States to proceed, in accordance with the Treaty of Rio de Janeiro, to a military occupation of Haiti in the name of the American republics. At the same time, a new Haitian government would be organized from among exiled Haitians and installed in Haiti. Within 24 hours this de facto government would be recognized by at least five American republics, including the United States. The first act of this government would be to invoke the aid of the OAS. Plans prepared in advance by the OAS would call for the integration of an inter-American army which could replace the North American marines in the maintenance of public order; the appointment of a High Commissioner, preferably some Latin American ex-President; a military counterpart for the reorganization of the Haitian armed forces (some thought having been given to an officer of the Chilean Corps of Carabineers); and a commission of technicians which would carry out functions in all the ministries of the new government.

According to the same source, the reason why Duvalier did not flee on May 15 was that two New York newspapers published the information about his plane reservations; fearful for his life and the lives of his family, Duvalier decided to cancel his plan of escape and risk whatever might befall him in Haiti.[24] If this story is true, Duvalier must have been pleasantly surprised to find that nothing whatever happened except the complete and unconditional about-face of his powerful American neighbor.

On June 14, Haiti recalled its ambassador from Washington and requested the recall of U.S. Ambassador Thurston. A month later the United States suspended the $2.8-million loan which was to have financed a jet airport. The surprising result of this action was that the Haitian government, its hand forced by the prospect of complete disappearance of the profitable tourist traffic, suddenly found it possible to corral from its domestic resources the funds and the labor required to build the airport. In February 1965 the new facility was inaugurated. It was high time; tourist 'expenditures in Haiti had fallen by something like 90 per cent since 1960.

As though its political and economic adversities were not enough, Haiti suffered in October 1963 another severe hurricane, Flora, which killed several thousand people in the southern peninsula, made more than 100,000 homeless, laid waste a number of towns, destroyed something like one-half of the exportable production of coffee and badly reduced the output of bananas and sisal. The United States supplied relief in the form of cash ($250,000) and 25 million pounds of food, transported in U.S. Navy vessels. Lesser hurricanes were experienced in 1964 and 1966.[25]

Having been confirmed in his stranglehold on the Haitian people and economy, Duvalier had no reason for compunction about the further elimination of opponents. In February 1964 he expelled 18 members of a Canadian Jesuit mission on "vague allegations of improper activities," and closed the Catholic seminary.[26] In April of that year he expelled the American bishop of the Haitian Episcopal Church. During the same month he agreed to accept the title of President-for-Life "in response to nationwide demonstrations calling on him to rule for life."[27] In January 1965, Msgr. Claudine Agénor, Apostolic Vicar for Haiti, was put under house arrest. In the same month more than 50 peasants were reported to have been shot because they were relatives of Haitian exiles who had returned from the Bahamas; the 15 exiles also were killed.[28]

In June 1967, Duvalier was reported to have sent into exile his own married daughter and her husband, Colonel Max Dominique, together with a younger daughter. Colonel Dominique was charged with conspiring with 19 other army officers to overthrow Duvalier. According to the American who had been in charge of training the Haitian army, the 19 accused officers were shot down by firing squads in the presence of both Duvalier and his offending son-in-law. The latter's three bodyguards and chaffeur were also executed. Four of Duvalier's ex-ministers were jailed, as was Clémard Joseph Charles, a Haitian banker who had been an intimate of the President and had grown wealthy thanks to this intimacy. Charles was also stripped of his wealth. A curfew was imposed, and 107 new refugees crowded into the foreign embassies of Port-au-Prince.[29]

In December 1967, when hunger demonstrations took place at La Fossette, near Cap-Haitien, Duvalier sent his militia and part of the presidential guard for a show of force and imposed a two-night curfew. He also ordered the closing of the Haitian-American Institute in Cap-Haitien and the departure of the American director of the institute.[30]

In November 1968 four of the most prominent citizens of Port-au-Prince (Oswald and Clifford Brandt, Georges and Jean-Claude Léger) were arrested "on suspicion of having helped Haitian exiles," but were later released.[31]

Notwithstanding all this, the international institutions and agencies continued to support the Duvalier régime in a financial and economic way. In March 1964 the IDB announced a 27-year 2 per cent loan of $2.36 million from its Fund for Special Operations in order to help finance the first stage of a program to improve and expand the water supply of Port-au-Prince and its suburbs, and also a $190,000 loan to pay for advisory services to an autonomous agency to manage the water service.[32] These loans had been vetoed by the U.S. government in January 1963, but now received its blessing.[33]

In November 1966 the IDB announced a 30-year 2¼ per cent loan of $1.3 million to help finance a Haitian program of instruction in agriculture and medicine, as well as an additional $125,000 for advisory services.[34] In June 1970 the same agency approved a further loan of $5.1 million to help finance the second stage of the program of improved and expanded water supply for Port-au-Prince and adjacent areas; with this went a $72,000 grant for advisory services.

The United Nations continued to maintain a full-fledged staff of technicians in Haiti to assist the country's economic "progress," despite the fact that the U.N. Resident Representative (Jean Richardot) had been expelled during the U.S.-Haitian showdown of May 1963, on the curious charge that he had shown unfriendliness by insisting—at the request of the U.N. headquarters in New York—that the government give exit visas to 31 members of the families of U.N. technicians. The expulsion of Richardot was particularly ironic because he was generally known to be one of the warmest friends the Haitian people had among foreigners.

Even the U.S. government, notwithstanding the announced 1963 cutoff in its aid, has continued to devote sizable sums (about $2 million annually) to assisting Haiti, mainly for malaria eradication, hurricane relief, and food distribution.

Many reports out of Haiti in recent years have emphasized the incredible amount of corruption. Some reports have incriminated Duvalier personally. On an annual salary of $20,000, he is said to have bought two mansions in January 1968 for $575,000 and then to have sold one of them to the state for $600,000. It is also alleged that the President awarded to himself some of the bonds issued by the state and arranged for himself or close collaborators to win the top prizes in compulsory lotteries organized by the state.[35] On the other hand, an American citizen (a famous Negro folkloric dancer) who has made her home in Haiti for more than 20 years and has had close relations with the country's successive Presidents, including Duvalier, in 1969 wrote that the latter

> is not nor ever has been motivated by avidity for material things or good living at the expense of the populace. . . . For one thing, I have had too much experience with the costs of supporting an "extended family." In my case it was a theatrical company, in Duvalier's case it is a private, newly established army, or, one might say, a whole class split off from upper proletariat and lower bourgeoisie and made into an army police power structure. This takes whatever financing might be filched from within or extracted in handouts from sources without. . . . So

I would say that while Haiti's present President may have been driven successively by need for personal aggrandizement, then power, then to hold the power, then fear of losing it, then fear for life, he has not been one of those to commit whatever the syndicated press and expatriated countrymen attest to his having committeed for material gain.[36]

Whatever the truth may be with respect to Duvalier's own conduct, the evidence of large-scale corruption in his administration is overwhelming, as attested by many observers. The sources of personal enrichment are said to have been numerous: misappropriation of tax receipts, use of the Tontons Macoutes to compel businessmen to contribute to "worthy" causes, acceptance of bribes from foreign entrepreneurs or investors in exchange for government monopolies or concessions, compulsory withholdings from the salaries of government employees, etc.

Even the U.S. government and the Vatican gave indirect moral support to the Duvalier régime in its later years: the first by its continuance of appreciable financial aid, by discouraging or preventing Haitian exiles from invading Haiti, and by encouraging private investments in Haiti; the second by sending a new papal nuncio to Haiti, notwithstanding its earlier excommunication of Duvalier and his acolytes.

It should hardly surprise anyone, under all the circumstances, that Haiti showed little or no genuine progress under François Duvalier. Indeed, most of the news from Haiti indicated that the country was steadily sliding backward, despite all the financial and economic aid received. Where the people have lost all hope, there cannot be that élan, that ambition, on the part of individuals which is an essential ingredient of progress. Many of the contracts signed with foreign entrepreneurs, moreover, lapsed as the entrepreneurs came to realize the difficulty, if not impossibility, of carrying their schemes into practical effect. Two examples may be cited:

In 1962 a concession was granted to the Valentine Petroleum and Chemical Company of New York City for the purpose of establishing (through a subsidiary) one or more oil refineries and one or more petrochemical plants. For both types of enterprise the subsidiary company was to have a monopoly, as well as for the export, import, and sale of crude or refined petroleum products. The Valentine company received from AID a guarantee of its investment, although its successful execution would have meant the forced departure from Haiti of the American (and European) oil companies which for many years had supplied Haiti with gasoline and other oil products. A year or two later, for unknown reasons, the Valentine representative was expelled from Haiti and the contract cancelled.

In December 1964 the government gave control of oil, shipping, and port affairs to one Mohammed Fayed, who had arrived from Kuwait in June and been made a Haitian citizen in November. He received the exclusive right to import and distribute petroleum products, once he had invested $1 million, chiefly in a refinery. He was to invest $5 million in the next four years in a variety of harbor improvements in Port-au-Prince, and he was to collect pilot and wharfage fees that formerly went directly to the government, but he was to pay a percentage of his profits to the government. He was named sole shipping agent for 12 steamship companies serving Haiti, thus being entitled to fees totaling between $200,000 and $250,000 annually. When two international shipping conferences protested to the Haitian government, a meeting was called, but Fayed failed to show up; missing with him was a large sum of money, according to press accounts.[37]

To what extent current conditions in Haiti constitute an open invitation to communists to seize control when the Duvalier family loses its stranglehold is uncertain. It has been argued that the communists have no interest in Haiti because there are no Haitians capable of managing the economy for them. I disagree with this theory, for two reasons: (1) I have personally known plenty of well-educated and highly intelligent Haitians who have all that it would take to manage the Haitian economy; at present, most of them are in exile abroad, but many (probably the majority) of them plan to return to Haiti eventually. (2) A communist state similar to present-day Cuba can, if need be, be run more or less successfully without a full staff of trained native administrators, as Castro demonstrated during the early years of his dictatorship.

At any rate, there have been reports to the effect that several Communists are already among the régime's administrators, perhaps awaiting their day. The two Communist parties in Haiti recently merged to form the Parti Unifié Communiste Haitien (PUCH—the Unified Haitian Communist Party).[38] A Cuban radio station has been broadcasting to Haiti a daily two-hour program in the Creole language and a one-hour program in French. The Voice of America does not beam any program to Haiti in either Creole or French. Before and during the advent of Duvalier, I, then living in Haiti, was often unable to get the Voice of America on my radio, even in English or Spanish, whereas Radio Moscow was seemingly all over the set. Since July 1965, however, a group of Haitian exiles in New York (the Haitian Coalition) have beamed a short daily program to Haiti in the Creole language.

After nearly 14 years of the rule of Papa Doc (as the President liked to be known) it was amply clear that the bitter medicine prescribed by him could not restore health and happiness to the people of Haiti. On the contrary, Haitians—both the masses and the élite—had been slipping ever deeper into the depths of agony and despair. The death of Papa Doc in April 1971 has opened a new chapter. As these lines are written, little is known as to the intentions of his 19-year-old son, Jean-Claude, who has "inherited" the presidency, thanks to a stratagem devised by his father. Even before Papa Doc, however, Haiti's progress was excruciatingly slow. The reasons for this failure of the Haitian economy to move forward vigorously, whether in response to the carrot or the stick, are complex and can be ferreted out only by means of a close examination of the main aspects of Haitian life and society. To such an examination chapters 7 to 22 inclusive are devoted.

■□■□■□ PART III

# Current Economic And Social Problems

# The Language Problem: French or Creole?

One of the most difficult and unavoidable hurdles that confront Haiti in its efforts at economic and social development is education. The educational problem, in turn, is intimately related to certain aspects of the country's unique linguistic and religious systems. As a preliminary to the analysis of Haiti's educational system, therefore, the present chapter considers the language problem, and Chapter 10 will discuss religion.

According to the Haitian Constitution, the official language of the country is French. Actually, however, only a small fraction of the population—probably not much more than 7 per cent—can speak and write fluent French. The rest of the population speaks (but does not write) a language or patois known as Creole. The census taken in 1950 revealed that 90.4 per cent of the population was illiterate. In the cities, which make up only a small percentage of the total population, the ratio of illiteracy was only about 47 per cent, but in the rural areas it was 92 per cent. Since instruction in the schools had been exclusively in the French language, the 1950 test of literacy must have been the ability to read simple French. Of the 9.6 per cent (of the total population) who could pass the literacy test, all available information indicates that a goodly number could hardly have been making constant use of that language. Indeed, the opportunities for putting a knowledge of French to use were, for the vast majority, few and far between. One problem in the rural areas has been that after acquiring the ability to read simple French, pupils have tended to forget it owing to the paucity of occasions for using it.

There are weighty reasons for calling Creole, as we do above, "a language *or patois.*" One reason is that Haitians cannot agree among themselves whether Creole is a separate language or just a sort of dialect. The easiest way to get into a heated argument with some members of the Haitian élite would be to say something about the Creole "language." Traditionally, and for the most part still today, the élite looks upon Creole as a kind of debased French.[1] In the past 30 years, however, a few members of the élite have broken away from this philosophy and have publicized their conviction that Creole is a genuine language, distinct from French in pronunciation and grammar, even though its vocabulary was in overwhelming proportion derived from French. The fact is that the Creole-speaking masses understand little or no French, and French-speaking foreigners upon arrival in Haiti find they cannot understand Creole. Members of the Haitian élite, however, not only understand it but use it constantly for communication with servants, workmen, etc. At times they use it even among themselves, especially when dominated by some strong emotion, for which Creole seems to supply the proper degree of pungency.

Some of those who hold that Creole is merely a French patois claim that it existed in a primary form even before the colonization of Saint-Domingue. According to a principal exponent of this view, Jules Faine, Creole is an outgrowth of a French maritime dialect (now extinct) which was brought to Saint-Domingue by the first buccaneers, freebooters, and colonizers. The maritime dialect in question, says Faine, was an amalgam of the dialects of several French provinces (Normandy, Brittany, Picardie, Anjou, and Poitou), and upon exposure in Saint-Domingue it absorbed a number of expressions from the English, Spanish, African, and American Indian languages. Since the Negro slaves in the colony had come from all parts of western Africa, they spoke many African tongues and had such difficulty in understanding one another that they adopted the lingua franca spoken by some of their masters. This was all the more necessary because the plantation owners followed a policy of separating slaves of the same regional origin as a precaution against attempts at rebellion. In the process of learning to communicate in the new language, the slaves greatly simplified it. The end product was modern Creole.

Faine points out that Creole is spoken not only in Haiti but, to a greater or lesser extent, in widely separated parts of the globe which are (or were) French possessions. He divides these areas into two groups: the American and the Indian Ocean groups. The American group includes, in addition to Haiti, Guadeloupe, Martinique, French Guiana, St. Lucia, St. Vincent, Trinidad, and Louisiana. The Indian Ocean group includes Réunion, Mauritius, and the Comoro and Seychelles Islands. The resemblance between the Creoles spoken in these two groups, says Faine, is greater than that between any two Romance languages. Such differences as exist, according to this theory, are due to the fact that in the American group Creole was influenced by the slaves imported from West Africa, whereas the Creole spoken in the Indian Ocean group shows the influence of Magache, a Malayan-Polynesian language.

Among those who affirm that Creole is a language in its own right, perhaps the most vigorous exponent in Haiti has been Charles Fernand Pressoir, who has written widely on the subject. According to Pressoir, Creole did not derive from a pre-existing maritime dialect, but derived directly from French, as it was spoken in France generally during the seventeenth and eighteenth centuries, as well as in Saint-Domingue. Pressoir rejects in the main the thesis that French provincial dialects were a primary source of Creole. He insists that Creole is simply a mixture of French vocabulary (simplified in form with numerous changes of pronunciation) and African grammar.[2]

All who have written on this question seem to agree that Creole is a pungent, graphic mode of communication with no words or syllables wasted. In its terseness it rivals Latin. Compare, for instance, the following:

ENGLISH:   He said he would give it to me tomorrow.
FRENCH:    Il a dit qu'il me le donnerait demain.
CREOLE:    Li té di la bam li démin.

The extent to which French *words* have been simplified in Creole may be guessed from the fact that the French expression "A quelle heure?" ("At what time?") becomes in Creole: "Ki lè?" As for the fine points of French *grammar*, Creole has pretty thoroughly dispensed with them by switching to a syntax so simple that it puts no strain on the memory or thought processes.

The deprecating attitude of most of the Haitian élite toward Creole can be accounted for on historical and racial grounds, even if one may not agree with it. In the colony of Saint-Domingue it was the French settlers who dominated the island and who, as already explained, did everything to keep the *gens de couleur* from enjoying equal status. Nevertheless, as free men, the mulattoes were far above the slave level and they naturally tended to imitate the white colonists in every way left open to them. One of those ways was the knowledge and use of the French language. When the French yoke was thrown off, the mulattoes suddenly found that the slaves were legally now their equals. Being a free man was no longer a distinction. Attachment to the French language and French ways suddenly became much more important as a means of maintaining a status of superiority over the ex-slaves. (Lightness of skin color was, of course, also a status symbol, and as such it enjoyed a premium.) Since the liberation, the élite (who are for the most part the mulattoes) not only have had their children educated in Catholic and private schools conducted by teachers whose native language was French, but have whenever possible sent their offspring to France for the higher levels of instruction. As a result most of the élite have an impressive command of the French language and of French culture in general.

In this situation Creole appears to the élite as a disturbing element. It is seen as the sign of ignorance, of poverty, of inferior status. Above all, according to this reasoning, it must not be dignified by calling it a language. Practically every Haitian constitution has therefore provided that French is the Republic's official language and that its use in all public services is obligatory. Significantly, the 1957 Constitution, which was drafted at the time of Duvalier's accession to the presidency, for the first time contained a reference to Creole. Its Article 35 reads:

> French is the official language. Its use is obligatory in the Public Services. The law will determine in what cases and under what conditions the use of Creole shall be permitted and even

recommended in order to safeguard the material and moral interests of citizens who do not have a sufficient knowledge of the French language.

This article was repeated without change in the 1964 Constitution. To my knowledge, however, no law on this subject has yet been passed.

Not only has all instruction in the public schools been given in French, but the use of Creole at court trials has not been permitted. No newspaper appears to have been printed in Creole until 1943, when a miniature sheet called *Konnesans* appeared under official auspices. Practically all books printed in Haiti have been in the French language, and until recent years nearly all Haitian writers wrote exclusively in French. The past few decades, however, have seen the gradual growth of a movement toward writing and publishing in Creole, and particularly toward the use of Creole in the elementary schools as a preliminary to instruction in French. Some would even go so far as to make Creole the country's second official language.

From the literary point of view, it is argued that there is no thought or sentiment that cannot be expressed in Creole as effectively as in French. Two present-day Haitian writers, F. Morisseau-Leroy and Franck Fouché, have attempted to demonstrate this by writing and presenting Creole translations of classical plays, such as Sophocles' *Antigone* and *Oedipus*.

As for the use of Creole in the schools, an important stumbling block has been the inability of interested parties to agree on how Creole should be spelled in order to facilitate learning and avoid confusion. This point is somewhat less important in the publication of literary works, and in the past each author writing in Creole has used his own orthographic system. The first attempt to supply a Creole textbook for school use appears to have been made in 1925, when Frédéric Doret published a French grammar with explanations in both French and Creole. French spelling, so far as possible, was used for the Creole text. In 1931, Rev. Victor-Emmanuel Holly published a grammar of the Creole language, using a phonetic spelling for words whose pronunciation differed from French. In 1936 a Sorbonne thesis by Suzanne Comhaire-Sylvain entitled *Créole haitien, morphologie et syntaxe* was published, using scientifically phonetic spelling. In 1939, Christian Beaulieu authored a Creole reader, using the French spelling for all words pronounced as in French.

In 1940, Rev. H. Ormonde McConnell, pastor of the American Methodist Church in Haiti, worked up a series of phonetic charts for teaching people to read Creole. For this purpose he used the phonetic spelling advocated by Dr. Frank Charles Laubach, the famous Congregational missionary who had introduced his methods of teaching illiterates to read in some 200 languages or dialects around the world.[3] Experimental classes using this method demonstrated that an illiterate Haitian could be taught to read Creole in three months. A single-sheet mimeographed bulletin in Creole was circulated to the new readers, and the Haitian government was invited to observe the results of the campaign. By April 1943 over 600 persons had been taught to read. At that time Dr. Laubach visited Haiti and completed the task of persuading the government to give its backing to the McConnell campaign. As a result an Adult Literacy Campaign was set up by the government, a series of small textbooks was published, and teaching centers were established throughout the country. Classes were held in the evening, and most of the teaching was done on a voluntary basis. A small Creole newspaper was published at government expense. In 1945, McConnell published his own book, *You Can Learn Creole,* for the use of English-speaking persons. Finally, in 1947, the government voted a law formalizing the literacy campaign, "to continue until illiteracy was wiped out."[4]

According to Charles Fernand Pressoir, the McConnell-Laubach system of spelling Creole did not win favor with the Haitian public, which thought it well suited to the needs of English-speaking persons but not of Haitians. Pressoir recommended several changes which brought the Creole spelling closer to the French orthographic system, and his recommendations were adopted. Thereafter the campaign went ahead on the new basis, through two channels: adult literacy classes held by the Department of Education and similar classes sponsored by the Department of Labor for workers.

The UNESCO Pilot Project in Basic Education (see pp. 67-68) also had its beginnings in 1947 and involved among other things the preparation of textbooks for teaching the illiterate to read Creole as an approach to French. McConnell's lack of enthusiasm for the UNESCO project as it unfolded is apparent from the following passage:

> A new method of teaching to read in Creole was prepared by UNESCO. It is known as the Gabriel method, and is essentially a translation of the Richards method. According to one of their staff, 43 pupils out of a total of 700 in the region learnt to read during a period of 12 months. (There are reasons to believe that the period in question should have been given as 24 months.) Even admitting that these people have learnt more than merely the capacity to read, it is obvious that as a pilot project to serve as a model . . . this experiment does not excite much enthusiasm if it is to be judged as a modern, quick method for abolishing illiteracy. . . . The Laubach method and chart have been so completely set aside that none of the U.N. experts who have come to Haiti in recent years seem to know that they ever existed. UNESCO may have achieved many other successes but . . . the results in combating illiteracy are sadly disappointing.[5]

To add to the confusion about the most suitable method of spelling Creole, the distinguished author of several Creole dramas and poems (Morisseau-Leroy) persisted in a system of his own devising, namely, the use of French orthography for words common to both languages, the use of a simplified etymological spelling for Creole words which are plainly of French origin, and the arbitrary spelling of other words according to a phonetic system "to which Haitians are accustomed."[6]

All this while most of the élite continued to pour scorn on the use of Creole for either literary or educational purposes. The U.N. mission of 1948, on the other hand, while lauding the potential benefits of literacy in the French language, argued that such literacy could most quickly and easily be obtained by first teaching children (and adults) to read Creole. "The linguistic and phonetic relationships between Creole and French are strong enough to make possible a rapid transition from the former to the French."[7]


□□□ 10

# Religion and Folklore

The Haitian Constitution of 1950, in its Article 20, provided as follows:

> All religions and faiths recognized in Haiti are free.
> Every person has the right to profess his religion, to practice his faith, provided that he does not disturb the public order.
> The Catholic religion, professed by the majority of Haitians, enjoys a special position as a consequence of the Concordat.

Article 27 of the 1957 Constitution clarified the first sentence above as follows:

> All faiths and religions are equally free and recognized.

On the other hand, it omitted the reference in the third sentence to a special position for the Catholic religion and substituted for it the following clause:

> No one may be compelled to belong to any religious organization or to receive any religious instruction contrary to his convictions.

The second sentence of the 1950 Constitution was maintained without change in 1957. The 1957 provisions with respect to religion were repeated in the 1964 Constitution.

This de-emphasizing of the Catholic religion was in character with the philosophy of President Duvalier, who, although he professed to be a Catholic, was a stout defender of the culture and rights of the masses, i.e., the primary adherents of vodou.[1] The new clause added by the 1957 and 1964 constitutions appears to be a warning to the Catholic priesthood to desist from its efforts to belittle and proscribe the vodou religion.

Nominally, nearly all Haitians are Catholics, whether they are members of the élite or of the non-French-speaking masses. The few who are not Catholics belong to one or another of several Protestant sects which in recent decades have been slowly gaining adherents in Haiti; among these are Episcopalians, Methodists, Baptists, Jehovah's Witnesses, and Seventh-Day Adventists.

In fact, however, only members of the élite are Catholics in the sense in which that term is used in Europe and the United States. The Creole-speaking masses are baptized in the Catholic Church and consider themselves Catholics, but the vast majority of them continue to practice and believe in all the features of vodou. In other words, they have accepted the Christian God and saints and integrated them into the vodou pantheon. To the Christian God they have assigned the supreme rank over and above the gods they brought from Africa, and they have identified the individual Christian saints with those of their own gods to which the saints appeared to bear the strongest resemblance.[2] In the vodou services, which are held in rustic temples throughout Haiti, considerable use is made of Christian prayers, saint images, the Holy Cross, etc., but otherwise the services are vodou pure and simple.

The Catholic Church, as the official church of seventeenth- and eighteenth-century France, of course came to Saint-Domingue with the French colonists. The latter, however, were noted in the main for their loose morals and their indifference to religion. Under the *Code Noir* they were required to baptize and instruct their slaves in the Catholic faith and to see that they attended mass on Sundays and religious holidays. In 1764 the Jesuits were expelled from Saint-Domingue on the ground that in their efforts to convert and instruct the slaves, they were undermining the foundations of colonial society. A governor of the colony is said to have remarked that "the safety of the whites demands that the Negroes be kept in profound ignorance."

Toussaint L'Ouverture laid down in his 1801 Constitution that the Catholic religion was the only one publicly professed, and he invited the help of the Church in stabilizing conditions in the colony. However, the priests had for the most part fled during the massacre of the whites, and it was not easy to lure them back. Dessalines took a different tack; he refused state support to any denomination, granted freedom to all cults, and refused to admit that any one religion was dominant. Christophe, Pétion, and Boyer re-established the official position of the Catholic Church, but Christophe and Boyer subordinated the Church to themselves personally, while Pétion specified that citizens should be free also to practice other religions. For whatever reason, the Papal See preferred to ignore Haiti during the country's early decades, and in the absence of a Catholic clergy it proved increasingly difficult to maintain any proper observance of the Catholic religion. Matters were made worse by the fact that unfrocked and bogus priests from other countries came to Haiti to fill both the religious void and their secular pockets.

In the meantime the ex-slaves were developing the vodou religion as an amalgam of African and Indian beliefs and practices. In 1847 vodou received for the first time official approval through the accession of Faustin Soulouque as President of the Republic (later as Emperor). This black ex-general, who had been chosen because of his ignorance and apparent harmlessness and who ruled tyrannically for 12 years, was himself a follower of vodou and encouraged the open practice of vodou rites.

It was not until 1860 that a concordat was finally signed between Haiti, under President Geffrard, and the Holy See. The concordat made provision for the creation in Haiti of archbishoprics, bishoprics, and dioceses; for the payment of an annual subsidy by the Haitian government to the archbishoprics and bishoprics; and for the appointment of the archbishops and bishops by the President of Haiti subject to their qualifications proving acceptable to the Holy See. The latter thereupon sent a commission to Haiti for the determination of dioceses, the allocation of clergy, and the founding of a seminary. An archbishop, 40 priests, and a number of brothers and sisters went quickly to work, but it was too late to stem the tide of vodouism.[3]

Some writers have described vodou in unflattering terms as

a set of savage superstitions and magic supported by erotic dancing and orgies. In doing so, they not only displayed ignorance or a penchant for distortion and sensationalism, but deeply offended many Haitians. Unfortunately, numerous American visitors to Haiti have read only such misleading accounts, or stories based upon them, and they frequently ask to be shown a "voodoo dance." This is somewhat comparable to a European tourist in the United States asking to be taken to some American church service, not for worship but simply to stand around, most likely with a camera, watching how others worship and taking occasional snapshots of them as they kneel in prayer or sing hymns. This comparison becomes more apt if one can imagine the Christian religion's having been formally outlawed and being an object of scorn and derision by the ruling class. Vodou is as much a religion as any other; as such, in fact, it is taken more seriously by its adherents than some of our Christian sects are by theirs.[4]

What, then, is the precise nature of vodou? It has been defined as "a set of beliefs and practices which claim to deal with the spiritual forces of the universe, and attempt to keep the individual in harmonious relation with them as they affect his life."[5] This definition is good so far as it goes, but it does not convey much of a picture to those who have no previous knowledge of vodou. Basically, vodou (this word, from Dahomey in Africa, means "spirit" or "god") is a combination of ancestor worship and animism, under a supreme master, the Christian God. It recognizes a series of lesser gods or spirits—some of whom it equates with the Christian saints—who personify such forces of nature or aspects of the common life as love, war, the sea, the serpent, the crossroads, the cemetery, etc. Other gods are simply the ancestors of the race, whose characteristics have perhaps undergone some unconscious modification (in the minds of their descendants) since their departure from the mundane life. The vodou gods (now called *loas, mystères,* or *les invisibles*) have most of the qualities and defects of ordinary human beings. They have moods, jealousies, vanities, pride, etc. What is more, they require sustenance, and supplying them with food and drink is a frequent concern of the faithful. But the outstanding fact about them may be said to be their ability to possess, or take temporary control of, the bodies of their followers. This they may do in the home or elsewhere, but most often the phenomenon takes place at the rustic temples (called *houmforts*) where vodou services are held once a week or more often.

A distinguished Haitian, Dr. Louis Mars, describes vodou as "the cult through which Haitian peasants worship the divinities upon whom depend fortune and misfortune, sickness and death. The man who has been fortunate enough to by-pass danger owes an act of gratitude to the Vodou, or spirit gods; misfortune is visited upon him, he believes, because he has failed to carry out his religious duties; he must plead for divine mercy. When this man begets a child, he will dedicate it to the Vodou by pouring lustral water over its head; when a member of his family passes on, specific rites will assure the soul's safe passage into the world beyond."[6]

The vodou religion is informal in the sense that there is no national or central body to define its doctrines or lay down rules of organization and conduct, nor any set of ordained priests or ministers, nor any seminary. It is based for the most part on small groups, each consisting of a family and its intimate circle of relatives and friends, which are known as *sociétés*. Each *société* has its *houngan* (priest) or *mambo* (priestess), who directs the religious services and, in addition, advises members of the *société* on matters of health and a variety of personal problems. The *houngan* or *mambo* is assisted in administrative matters by the president of the *société*, and in the services by a laplace (master of ceremonies), a *houngenikon* (a male or female song conductor), a number of *hounsis* (women who have been initiated into some of the techniques and traditions of vodou), and various minor aides. A further essential part of the *houmfort* staff is a trio of expert drummers. The office of *houngan* or *mambo* is hereditary, passing from the head of the family to the most qualified junior member.

A typical service will consist of prayers and songs, the tracing of a *vevers* on the earth floor, and the sacrifice of one or more chickens, or perhaps a goat, in honor of one of the *loas*. The *vevers* is an intricate and symmetrical design made by the *houngan's* (or *mambo's*) skillful release of a thin stream of cornflour from his (or her) hand. There are traditional designs for each of the *loas*. After the religious service all present repair to an adjoining peristyle for the dancing. The dances are carried out single-file, to the throbbing of the drums. It is usually in the course of the dancing that possession of one or more devotees by the *loas* occurs, although this may also occur during the religious service. The person possessed is said to be "mounted" by the *loa* and is referred to as the *loa's* "horse." According to practically all accounts, the "horse" loses his personal consciousness, and his body momentarily becomes in effect that of the *loa*. His gestures, manners, and voice often change radically and are recognized as those of the particular *loa* in possession of his body. Possession may last anywhere from a few moments to several hours or, rarely, several days. The possessed person, upon regaining his own personality, is said to have no recollection at all of what he did or said during possession.

There are apparently hundreds of *loas*, but probably not more than a few dozens are known to all vodou worshippers. Various attempts have been made to classify the *loas* according to origin, characteristics, and rites, but no agreement on the best method of classification has been reached. There is, moreover, more than one set of rites for the practice of vodou. The Rada rites, which are the principal ones, are inheritances from Africa only, while the Petro rites derive in part from Indian customs. There are also the Congo rites, brought over from Africa.

Among the best-known *loas* are Legba, keeper of the gate and guardian of the crossroads (whose powers are invoked at the start of each vodou session); Damballah, the venerable snake-god and rain-maker; Agwé, king of the seas; Ogoun, warrior hero and statesman; Erzulie, goddess of love and beauty; Azacca, god of agriculture; and Ghédé, lord of the cemeteries and the underworld. In the eyes of vodou worshippers, many of the *loas* identify with certain of the Christian saints. Legba, for example, is usually identified with St. Peter (although some see his counterpart in St. Anthony or St. Christopher). Damballah's Christian appellation is said to be St. Patrick. Agwé is equated with St. Ulrique. Ogoun's Christian cognomen is St. Jacques. Erzulie is none other than the Holy Virgin!

In addition to the *houmfort* services, vodou is practiced in peasant and other homes, or in domestic annexes called *tonnelles,* where there is usually a small altar, or at least a table bearing some of the sacred objects (*loa* emblems, a crucifix, a vase of flowers, lithographs of the saints, etc.). Altars of this sort are used for the worship of the particular *loas* who are "served" by the house inmates and whose protection they invoke. The similarity to early Greek and Roman religious practices is striking. The family's *loas* are inherited from its ancestors. Each member of a Haitian peasant family has his own personal *loa*, who is known as his *maître tête* (the master of his head). At the time of a child's baptism into the vodou religion, he is possessed by his *maître tête*. Throughout his life he will look to his personal *loa* for guidance and protection.

A truthful analysis of the vodou religion cannot dismiss peremptorily the charges of magic and superstition which some observers have made. Even religious experts have difficulty in drawing a perfectly clear line between religion and magic, or between religion and superstition. However, there cannot be much doubt that vodou, though a true religion, also contains some elements of magic and superstition.[7] To take an example, there is a vodou practice called *retirer d'en bas de l'eau,* i.e., recalling the spirits of the dead from below the waters where they are supposed to have gone at the time of death. This ceremony is performed one year and a day after death. Should a deceased person not be thus recalled, he would become "a wandering and evil spirit which would avenge itself against its relatives by inflicting upon them all sorts of vexations and illnesses. Consequently the vodou worshipper will sell his possessions, if necessary, in order to meet such an obligation."[8] Here is how one witness of this ceremony has described it:

> . . . We were part of the crowd pushing back to make way for the *mambo* followed by *la place* with the sword, flag bearers

and a long file of white-clad *hounsi* with their long colorful strands of ceremonial beads. Seven of the *hounsi* bore on their heads cloth-wrapped earthen jars which they steadied with their hands.

"The jars are the sacred *govi*," Reser hurried to explain, "mystical containers prepared to receive the spirits of the dead."

. . . The *mambo* was leading her solemnly chanting retinue around the altar and then escorted them out to where the white cloth enclosure had been formed.

. . . Soon we stood before a crude canopy of cloth about six feet long, three or four feet wide and perhaps six feet high. . . . Reser called it a *card*. He informed us that inside was a tub of water to which had been added wines, liqueurs, small cakes, an egg, leaves of mombin and lalo-guinin, and that the *mambo* had previously made a *veve* of corn meal on the tub. . . .

The seven *hounsi* lay down on the ground in front of the *card* or canopy, each clasping a sacred *govi* in her arms. They lay close together, their bodies touching. Then they were covered completely with a white sheet. This done, the *mambo* stepped inside the *card*, and the flap was fastened down.

. . . The voice of the *mambo* intoned an invocation in Creole. . . . She began calling upon Catholic saints and Voodoo *loa*, and the crowd, led by Reser, responded. . . .

This litany was repeated for the various deities, for both Christian saints and African *loa*. . . . Then the *mambo* called for a *govi*. There was a rustling beneath the sheet, and the hands of a *hounsi* held up a sacred vase. This was passed in to the *mambo*.

. . . All at once a sound came from inside the cloth enclosure. It was a sudden babbling of water like a brook rushing over stones. Then there was a brief instant of quiet, out of which came a man's voice, deep and gasping.

"He's speaking from the island beneath the sea," Reser said quietly. "The first soul is being released."

The spirit voice speaking in Creole called the name of one of the worshippers. A woman in the crowd responded eagerly. Then a message came for her veiled by the water's sound. . . . Reser explained that the departed souls were not only giving messages, but that they were being liberated from their "purgatory" of bondage and assisted in the attainment of a happier, fuller life.

At the end of about five minutes the *govi* was returned to the *hounsi* under the sheet. Each *govi* would, in turn, be presented to the *mambo,* and the spirit of a departed loved one would be conjured from below the water. Each would give messages and advice and go on to its liberation. . . .

. . . The voices "from the dead" and the human voices carried on their dialogues. . . . He [Reser] believed unquestioningly that these muffled utterances were those of discarnate spirits. Some had been invoked, but others came through by their own striving force, begging to be liberated and asking the *mambo* to take pity upon them and "raise them up. . . ."[9]

Ceremonies like the above are a strain on the credulity of anyone outside the influence of vodou. There are other features of the vodou religion which similarly partake more of the nature of magic and superstition than of straight religion.[10] Possession by the *loas,* however, is not such a feature. Those who have made a close study of this phenomenon are agreed that (except for isolated instances) no trickery, no magic, is involved.

Several writers distinguish between religion and magic on the ground that religion involves an effort to invoke the guidance and protection of the gods, who will decide for themselves whether the petitioner's plea should be granted, whereas magic involves an attempt to *compel* God, or the gods, to bring about the desired action, whether or not it is moral and right. As stated by Maya Deren,

. . . the magician acts directly upon reality and produces *results* by his actions; the hungan acts as interlocutor between supplicant and loa, who *reward* the performance of the ritual service. One is man-made magic; the other is god-made miracle. In magic, the magician is the supreme power; in Vodun the loa are the supreme power.

The loa of Vodun, like the divinities of all religions, are not only supernatural forces; they are also a supra-human moral authority. They have standards of good and bad, of right and wrong. To worship the loa is to celebrate not only their power but also their moral nature and the justice with which they dispense their miracles; and since the loa do not depend upon man, there is no sacrificial offering which could or would induce them to abandon their moral standards. . . .[11]

Just how this principle can be applied in the case of the ceremony of recalling the spirits of the dead is not clear. Few if any non-vodouists will believe that the voices heard during the ceremony were actually those of the deceased. The high reputation of most *houngans* and *mambos* makes it unlikely that deliberate deception is involved. Some might ask whether it is not a case of involuntary or unconscious deception, i.e., self-delusion on the part of the *houngan* or *mambo,* producing in some fashion voices that can be mistaken for those of the deceased and having them say the things that seem best fitted to the occasion.

Manipulative magic of the sort described by Maya Deren is carried out in Haiti by men called *bocors.* These magicians or sorcerers or witch doctors may be resorted to for pretty nearly any type of problem, including cures for illness, winning the affections of a coveted person of the opposite sex, and putting a hex on an enemy. In the curing of illness, *bocors* compete with the *houngans,* who also have a special knowledge of herbs and their curative effects. The *bocor* of course benefits from the widespread prevalence of superstition, in that the superstitious often have recourse to his knowledge and techniques to ward off the misfortunes they apprehend—especially if they have a guilty conscience which tells them that the misfortunes are deserved. The *bocor* will supply charms against the evil eye, a *ouanga* which will bring bad luck to one's enemy, or a *garde* to combat the evil effects on oneself of an enemy's *ouanga.* Or he will supply a thing called *drogue* that is supposed to make one impervious to gunshot or weapon blow; should the *drogue* fail of its effects, it is assumed that counter-magic was the cause of failure.[12]

As is only natural, in view of the prevailing degree of illiteracy and ignorance, superstition is widespread in Haiti. Most members of the lower classes believe in such things as *zombis,* demons, werewolves, and *bakalous.* A *zombi* is someone who was presumed to have died, was buried, and was then resurrected to become the silent and permanent slave of the evil person who engineered his "death." Although no such instance has ever been proven, the myth is taken for the fact. So fearful have some of the more unenlightened been lest a deceased relative become the *zombi* of an enemy that they have sometimes allowed a knife to be plunged into the corpse to ensure actual death, as opposed to a state of possibly temporary unconsciousness which would make resurrection possible. Demons and werewolves are persons who turn themselves into animals for the purpose of eating the flesh and drinking the blood of humans. *Bakalous* are evil spirits who are said to make devilish bargains with people, bestowing upon them some greatly desired power in exchange for the death of a member of their family, then another and another.[13]

Haitian folklore is by no means confined to such things as magic, *zombis,* demons, werewolves, and *bakalous.* There are also highly agreeable aspects, including hauntingly beautiful music and delightful folkloric dances. In this chapter, however, we have touched only on those aspects which are in some way related to the problem of education, the subject of our next chapter.

# □□□ 11
# Education

Up-to-date statistics on Haiti's educational system are scanty and unreliable. It is unlikely, however, that accurate data on the situation as it exists today would show major changes (other than those due to population growth) from the situation which existed in the fiscal year 1951-52, for which reasonably accurate and detailed data are available. The 1951-52 figures were published by the Haitian Institute of Statistics.

At the same time, the institute published the data on illiteracy in Haiti which had been obtained as part of the national census of August 1950. In the country as a whole, 90.4 per cent of the population was found to be illiterate. For males the ratio of illiteracy was 88.7 per cent, for females 91.9 per cent. In the city of Port-au-Prince, however, only 46.3 per cent of the population was illiterate (38 per cent of males, 52.2 per cent of females). Smaller towns showed an illiteracy rate of 49 per cent, while in villages the rate was 60 per cent. In the purely rural areas, 92 per cent of the population was illiterate. These ratios are, of course, appalling, and they are among the worst in the world.[1]

In 1951-52 there were 1,522 schools of all kinds in Haiti. Of these, all but 60 provided only primary instruction. The others were secondary schools (13 of them public and 20 private), professional schools, normal schools, etc. Ten years later the number of primary schools had risen to 1,593, and the number of secondary establishments and normal and professional schools had increased to 108; there were also 965 schools for adults and 15 university schools.[2]

The teaching staff for the whole school system in 1951-52 numbered 4,263. This gives an average of less than three per school, indicating the diminutive size of most of the schools. Only 469 teachers were assigned to secondary and other schools above the primary level. By 1961-62 the teaching staff in the whole school system (other than adult and university schools) totaled 6,783, or an average of four per school. In the 1,593 primary schools, the teaching staff numbered 5,551, an average of 3.5 per school.[3]

The total number of pupils in 1951-52 was 162,338, of whom all but 7,228 were in primary schools. Comparison of the teaching staff in primary schools (3,794) with the number of primary pupils (155,110) gives 40.9 as the *average* size of classes in 1951-52. In many instances this meant 50, 60, or more per class. By 1969 the average class size had risen to 46 for the country as a whole and to 61 in the rural public schools. Some rural classes had more than 80 pupils.

Since the population of Haiti in 1951-52 averaged around 3,200,000, the total number of pupils was then equivalent to 5 per cent of the population. If, as a former Minister of Education stated in 1952, the number of persons aged between 5 and 19 made up 33 per cent of the population, it follows that only about 15 per cent of those eligible for school attendance were actually going to school.[4] By 1969 the percentage of school-age children in school was reliably reported to have dropped to 11.6 per cent.

Under Haitian law, education is compulsory and free between the ages of 7 and 14, and children may receive free instruction from the age of 4. From data given by the Institute of Statistics, one may deduce that the percentage of children within the age range 4-14 who were enrolled in the schools was (in 1951-52) something like 75 per cent in the urban communities and less than 11 per cent in the rural areas.[5] It is clear that the law "compelling" school attendance was without much practical effect. The situation was even more serious than these figures indicate if one takes into account absenteeism and dropouts. The average daily attendance at urban primary schools in 1951-52 was 59,200 out of a total enrollment of 67,576, while at rural primary schools only 57,358 out of an enrollment of 76,190 were in actual attendance, on the average.[6]

These quantitative data are bad enough, but what makes Haiti's educational problem really desperate is the poor quality of most of the instruction imparted in the primary schools, combined with the fact that it is given in a language (French) which few of the pupils comprehend, at least in the early stages of their schooling.

Haiti's educational system is modeled after that of France. Boys and girls attend separate schools, at least at the primary level. Sports play only a minor role, and extracurricular activities are practically unknown. The primary schools offer six years of study, upon the satisfactory completion of which the *certificat d'études primaires* is granted. At some schools a further three years of study entitle the successful candidate to the *brevet élémentaire,* while another two years successfully completed bring him the *brevet supérieur.*

Secondary schools consist of *lycées,* which are owned and operated by the state, and *collèges,* which are privately owned high schools. Until 1918 these schools gave a purely classical type of education, with emphasis on the Greek, Latin, and French languages. For many years before 1918, however, competent Haitian educators had increasingly criticized this concentration on classical erudition to the exclusion of practical knowledge which would be useful in the workaday world. In 1905 a committee of educational experts was appointed to study Haiti's school system and recommend reforms. This committee recommended splitting secondary-school instruction into two cycles. Greek and Latin were to be omitted from the first cycle, to which was to be added a course in agriculture. The second cycle was to have two alternative sections, one devoted to the humanities, the other to the physical and natural sciences. In justification of this reform, the committee said in its report:

> In short, we have pursued a double aim: an educational aim and a utilitarian aim. Education should be directed first to the development of all of the faculties of mind and heart; to arrive at this result we believe that the literary humanities as well as the "scientific humanities" can and should contribute. But the young man who leaves the *lycée* will enter upon an active life. He will have to struggle in order to make a place for himself in the sun. He will have to function within a social group which must itself struggle against other groups which are better armed or more competent. What would be the value of an education which did not prepare those trained by it for this dual combat: individual competition, international competition; which left them ignorant of the enormous power that science bestows on man over nature; which failed to show them the work of renewal and transformation that the world goes through thanks to modern techniques? Thus, without any sacrifice from the educative point of view, we have not been afraid to orient people's minds toward utility. . . .[7]

As we saw in chapter 5, the American occupying authorities not only criticized the excessively literary nature of Haitian school instruction but took drastic measures to change it. They were perhaps unaware that the Haitians themselves had long ago tried to steer their educational system into more practical channels, as demonstrated by the above-mentioned report.

Unfortunately, the Murville-Férère commission's recommendations were not put into practice, owing mainly to a change of Finance Minister. On the other hand, a new commission which was appointed in 1914 for the same general purpose made similar recommendations. In 1918, Dr. Dantès Bellegarde, who had been a member of both commissions, became Minister of Education and in that capacity was able to put through the desired reform. Thereafter, completion of the first cycle, of three years' duration, led to the award of the certificate of first-degree secondary studies, while upon completion of the second cycle (of four years' duration) the student was awarded the baccalaureate, or certificate of second-degree secondary studies. While in office as Finance Minister, Dr. Bellegarde instituted a number of other reforms, including the creation of a School of Building Trades and an Industrial School, and the organization of a vocational department in one of the boys' schools, now known as the J. B. Damier School. He was, in fact, working along lines similar to those of the occupying authorities. The latter, however, took every opportunity to snub the Minister of Education and veto his plans.[8] Had they, on the contrary, joined forces with Dr. Bellegarde, they could have achieved far more and would have left a favorable imprint on the minds of most Haitians, at least so far as educational problems are concerned.

Dr. Bellegarde's 1918 reform of the curriculum of secondary schools remained, for the most part, in effect until 1929, when a Minister of Education who was partial to Greek and Latin restored the uniformly classical curriculum. Since then other changes have occurred. At present, students in the public secondary schools are allowed a choice between classical studies—a combined science and modern-language section—and a technical section. Completion of one of these sections and successful passing of two official examinations (one at the end of *Rhétorique,* as the sixth year of study is called, the other after *Philosophie,* the seventh year) lead to the baccalaureate (Certificate of Secondary Studies). The baccalaureate examinations are so difficult that it is not unusual for more than half of those taking the first examination to be rejected, while anywhere from 10 to 50 per cent of those taking the second examination fall by the wayside. Only the few who expect to go on to college try for the baccalaureate. The Haitian baccalaureate is accepted by the school authorities of France as the equivalent of their own.

Haiti's educational problems revolve primarily around its peasantry. As will have become evident to the reader by now, Port-au-Prince, with its university, agricultural school, *lycées,* Catholic and private schools, vocational schools, normal schools, military academy, apostolic school, Bureau of Ethnology, Centre d'Art, etc., has a sufficiently modern system to justify an absence of any particular concern. There is more of a problem in the smaller towns. But the major problem is how to bring enlightenment to the rural areas.

The obstacles to educational progress in rural Haiti may be discussed under six headings: (1) language difficulties; (2) a shortage of teachers; (3) the inadequate financial resources of the state; (4) the poverty of the people; (5) the random pattern of population dispersion; and (6) health hindrances.

Little need be added to what was said in Chapter 9 about the problems growing out of the existence in Haiti of two languages: one (French) which the élite insist is the only possible official language for Haiti, another (Creole) which is the only one the masses know. The language difficulties in the school system are threefold: (a) the pupils cannot comprehend, or they have great difficulty in comprehending, what their teachers are saying to them in French, and they have no opportunity to use or practice the French language at home or in their local neighborhoods; (b) the teachers are required to instruct in the French language, which they may or may not be competent to do; whatever degree of competence they do possess in French they are proud to show off as proof of their scholastic achievements and of their claim to membership in the élite; there is thus no likelihood of their lapsing voluntarily into Creole to facilitate the learning task of the pupils; (c) there were until 20 years ago no textbooks in Creole; the few which now exist are only a drop in the bucket of what would be needed if instruction were to be generally given in Creole, even if only in the lower grades; moreover, these few textbooks do not all use the same spelling system, thus making for confusion in the learner.

The shortage of teachers in Haiti is such that even if the funds suddenly became available to build enough schools to accommodate all children of school age, only a fraction of such schools could be put into operation. Teachers, in other words, are the main limiting factor. This is true even if one assumes that additions to the teaching staff would not be of better quality than the present staff, whose qualifications often leave much to be desired. The shortage would be infinitely greater if all schools had to be staffed with well-trained professional teachers. Many of the rural teachers have had no normal-school training, and many do not even hold the baccalaureate degree. Many persons, despite a lack of interest in education, take a teaching job as a stopgap while waiting for employment in business or government. The work of rural teachers has few attractions. The pay is extremely low (the maximum in recent years has been $50 per month; it was much lower formerly), and there is no tenure. For an educated person, life in the Haitian countryside can be a dreary affair, since there is no access to cultural activities, such as concerts, lectures, theaters, museums, and social gatherings.

As a third obstacle to educational progress, the Haitian government does not enjoy the financial resources that it would need for a really large-scale expansion and improvement of the school system. Out of total annual revenues fluctuating usually between 20 and 30 million dollars, the government has traditionally allotted roughly 10 per cent to education. Revenue devoted to military expense has been much higher than 10 per cent, and one may certainly ask why education should be starved for the benefit of the military. But even if education's share of total government revenues were doubled, the increase would amount to only 2 or 3 million dollars per annum—hardly more than a start at solving Haiti's monumental education problem. Not only must schools be built in the hundreds or thousands, but teachers must be trained, hired, and paid at better salaries than are now the rule; most existing schools must be refurnished or repaired, or both; textbooks must be written, printed and distributed; libraries, laboratories, audio-visual equipment, and canteens must be installed.

If the government is poor, so are the people whose children require education. In many, if not most, peasant families, children who go to school must do so on empty stomachs because the family cannot afford more than one or two meals a day.[9] How can children so undernourished have the stamina of mind and body to sit through a day at school and absorb much learning, especially when it is transmitted in what is to them a "foreign" language? In a sample survey conducted by the Haitian Institute of Statistics, more than 40 per cent of the teachers (in some areas more than 75 per cent) reported having observed a state of malnutrition among their pupils.[10]

Apart from the food problem, there is the matter of dress. Haitian children up to the age of puberty are customarily allowed to go naked, but in school they must wear clothes. Many peasant families either cannot afford to clothe them properly or prefer to keep them at home in order to avoid this expense. There is also the cost of textbooks, which the state does not bear.

The Haitian countryside has few villages. The population is widely dispersed among the mountains and valleys. It is customary for the children, when they marry, to build a home within a stone's throw of the bridegroom's family. Thus the typical country scene is of clusters of four, five, or six huts scattered here and there. There are also many individual isolated homes on the mountainsides. This unique population pattern makes the choice of convenient school sites difficult. No matter where a rural school is set up, only a few families can be within easy walking distance of it. Many children must walk several miles to and from school, often up and down steep mountain slopes, sometimes under a broiling sun, at other times in a heavy downpour. Considering how many of them do this on an empty or near-empty stomach, it is all the more remarkable that they should have the strength and the courage to attend school. Even more remarkable, they are usually able to laugh and smile through 'it all. The reader may ask, "Are there no school buses?" The answer is, "No." To begin with, there are very few roads in the Haitian countryside, and those few are usable only in the dry seasons. None, of course, is paved. For the most part, the children reach school via mountain or valley trails.

Finally, the poor health of most Haitian children is an additional hindrance. In the above-mentioned sample survey, about one-fourth of the teachers reported skin eruptions among their pupils, more than 10 per cent reported dental caries, some 8 per cent reported intestinal worms, and more than 80 per cent reported other evidences of ill health. What the latter may have consisted of is not known, but we do know that the most common diseases in Haiti have been tuberculosis, malaria, syphilis, yaws, and influenza. Clearly, when ill health is added to undernourishment, children who have to walk miles to attend an overcrowded class conducted in a strange language by an untrained teacher using textbooks unrelated to the world they live in are not going to derive much benefit. Topping off all these difficulties is the total absence of electric lights in rural areas, making homework impracticable.

The United Nations and its specialized agency UNESCO have both given Haiti advice and assistance in overcoming its educational handicap. In Chapter 6 we told of UNESCO's action in setting up, jointly with the Haitian government, a pilot project in fundamental education in the Marbial Valley. The term "fundamental education" was defined as follows in 1950 by a mixed committee in Paris:

> By "Fundamental Education" is understood that minimum of general education which has as its purpose helping children, and adults deprived of the advantages of a school education, to understand the problems of the environment in which they live, to form a correct idea of their rights and duties, civic as well as individual, and to participate more effectively in the economic and social program of the community of which they are a part.
>
> It is "Fundamental" in the sense that it confers the minimum of theoretical and technical knowledge that is indispensable for attaining a sufficiently high level of life. Without it, the activities of specialized services (hygiene, agriculture, etc.) could not be fully effective.
>
> It is "general" in the sense that this theoretical and technical knowledge is not transmitted simply for its own sake. Fundamental education has recourse to more active methods; it concentrates interest on the concrete problems presented by the environment and, in doing so, aims to develop both the personality of the individual and social life.
>
> It has reference to children who cannot benefit from adequate primary instruction and adults who have not had the opportunity to get an education; it uses appropriate means to further their development thanks to individual effort and social life.[11]

UNESCO announced that the specific aims of the Marbial pilot project were to try out [the] most advanced techniques of Fundamental Education, test new educational materials [improved textbooks, visual and oral aids] and use education to raise social, economic and health levels.[12]

The project involved setting up a two-year teacher-training center, two rural primary schools, and ten adult centers for teaching literacy in Creole. It was expected that the World Health Organization would assume the responsibility for health education and for a campaign against malaria, yaws, and hookworm, while the United Nations Food and Agriculture Organization would operate a model farm and demonstrate crop rotation and veterinary practices. Unfortunately, UNESCO went ahead with the project before reaching an agreement with WHO and FAO, with the result that WHO contributed only the services of a doctor and a nurse for a one-year period, while the FAO proved unwilling to participate at its own expense. Nevertheless, the project was useful as a demonstration of what could be done on a larger scale, and as a training center for teachers of fundamental education in other parts of Haiti. In January 1954 the Marbial project was taken over by the Haitian government and its operation entrusted to the Adult Education Division of the Ministry of Education.

The United Nations study mission of 1948 made extensive recommendations for improving Haiti's educational system. The mission's report contained four major recommendations in education, supplemented by ten more detailed suggestions. The major recommendations were:

1. An intensive national effort to reduce illiteracy.
2. The preparation and publication of a series of basic readers for the literacy campaign, and of a minimum series of elementary school books for all the school children in Haiti.
3. The initiation of a practical industrial training and apprenticeship program.
4. The extension of the rural community school program.

On all of these points, appreciable progress has been made since 1948, but much more intensive efforts are required.

With respect to the first point, the U.N. mission, while praising the advantages of the French language as "a suitable instrument with which to share in scientific and technological progress of the modern world," pointed out that it seemed logical "to develop a method of teaching French to the rural population which is based on previous ability to speak, read, and write the native language," and that "the linguistic and phonetic relationships between Creole and French are strong enough to make possible a rapid transition from the former to the French."[13] The Haitian government has not yet taken this basic decision to teach literacy in *all* schools in the Creole language and to move on from there to the teaching of French. It still relies on special classes for literacy instruction in Creole, instead of generalizing this type of instruction throughout the school system.

Only a few textbooks have been printed in the Creole language. If literacy instruction in Creole is to be generalized, a far greater effort is necessary to produce enough Creole textbooks of the right sort, i.e., related to the national environment rather than to French or classical conditions.

The U.N. mission's third recommendation may be said to have been faithfully followed; a practical industrial training and apprenticeship program has indeed been initiated. Numerous experts were obtained from the Bureau of International Labor during the fifties and sixties to teach young Haitians in such practical fields as carpentry, metalwork, plumbing, leather-tanning, wheelmaking, automobile mechanics, and electricity, and to prepare others to teach these skills. The J. B. Damier trade school was reorganized, similar schools were opened in several provincial towns, and modern equipment and tools were received from ILO for use by the students. This good beginning should be followed up by intensive and expanded efforts. A recent initiative of the West German government will apparently make such a follow-up possible (see p. 206).

The fourth recommendation made by the U.N. mission—extension of the rural community school program—has also been applied, at least within limits. The U.N. mission's report explained the need for community schools as follows:

> . . . Without community centres or cores, essential public services for the protection of education and of agricultural production

are impossible. In order to enlist all Haitians in the programme of national rehabilitation, the organization of villages or rural centres is a necessity. Any scheme for the development of rural communities must be accompanied by a nation-wide effort to provide a minimum of fundamental education for the rural people of Haiti. Such educational efforts should consist in teaching the peasants the simplest notions of hygiene, government, science, tools and machines, and how to use the skills of reading and writing in their daily activities.[14]

The aims of this sort of program are clearly similar to those of UNESCO's fundamental education program, on which, as we have seen, Haiti was already making a start in 1948. The setting up of community centers, moreover, is useful for the purpose of "community development" programs, which endeavor to organize local communities for the purpose of achieving through self-help the improvements they need. The U.N. in the fifties provided Haiti with a community development expert, who succeeded in bringing about the creation of a community development office in the government. With the cooperation of ILO and UNICEF, the Duvalier government in 1966 set up a number of Centres d'Artisanat Rural which, in addition to instructing peasants in the production and use of new types of tools, were expected to demonstrate how rural communities could build schools, dispensaries, etc., through their own efforts. In 1954 the Haitian government and the ICA jointly launched a new *servicio* called SCHAER (Service Coopératif Haitiano-Américain d'Education Rurale), which had as its main purposes training rural teachers and promoting the creation of community schools along the lines described in the U.N. mission report. SCHAER cooperated with a Rural Normal School which the government organized in the outskirts of Port-au-Prince in 1954, and it organized seminars for rural teachers in various parts of Haiti. In this program it had the help of two other *servicios,* SCISP and SCIPA, as well as the cooperation of a U.N. expert.

On the whole a good start has been made at improving Haiti's educational system, but it is only a start. A vastly greater effort is needed, and this means more of everything: schools, teachers, textbooks, and money. The community school is undoubtedly the right approach, but it should involve the use of Creole for the first year or two of instruction before making use of the French language. If community schools cannot be built everywhere simultaneously, there is no apparent reason why classes cannot be held in churches, *houmforts,* or other structures which are not in daily use, or even under the thousands of beautiful, shady mango trees with which Haiti is blessed. It should furthermore be possible to build hundreds of community schools by organizing rural inhabitants into *coumbites* for this specific purpose. The *coumbite* (an informal working group of neighbors) is a popular device to which Haitian peasants resort when faced by tasks which require numerous hands, such as the building of a home and the harvesting of a crop. It may be compared to the American husking or quilting bee.

The provision for education in the national budget should be raised substantially by cutting other less essential items and by reducing opportunities for graft through better budget administration. All possible financial help for education should be sought from the international agencies, particularly the IBRD and the IDB, as well as from the U.S. government and American philanthropic organizations. But, as the above enumeration of difficulties indicates, the educational problem cannot be fully solved if it is tackled separately and in isolation from the problems of nutrition, health, roads, transportation, and general poverty.

# 🔲🔲🔲 12
# Agriculture

The description and analysis of Haiti's agricultural system are made difficult by the absence or unreliability of statistics on production, consumption, and domestic trade, and by the incompleteness of data on existing resources. The Haitian Institute of

Statistics, which was set up in 1950 with the help of a United Nations expert, has been able to fill only a part of this void.

As already noted, Haiti is so mountainous that only about 21 per cent of the land consists of plains with an altitude of less than 600 feet.[1] The mountains run in a northwest-southeast direction, except in the south, where they run east-west. Since the prevailing trade winds come from the northeast, the northern (or northeastern) slopes of the mountains receive a relatively heavy and frequent rainfall, while areas on the other side of the mountains receive much less precipitation or are in fact quite arid. Thus Haiti enjoys a variety of climates determined by local differences in elevation, precipitation, and temperature. The climatic variety, in turn, makes possible the production of varied types of commodities. Haiti is therefore hardly typical of what a small tropical country is often thought to be—a one-crop economy—even though a single product (coffee) makes up an undesirably large proportion of its exports. There is a potential of widely diversified exports.

Another unique feature of Haiti is its physical contours. The country consists, in large part, of two very long peninsulas that jut out, pincerlike, from the western side of Hispaniola. The northern peninsula is shorter and much wider than the one to the south. The two peninsulas are separated by the Gulf of Gonave. East of the gulf, between the bases or hinterlands of the two peninsulas, lie the Artibonite Valley, a mountain chain (Chaine des Matheux), and the Cul-de-Sac (Dead End) Valley. The last-named is only about 12 miles wide and 20 miles long. Port-au-Prince, the capital and principal port, lies in this valley, facing the gulf. There are a few offshore islands, the principal ones being La Gonave, in the gulf, and the Ile de la Tortue (Turtle, or Tortuga, Island) off the north coast. Owing to its peculiar configuration, Haiti has a long coastline dotted with numerous ports. Despite the country's diminutive size, distances by road can be surprisingly long, so that land travel, already impeded by the mountainous terrain and primitive roads, is cumbersome. Coastwise shipping has therefore shown a considerable development.
Land erosion had begun even during the colonial era, as the

French chopped down much of the forest for buildings, domestic fuel, etc., thus permitting the mountain soil to descend into the valleys and rivers, much of it to be swept out to sea. Erosion did not become serious, however, until the nineteenth century; it has since become one of Haiti's most acute and urgent problems. Not only has the amount of fertile land been greatly reduced, but rain-water now pours down the mountainsides to create damaging and dangerous flash floods, disrupting agriculture, trade, and traffic.

The French colonists had built roads and irrigation and drainage systems throughout the country and set up 3,150 indigo farms, 3,117 coffee plantations, 793 sugar estates, 789 cotton farms, 182 rum distilleries, and numerous other enterprises.[2] None of this remains in its original state, although the ruins of some of the ancient structures have been used as the basis of modern facilities. The French system of land tenure was one of large estates, each owned by a French family and worked under its supervision by the Negro slaves. With the departure of the French, much of the land was distributed in farm-size parcels to veterans of the liberation army. The Haitian legal system, based on the *Code Napoléon,* divided the inheritance of property among all the children of the deceased owner, including his "illegitimate" children, who were sometimes numerous. As time went on, therefore, family holdings became smaller and smaller. By 1950, about 40 per cent of all agricultural holdings had an area of less than one *carreau* (3.19 acres), 70 per cent had an area of less than two *carreaux,* and only 6 per cent had an area in excess of five *carreaux.*[3] What is more, these holdings were often split up into two or more plots at some distance from one another, as a result of sales and exchanges between relatives and other owners.

The 1950 census revealed that more than 80 per cent of the peasants occupying Haitian farmland were, or at least claimed to be, the legal owners of their land. The remaining occupants were split up between (1) those holding leases from the state; (2) those leasing from private owners; (3) those managing land 'for the account of others; and (4) sharecroppers on a 50-50 basis. It is probable that many of those who claimed legal ownership were in fact squatters on government land. In two communities, for instance, only 51 per cent of the occupants were reported as owners, while 40 per cent were shown as "occupants without a title." There are no official cadastral records in Haiti, so that a chaotic situation exists with respect to the actual ownership of land. The resulting insecurity of tenure is one of the numerous obstacles to progress in Haitian agriculture. The government attempted in 1934 to bypass this obstacle by passing the *Loi sur le Bien Rural de Famille* (Law on Family Rural Property), under which a family could acquire ownership of a government plot by exploiting it profitably under certain conditions over a five-year period. However, the application of this law

> has been difficult chiefly because of the inadequate agricultural education of the peasants and their lack of capital or credit. . . . The mere promise of a gift of land, even the actual conferring of land ownership, may amount to nothing and actually be an evil instead of a blessing, if it is not adequately supplemented by effective education and the provision of credit facilities and a convenient advisory service. The general ignorance of the Haitian peasant, his reluctance to adopt new methods, and his lack of confidence and capital are indeed great obstacles with which the law of January, 1934, unfortunately had not reckoned.[4]

The Haitian peasant, who makes up something like 88 per cent of the total population, sometimes gives the impression of indolence and laziness. This is due in part to malnutrition and disease. When well nourished and free from illness, he reveals himself as intelligent and capable of hard work. However, he has little foresight, and no conception of such terms as "progress" and "development." If he can eke out a bare subsistence for himself and family, he is satisfied; unfortunately, the instances where he cannot do this are far too frequent. And even if he can, he has usually no reserve of cash or commodities with which to face such emergencies as hurricanes, floods, and droughts. So general is poverty in the Haitian countryside that even if a peasant family does acquire some slight surplus over and above its daily needs, it is reluctant to disclose the fact, for fear of arousing envy and inviting theft.

In his thoughtful treatise on the Haitian economy, Paul Moral makes the following interesting comparison between the output of the colonial régime and that of independent Haiti. The total value of exports from Saint-Domingue on the eve of the French Revolution was $75.4 million; that of Haiti's exports today is only $31 million.[5] In 1789 the owners of 8,500 plantations in Saint-Domingue having an area of 1,235,000 acres exported, with the help of 400,000 slaves, 24,000 tons of white sugar and 47,000 tons of raw sugar, 38,500 tons of coffee, and 3,500 tons of cotton. At present 560,000 peasant families exploiting somewhere between 1,480,000 and 1,730,000 acres produce for export 15,500 tons of sugar, 25,000 tons of coffee, 1,000 tons of cotton, and 24,000 tons of sisal.[6] This is, of course, an oversimplification, but it does bring out a brutal fact: today's vastly greater population, with access to scientific methods unheard of in 1789, appears unable or unwilling to equal the achievements of the colonial economy of almost two centuries ago. It underlines further that *if* the right measures were adopted, the Haitian economy of today could, without the shadow of a doubt, produce far more, probably several times more, than it is actually producing. In other words, economic development is not by any means an impossible dream for Haiti, once the problem is thoroughly understood and a national determination reached to solve it. It would be absurd to say that an economy of free men today cannot accomplish more than a very much smaller slave economy achieved two centuries ago.

What, then, are the problems and the potential of Haiti's agricultural crops of today? We shall treat first those commodities which are produced primarily for export, although in each instance there is a certain (but often unknown) amount of local consumption.

Haiti's most valuable crop is coffee. All but 1.3 per cent of Haiti's coffee producers today occupy plots of 5 *carreaux* (16 acres) or less. No less than 72.8 per cent of them have plots of only 1 *carreau* (3.19 acres) or less. In further contrast to colonial times, today's coffee is not grown out in the open, exposed to the sun; it is grown in the shade of trees—often banana trees. It is grown from sea level up to an altitude of 5,000 to 5,500 feet. At least 60 per cent of Haiti's area is considered well suited to produce a fine type of coffee. About two-thirds of total production now comes from the southern peninsula.

The peasant pays little attention to his coffee bushes. He does not trim and prune them, as the colonial settlers did. He does not even plant bushes, simply allowing new ones to grow up from the berries that fall to the ground when rats eat the outer pulp. Instead of picking the red berries, the peasant with one quick movement of the hand sweeps off all the berries, ripe and unripe, from each branch. Weeding and cleaning take place only once a year. Thus only a small and variable yield is obtained. The peasant's methods of preparing the beans for market are also defective. A long and detailed law known as the *Code du Café* regulates, at least in theory, most aspects of the cultivation, preparation for market, transportation, sale, and export of coffee. This law provides for eight standard types or qualities of coffee for export and levies a tax which increases as the quality decreases (the two best grades being exempt from the tax). According to the 1948 report of the U.N. study mission, this law, combined with quality policing by Ministry of Agriculture inspectors, had not accomplished the desired result, the quality of Haitian coffee had therefore suffered, and complaints had been received from foreign purchasers. Moreover, according to the report, scarcity and high prices of foodstuffs had turned the peasant's attention away from coffee to the production of food crops, and in some areas coffee bushes had been cut down and replaced by food crops, "which provide a greater feeling of security and are subject neither to policing for quality nor to taxation."[7] While coffee is still Haiti's leading export, its relative importance has declined in recent years. It is clear that with proper procedures, the country could increase substantially the quantity of coffee it produces, undoubtedly with some improvement in quality.

Sugar is next in importance as an export crop. Following the destruction of the sugar mills during the revolution, there were no further exports of sugar, although this commodity had made up 48 per cent of the value of all colonial exports. Not until the latter part of the nineteenth century was sugar again exported, and it was only a trickle. Sugar cane continued to be grown, mixed with other crops on peasant plots, and was transformed into syrup, *rapadou* (brown sugar), *tafia* (a drink containing 10 to 15 per cent alcohol), and *clairin* (25 to 30 per cent alcohol), all for domestic consumption. In 1916 an American company known as HASCO (Haitian-American Sugar Company) set up a modern sugar mill on the outskirts of Port-au-Prince for the processing of sugar grown in the Cul-de-Sac Valley and part of the southern peninsula. Exports gradually resumed. In the ten fiscal years ended in 1926, an annual average of 4,637 metric tons of raw sugar was exported; in the two following decades the annual average rose to 18,250 and 30,925 tons, respectively.[8] HASCO's exports of unrefined sugar, however, make up less than half its total production. The rest, including a small quantity of refined sugar, is sold in the domestic market under strict government regulation of its price and distribution. About 100,000 hectoliters (2.6 million gallons) of molasses is also produced. Altogether, HASCO processes the cane from some 27,000 acres, of which less than 40 per cent are exploited directly by HASCO; the remaining acreage is that of independent growers.[9]

Following the 1951 visit of an FAO sugar expert, who reported favorably on the feasibility of further sugar mills in Haiti, the Magloire government took steps to encourage the setting up of new mills in various parts of the country. The so-called Dessalines mill was built by Cuban interests in the Cayes area. The Centrale Sucrière Nord d'Haiti, a mill which had been partly set up on the north coast by (of all things) the Congregation of the Immaculate Heart of Mary, was scheduled for completion. A private Haitian company, HARICO (Haitian Sugar Refinery Company), was granted a concession for operating a refinery at Jérémie, on the north coast of the southern peninsula. Two or three smaller mills were planned for other areas. The only one of these projects that became operative was the Dessalines mill at Cayes, and it quickly ran into difficulties, attributed largely to mismanagement. In 1956 it was taken over by the government and entrusted to the care of IHCAI, the Agricultural and Industrial Credit Institute. The Dessalines plant raises part of its own cane and buys the rest from nearby peasant growers; its output is small in relation to that of HASCO.

Surveying the difficulties encountered in getting new sugar mills into profitable production, Moral comments:

> All these unsuccessful projects seem to present as a common factor a very faulty appreciation of the conditions for setting up and operating a modern sugar mill in a rural environment which though favorable to the cultivation of sugar cane and in fact producing worthwhile quantities, lacks three essential elements, namely: an irrigation network, a system for collecting and routing the crop, and the regrouping of the cane. . . . One of the prime causes of the Dessalines mill's setback in the Aux Cayes region was the absence of a regular and massive supply of the raw material, the dispersion of producers, and the multiplicity of transactions. . . .[10]

Further difficulties were entailed by the fact that Haiti did not, until recent years, enjoy more than a ridiculously small quota for sugar exports to the United States, and thus was forced to dispose of practically all its sugar at the lower price prevailing in the world market. It is questionable whether any of the mills erected or planned in Haiti since 1950 can turn a satisfactory profit at the world market price. Until the advent of Castro, Cuba received something like 96 per cent of the total U.S. sugar import quota, leaving only driblets for such producers as Haiti, El Salvador, and Nicaragua. Even the latter two countries were consistently favored over Haiti. During the mid-fifties the U.S. annual quota for Haiti averaged only about 2,500 tons. Since the disappearance of Cuba as a source of U.S. sugar imports, the Haitian quota has been gradually increased. For 1971 it is 25,892 tons.

Competent observers agree that Haiti could greatly expand its sugar exports if an efficient plan for this purpose were put into effect. The United Nations 1948 mission found that sugar-cane yields in Haiti could be increased through better use of irrigation water, the use of fertilizers, and more widespread use of improved varieties of cane. Holly states that so long as "opportunities for work and prices are satisfactory, and the planters receive help and advice on their methods of production, the system is quite sound and advantageous. Haitian soil can be well fertilized by foreign capital, and Haitian labor directed by wise and skillful experts, but by these only."[11] Moral concludes that "the creation of new sugar mills should certainly be among the prime objectives of economic policy, provided there is serious evaluation of the financial, technical, and agricultural conditions for the success of such enterprises."[12] The Haitian Institute of Statistics has expressed the opinion that by doubling the acreage devoted to sugar cane and employing fertilizer and better methods of cultivation, total output could be quadrupled (from 500,000 to 2 million tons).[13]

Furthermore, as the U.N. mission of 1948 pointed out, HASCO possesses facilities for producing high-grade rum, but does not use them because of unfavorable legislation. Haitian rum is not exported, much to the regret of Americans who have learned while in Haiti to appreciate its outstanding quality.[14]

Before World War II, Haiti's production of sisal fiber was not significant, and the value of sisal exports was well under $1 million. During the war the volume of such exports rose moderately, and their value increased to slightly less than $2 million. After the war, with rising demand and prices, sisal zoomed to second rank among Haiti's exports, with a value of $8.1 million. In fiscal 1949, with a total volume of 29,710 metric tons valued at $9.3 million, sisal made up 30 per cent of the value of all exports. Haiti's sisal boom continued until 1952, when the world price collapsed. Thereafter sisal shipments declined in both volume and value as Asiatic and other prewar sources of fiber supply resumed shipments. Nevertheless, sisal continued until 1968 to be Haiti's second most valuable export; it is now in fifth place. Sisal fiber is used primarily for binder twine, rope, and cordage. It is also used in Haiti for a variety of handmade articles (handbags, rugs, hats, shoes, etc.), primarily for the tourist trade.

The first production of sisal in Haiti was by the two American companies to whom concessions were granted in 1927—the Haitian-American Development Corporation (known as the Dauphin Plantation) and the Haitian Agricultural Corporation (HACOR), both on the north coast (see p. 45). The Dauphin

Plantation covered some 14,000 acres, the Haitian Agricultural Corporation some 2,200. In 1942, SHADA (see p. 64) took up the cultivation of sisal, centering its activities mainly on the west coast. As the postwar boom in sisal developed, a number of large private entrepreneurs undertook the planting of the fiber in various parts of Haiti.

The soil and climate of most of Haiti are particularly well suited to the cultivation of sisal, which grows best in warm and arid or semiarid regions and in limestone soil. It requires, moreover, no irrigation. At the height of the postwar boom some Haitians (including Senator Déjoie, an experienced agronomist) were so impressed with the possibilities that they urged the immediate establishment of sisal nurseries all over the country with a view to making Haiti the world's greatest producer of this product. Actually, Haiti's exports rank third, after Kenya's and Tanganyika's. The Magloire government fortunately preferred to proceed cautiously, established only one such nursery, and carefully avoided introducing sisal in areas where conditions favored coffee, sugar, and other crops. This caution may have been motivated by memories of the SHADA rubber-growing debacle.

It does not appear that much further expansion of sisal-growing in Haiti would be feasible or desirable, but present levels of production have been a distinct boon to the economy and should be maintained, so long as the world price level for sisal makes its production profitable.

In contrast to sisal farming, the production of bananas requires a moist climate, such as one finds in many parts of Haiti. Until this century, bananas were grown in Haiti only for local consumption, and they continue to be one of the most important food items locally. Although small shipments were made abroad in the twenties, it was not until 1935 that systematic exports began. In that year a monopoly of exploitation and export was granted to the Standard Fruit and Steamship Company of New Orleans, which had its own steamers for transporting the bananas to the United States. Standard Fruit itself leased 3,700 acres in the Artibonite Valley and purchased the output of peasant producers. In fiscal 1937, 1.3 million stems of bananas were exported, representing

4.2 per cent of the value of all exports. By fiscal 1941 bananas had risen to second place among Haiti's exports, their value representing 23.5 per cent of the total. This remarkable success continued until, in fiscal 1947, the quantity of bananas exported was no less than 7.3 million stems, with a value of $6.1 million.[15]

Unfortunately, political maneuvering killed the goose that had been laying the golden eggs. Beginning in 1943, regional concessions were granted to newly formed Haitian companies. In 1946, Standard Fruit was deprived of its monopoly on the ground that it had not carried out all its obligations under the contract. Among such obligations were irrigation; loans to the peasant growers; and provision of buying posts, storage facilities, wharves. Banana exports declined in fiscal 1948, when only 3.5 million stems, valued at $2.8 million, were shipped abroad. Each successive year saw a further decline, until by fiscal 1953 the export of 418,000 stems brought in only $263,000. In the meantime Standard Fruit had left Haiti, and the Haitian companies with regional monopolies went out of business one by one. According to Moral,

> These unsound companies hastened to forget their obligations, contrived to buy at the lowest possible price and even dupe the small grower, and introduced the most complete anarchy in the matter of delivering cargo to the ships.[16]

In 1952 the Magloire government resuscitated and refinanced what had been the largest of the Haitian companies engaged in the banana trade, namely, HABANEX (Haitian Banana Export Company), and for a brief interval there was a mild resurgence of banana shipments, but within three years HABANEX was declared bankrupt and the effort to revive banana exports was taken over by IHCAI. The latter launched an energetic program of extension of banana plantations, but it ran out of funds for this purpose when the political chaos of 1957 resulted in a financial crisis. In 1958 the Duvalier government granted a concession to an American company called the West India Fruit and Steamship Company, entitling it for 15 years to exploit up to 19,000 acres of land in northern and central Haiti for banana cultivation and export. There is no indication that this contract ever became effective.

The mishandling of the banana trade by successive Haitian governments has been nothing less than a tragedy, since it is universally agreed that much of Haiti's climate and soil is ideally suited to banana production, while the country's nearness to the world's leading banana market gives it a decided advantage over most competitors in the banana trade. It has been estimated that Haiti could devote 74,000 acres of land to the commercial exploitation of bananas and that this would yield some 20 million stems annually, or nearly three times the quantity exported in the best year, 1947.[17] But this would undoubtedly require giving a monopoly to a single foreign company, similar to the monopoly which Standard Fruit had. The banana is a fragile fruit which is easily damaged, and peasant methods of transport (on men's heads or donkey's backs, followed by truck haul or sailboat transport) entail considerable risk. There is also the danger of Panama disease or *sigatoka,* both of which have caused considerable losses in Haiti. Proper spraying on small peasant holdings is difficult. Finally, the peasant growers, unless carefully supervised, make many mistakes in banana planting, the commonest ones being

> improper selection made among the suckers; no serious care taken to remove them from the parent; careless placing of them in very small holes in a soil superficially turned over with hoes; inadequate spacing of the distances; and as little attention is given to pruning out the numerous suckers which appear around the main plant, the trees are overcrowded, thus competing with one another.[18]

Under such conditions, states Holly, "a high percentage of fine bunches of fruit is rarely obtained, except where soil and climate are particularly favorable."

Another agricultural staple which Haiti produces is cotton. The cotton plant grew in Hispaniola even before the arrival of Columbus and was exploited by the early colonists. In 1789 cotton exports from Saint-Domingue made up 14 per cent of the value of total exports. Following the revolution, practically no cotton was shipped, except during the American Civil War when the United States temporarily ceased to be a source of supply. It was not until after World War II that independent Haiti began the export of cotton; possibly the presence of American marines (most of whom appear to have been from the South) had something to do with this. Cotton exports remained important until the early fifties, amounting at one time (1935) to 21.5 per cent of the total value of Haiti's exports. Cotton was the second leading export during the interwar period.

The main reason for the decline in cotton exports since the early fifties appears to have been the Mexican boll weevil, combined with the fact that the small peasant growers could not be taught or induced to give proper care to their plants. Other causes of the decline were the loss of the British and European markets because of trade and exchange controls, the switch of peasant interest to other crops requiring less attention, and the beginnings of a cotton-textile industry in Haiti which could absorb most of the locally produced cotton. Here, Moral points out, was an industry which could satisfy at one and the same time the needs of domestic producers of raw cotton and domestic consumers of cotton cloth, both products being in a rudimentary form.[19]

For many years Haitian technicians endeavored to improve the quality of Haitian cotton by introducing new strains and teaching the peasants how to care for their crops. These efforts were finally abandoned as hopeless. Holly points out "both the necessity and the limitations of agricultural techniques and the necessity for constant care which requires intelligence and extensive cooperation from the individual peasants if any lasting results are to be obtained." He adds:

> For about five to seven years, beginning in 1929, the work of selection was carried out carefully, intelligently, and, in the experimental fields, successfully. A steady improvement went on in the length, texture, and other qualities of the fiber. But the Haitian peasant, apart from the selected seeds which he received now and then, was quite indifferent to what was happening. . . .[20]

Most of the cotton grown in Haiti is of the perennial, long-staple sea-island variety, which is peculiarly susceptible to the boll weevil. For this reason the technicians' attempts centered on introducing the American annual varieties. But the peasants were used to the much easier cultivation of perennial cotton and were unwilling to switch to an annual type which required much more work, as well as expense for spraying equipment, etc.

Two cotton by-products—cottonseed and cottonseed cakes—have been exported by Haiti to a certain extent. The export of cottonseed was stopped in 1939, and it is now crushed for oil for domestic consumption. Some of the cottonseed-oil cake is used locally for feeding cattle, and more of it should be, according to the U.N. mission of 1948. The mission also pointed out that cottonseed meal is an excellent fertilizer.

On the whole, cotton and its by-products are unlikely to become a leading Haitian export in the future, but a considerable expansion of the present output should be possible for the supply of domestic needs in cotton cloth, oil, fertilizer, and cattle feed. Such an expansion was undertaken under a cotton-rehabilitation program inaugurated by the Development Institute (IDAI) in 1962. In addition to promoting this crop, IDAI helped establish a number of household cotton industries and opened a workshop for the training of cotton operatives. Through a subsidiary, the Société Nationale d'Equipement (SEN), IDAI set up agricultural centers and storage facilities for cotton and other farm products. By 1965 such centers, supplied with electric power, were in operation in five communities. As a result of IDAI's program, there has been a substantial increase in the number of cotton growers and in cotton acreage, and the 1969 cotton crop was reported to be the largest ever produced.[21]

Little attention was devoted to cacao production during the colonial period, and it was not until about 1850 that cacao output was expanded to meet a growing world demand. Around the turn of the century, Haiti exported annually between 2,100 tons (1890) and 3,400 tons (1912), mostly to France. As new sources of production were developed (Africa, Latin America), Haitian cacao exports declined until the mid-thirties. They have shown very little increase since then, fluctuating for the most part between 1 and 3 per cent of the value of total exports.

Since World War II, efforts have been made to stimulate cacao production and also to provide a domestic outlet in the form of processing plants. These efforts have so far proved fruitless, despite some areas of Haiti being highly suited to cacao production. The main difficulty lies in the faulty methods used by the peasant growers. Since Haitian cacao plantations are

> shady, overcrowded, and damp, ferns, mosses and other epiphytes grow on the stems and the branches and the fruit. The Haitian peasant very seldom, if ever, thinks of removing these hindrances which injure the trees and prevent the proper production of crops.[22]

Moreover, according to Holly, the peasant often injures his trees by pulling or twisting the pods off, thus tearing away some of the eyes which would otherwise produce the next crop from the base of the stalks. He does not follow the recommended practice of using the shells and mucilaginous materials as manure in order to return important nutrients to the soil, nor does he follow recommended methods of fermentation and drying. His average yield, therefore, is only 2 or 3 pounds per tree (as against 8 or 9 pounds in nearby Surinam), and he can offer only an inferior product with a bitter taste.[23]

The U.N. mission of 1948, while agreeing that peasant neglect was the principal cause of the failure of cacao production to expand, mentioned some additional factors: the instability and decline of cacao prices, the rise in foodstuff prices, the insecurity of land tenure, praedial larceny, and defects of the Haitian purchasing system. Still another negative factor is the comparative frequency of severe hurricanes in the southern peninsula (the principal cacao-growing region), combined with the peculiar susceptibility of cacao trees to wind damage.

The U.N. mission felt, nevertheless, that Haiti's position as an exporter of cacao could be regained by special efforts. For example:

> Secure tenure of the land must be guaranteed to the holders of lowland slopes suited to the production of cacao, on condition that the land be used in a manner which will protect the soil and produce cacao of high quality exclusively. Specially-trained extension agents should be detailed to cacao-producing areas, to teach and demonstrate proper methods of propagation, shading, pruning, disease control, harvesting, and processing. . . . Simple

devices for fermentation and drying, such as those formerly distributed . . . should again be provided. Cacao should be bought, if necessary, directly by the government, according to a scale of prices which provides an incentive for high quality.[24]

The mission further suggested that cacao be substituted for coffee now being grown in certain parts of the southern peninsula, and that at least 2,500 acres be planted to cacao in several other parts of Haiti where the climate is particularly favorable.

Essential oils, obtained by distilling certain plants and fruits, have been produced in Haiti only since about 1937. It was not until fiscal 1952 that such oils were exported in an annual amount exceeding $1 million. In that year they made up 2.2 per cent of the value of total exports. Essential oils are used in the manufacture of perfumes, soap, flavoring extracts, and certain medicinal products. The principal Haitian essential oils are vetiver, lemongrass, lime, amyris, petit-grain, neroli, sweet basil, and citronella. The pioneer Haitian producer of essential oils was Mme. Ganot, who was followed, on a more extensive scale, by the late Senator Louis Déjoie (the defeated presidential candidate in 1957). The oil plants were at first grown on peasant plots and bought by the processing plants. Later, scientific plantations were developed. Exports went initially to the United States but later also to France. By 1966 annual exports of essential oils had risen to about $2 million. A decline in essential-oil prices in 1968 caused the government to put IDAI in charge of this industry. With the assistance of a U.N. chemical engineer, control of the quality of exports was established. In 1969 the value of essential-oil exports increased to about $3 million despite some reduction in volume. As a subsidiary advantage of IDAI's control of the industry, export licensing is made conditional on the manufacturers' refraining from the use of wood for fuel, thus reducing the rate of deforestation.

The castor bean, which thrives in Haiti (particularly in the northwest), was until the twentieth century used only for domestic purposes (lamp oil, cosmetics, home remedies). It was not exported in quantity until World War II, when it suddenly became a strategic material needed for airplane motors. Thereafter shipments of castor beans declined, but they increased again with the

Korean war, being valued at slightly more than $1 million in fiscal 1951 (2.1 per cent of total exports). With the continued growth of plane traffic, there would seem to be an assured future market for castor beans, and the possibility of processing the beans into oil in Haiti should be explored.

Rubber-growing in the form of the cryptostegia vine was tried in Haiti in 1940 and proved a dismal failure (see pp. 64-65). Simultaneously with the cryptostegia program, however, SHADA began the development of a long-range plantation program based on the Hevea type of rubber. This program involved an initial planting of 7,500 acres of trees from which seedlings would be furnished to peasant growers, and the eventual planting of 70,000 acres to yield 35,000 tons of rubber annually. It takes seven or eight years to get Hevea trees to produce. Actually, SHADA planted only a little over 4,000 acres, fairly evenly divided between Bayeux on the north coast and the Jérémie area of the southern peninsula. The first exportation of rubber was in fiscal 1951—a mere 5 tons. Thereafter annual shipments gradually rose to about 200 tons.

The 1948 U.N. mission recommended the expansion of Hevea rubber production, primarily on peasant holdings:

> As a crop for small landowners rubber has definite possibilities in Haiti. Experiments made by the United States Department of Agriculture experiment station at Marfranc show that manioc, malanga, coffee, and other plants can be successfully grown as an intercrop with rubber. Similar work at stations in other countries has shown that maize and other food crops can be grown profitably between the rows of young rubber trees and can provide income or a subsistence until the rubber can be tapped. . . . Since the cost of maintaining rubber trees, once they are planted, is small, and since rubber as a permanent cover fits in well with a programme for control of erosion, it is recommended that rubber planting be encouraged as the central activity in suitable agricultural development areas.[25]

There is no evidence that these recommendations have yet been followed, although in 1956 the Magloire government did announce that 1,750 additional acres on the north coast were being planted to rubber.

Around 1870–80 honey—a peasant product—was exported by Haiti in appreciable quantities, but in recent times shipments have been inconsequential, apparently because of poor prices, absence of modern techniques, and deforestation. Prospects for the future do not seem to warrant special efforts to expand the production of this item. The situation is similar with respect to orange peel, also produced by peasant families.

A unique Haitian export is temperate-zone flowers, although the amounts earned at present make no substantial difference in the country's balance of trade. This type of business was started by, and remained the exclusive domain of, an American citizen (Atherton Lee) who, after a career in tropical agriculture around the world, retired to a 4,500-foot-high farm at Kenscoff, a mountaintop suburb of Port-au-Prince. There he grew many varieties of temperate-zone flowers, and he shipped them to Puerto Rico, Venezuela, and other parts of the Caribbean. Whether this type of export is capable of much expansion is questionable, but the success so far enjoyed is revealing of what can be accomplished in Haiti through ingenuity, scientific methods, and persistence.

Among the agricultural commodities that Haiti produces primarily for domestic consumption are rice, corn, cassava, millet, sweet potatoes, peanuts, tobacco, and a variety of fruits.

Rice is especially important because, mixed with beans, it is the most popular Haitian dish, particularly in the towns. Over the years consumption has exceeded the domestic production, so that imports have usually been necessary. In the decade 1917–26, for instance, annual imports of rice averaged over $300,000 in value. Since then imports have declined, and in some years have been replaced by small-scale exports. In the past twenty years Haitian production of rice has expanded to make the country normally self-sufficient, thanks in the main to the start of irrigation in the Artibonite Valley and to the experimental farm operated there by ODVA (the Artibonite Valley Authority) with the help of SCIPA. New strains of rice have been introduced, the land has been carefully prepared by machinery, the paddy water has been regulated, and participation agreements with the peasants have been made. By 1959, Haiti's rice production was said to be not far from double the output of a decade earlier. An FAO estimate places the crop at 43,000 metric tons in both 1966 and 1967.[26] The U.N. mission of 1948 recommended that the rice-culture methods used in the Artibonite Valley be applied also in parts of the northern plain which appear to be well suited to rice production. If this were done, Haiti might well emerge as a steady exporter of rice.

Corn is also important as a cereal crop in Haiti. Enough of it (about 250,000 metric tons) is produced to satisfy home consumption and permit of small exports to neighboring islands. Improvements in techniques might well make possible large-scale exports.

Although not listed above, wheat is deserving of comment. For many years Haiti has been accustomed to import 4 or 5 million dollars' worth of wheat flour annually. Experiments carried out by Senator Déjoie and others in the fifties showed that a very good quality of wheat could be produced profitably in Haiti at an elevation of about 5,000 feet, at which level there are many thousands of acres of unused land. By careful planning and organization, therefore, it should be possible to bring about the production of enough domestic wheat to reduce substantially the amount now being spent annually on imported wheat. It is understood that the Haitian flour mill (see p. 82), which has been processing imported wheat, has agreed to buy whatever Haitian wheat may be offered to it, on the basis of the samples it has examined.

A staple food item in Haiti, particularly among peasants and children, is cassava, a perennial shrub, from which are made cassava meal, flour, bread, and starch. Enough cassava is grown to feed the population and permit of small exports to Curaçao and the United States. The peasant growers obtain only a very low yield (less than 3 tons per acre, as against an average yield of 4 to 10 tons on the Gold Coast and in Nigeria). Commenting on this, Holly asks:

> Cannot a prudent selection of our varieties and of our cuttings, together with the use of fertilizer and manure, increase considerably the yield of the Haitian plantations? Such a result

implies hard and intelligent work, as anything worthwhile requires planning and effort. But the issue cannot be evaded. To avoid it or to renounce action altogether is to miss a great opportunity to educate the peasants and to improve our export trade. . . .[27]

Still another cereal that is grown and consumed in Haiti on a massive scale is millet, known locally as *petit mil*. The estimated output of this grain in 1966, and again in 1967, was 190,000 metric tons. It is neither exported nor imported.

A perennial plant which supplies Haitian peasants with a staple food is the sweet potato. Here too the yield obtained in Haiti appears to be well below that which is normal elsewhere (1½ tons per acre, as against an average 4 to 5 tons in other countries). The plant is subject to various diseases. Harvesting often results in damage to a part of the crop, and the product is very perishable.[28]

Tobacco became important as a native crop around the turn of the century, received a certain impetus from the American occupation, was helped along by the creation in 1946 of a Régie du Tabac (state tobacco monopoly), and has enabled Haiti gradually to cut down on its imports of tobacco products. The Régie manufactures several types of cigars and cigarettes for city consumption (the peasants still making their own). The U.N. mission of 1948 concluded that Haiti's tobacco production could be greatly improved and that the country's varied climates were favorable to the cultivation of several types of cigarette tobacco as well as a good cigar tobacco. It warned, however:

> Only systematic development of the tobacco industry under the central direction of a tobacco expert can be expected to bring about a substantial improvement of Haiti's tobacco supply. . . . An increase . . . should be directed principally toward local consumption. However, in certain areas it is possible in the course of time to develop for export a high-grade tobacco for cigar-filler and even for wrapper. There is also the possibility of developing a fine cigarette leaf.[29]

A Canadian cigar-smoker has paid the following high tribute to the quality of Haitian cigars:

Despite the high quality of native tobacco, too many Haitians prefer, in order to be in style, Havana cigars and American cigarettes. Why do the good Haitian cigars, in my opinion, excel the best Havanas? Less aromatic and much milder, they win hands down because of their unequalled flavor and aroma. Only certain special cigars of Brazil and Colombia seem to equal them. . . .[30]

The U.N. mission recommended that tobacco culture be taken up "as a cooperative enterprise within agricultural development projects which can provide adequate technical supervision" and that cooperating farmers should be provided with seedlings from a central nursery. The Duvalier government may have had these recommendations in mind when it contracted with an American group calling itself the Haiti Tobacco Company to provide the funds, fertilizer, and materials for setting up experimental tobacco centers at four points in northern and central Haiti and a number of similar centers in the southern peninsula. According to the Haitian press, these experimental farms were to be scientific laboratories for determining the type and quality of tobacco best suited to local and export requirements, and the Haiti Tobacco Company undertook to purchase any surplus production over domestic needs. The Régie would help set up cooperative organizations at the producing centers with a view to promoting standardization of the product, while Haiti Tobacco was to help establish a system of technical aid and supervised credit for the growers.

Bamboo—a plant that grows in various parts of Haiti but is put to only limited use—was recommended by the U.N. 1948 mission for large-scale exploitation. The uses of bamboo, said the mission, are almost endless, ranging from construction material to agricultural implements, domestic utensils, a palatable vegetable food, animal forage, and a source of cellulose and paper pulp. It could also provide a quick-growing cover for vulnerable soils. One may hope that this advice will sooner or later be heeded.

Haiti produces a variety of tropical fruits: mangos, papaya, avocados, pineapples, grapefruit, oranges, lemons, guava, cachiman, sapotilla, corossol, cayemitte, etc. However, because of the poor transportation facilities, these are not available, even in the domestic markets, except when in season. It is clear that much could be done by proper organization to create both domestic and foreign markets for these fruits, either fresh or in preserved form, or both. The same may well be true of the diminutive peaches which grow at high elevations; while they cannot be eaten fresh, they are exceptionally tasty in preserved form.

From the above review of Haiti's principal existing and potential crops, one must conclude that the main stumbling block to progress has been and continues to be the human element. The problem is twofold: (1) peasant ignorance of modern methods and, what is worse, of the meaning and necessity of development; and (2) failure of the Haitian government and its technicians to make and to carry out consistently a comprehensive agricultural plan based on potentialities and priorities. It may be argued that a further important stumbling block has been the absence, until recently, of agricultural credit facilities. Certainly the problem has been complicated by this factor, but the dearth of credit is in reality a secondary obstacle. An ample supply of agricultural credit could not have made up for the backward methods of the peasantry nor the mistaken attitudes and actions of the government. On the other hand, an enlightened peasantry supported by intelligent government planning and action would have produced far better results, even without agricultural credit facilities.

With respect to (1) above, we have already discussed (Chapter 11) some aspects of the rural education problem, particularly the efforts that have been put forth to solve it through fundamental education, community development, and community schools. These efforts, we pointed out, are all to the good, but they are only a start. It is important that they be vastly expanded at the earliest possible moment if the Haitian peasantry is really to be brought into the modern world.

Apart from the elementary rural schools, intermediate agricultural education is given at the secondary schools of Chatard (in northern Haiti) and Lesson (in the southwest). A third school of this type (Laborde, in the south) was destroyed by the 1964 hurricane. The Ecole Normale Rurale at Damiens, also of an intermediate type, is a training school for country teachers. The

Chatard and Lesson schools each have fewer than 40 students. Entrance is at the age of 15 or 16 after selection from among the best graduates of the elementary country schools throughout Haiti. Besides agricultural subjects, the curriculum includes various academic subjects, manual work, music, and religious and civic instruction.

The Ecole Normale Rurale was created in 1954, although some preparation of rural teachers had previously taken place within the National Agricultural School (described below). The students, who enter between the ages of 15 and 20, are those who receive scholarships from among existing schoolteachers (particularly rural teachers) or from among those who hold the *brevet simple* or who have completed three years in a secondary school. The course of study lasts three years. The first year is devoted to consolidation of academic knowledge, the second to a mixture of academic and pedagogical studies, and the third to pedagogical studies and practice teaching. The school is located on the extensive grounds of the National Agricultural School.

The National Agricultural School, originally called the Central School of Agriculture, was set up by the American occupation authorities in 1924 as part of their attempt to divert the Haitian school system from purely academic into practical channels (see pp. 39-41). The plan was to emphasize agricultural practice and manual work. But, writes Holly,

> as the years passed, the training of well-qualified Haitian specialists to help the American experts in the technical departments became so urgent that the theoretical and academic studies were increased. Many students were sent abroad to American universities, where they specialized and obtained degrees. In 1931, at the "haitianization" of the Technical Service, these students were ready to fill the gap left by the American experts and become the heads of the various sections and the professors at the Central School.[31]

The National School of Agriculture is now a part of the University of Haiti. It is located on a beautiful tract of more than 300 acres at Damiens, six miles from Port-au-Prince. It has various laboratories, a library, a museum of geology and natural science, a collection of insects, a herbarium, a shop for carpentry and blacksmithing, nurseries, a dairy, dormitories, and offices for technical staff of the Ministry of Agriculture. Admission is by competitive examination among students, aged 18 to 23 years, who have a certificate from one of the last two years of secondary school. The plan of study covers three years, leading to the degree of Agronomist. The curriculum includes all the main sciences related to agriculture, rural economy, veterinary medicine, and forestry, and actual practice in cattle-breeding, dairying, pig-keeping, poultry-keeping, bee-keeping, etc.[32]

The technicians of the Department of Agriculture also engage in a certain amount of adult education, either through farmer associations or through informal meetings of farmers and parents. Lectures deal with farming techniques, local problems, or the meaning of new laws. There have been frequent distributions of seedlings.[33]

Despite all this, the Haitian peasantry remains steadfast in its traditional ways, apparently unimpressed by modern techniques and theories. Writes Holly:

> Indisputably, the system is excellent. But it is rather astonishing that such a scheme, so simple and apparently well fitted to our rural conditions, has been practically inefficient and has yielded poor results, as is more than obvious by the continued state of backwardness of our rural population and the general ugliness of our countryside. Anyone who takes a simple trip into the country would hardly believe that the marvelous system of agricultural education . . . had been carried on for more than twenty years.
>
> How is it that so well-devised a tool has up to now been so powerless, so unable to raise the material and spiritual welfare of the peasants or to help them build up the countryside which the soil, the climate, and the natural beauty of the island can so easily support?[34]

His conclusion is that the failures are due to both psychological and material drawbacks.

From the psychological viewpoint, Holly alleges that successive governments lacked a sincere desire to give really effective help to the rural population. Indeed, he says, there was a positive unwillingness to educate the rural people and raise their standard of living. "The farmers were always considered as a means to produce wealth for the nation, but their personal and private interests, as individuals and as a class, were never unselfishly considered." Since the Lescot administration, this has changed:

> But this former lack of desire to build up our countryside, this absence of pride and love for the country as a whole, this unwillingness to help the rural people or to consider them as persons and individuals to be helped rather than as means for production, and also perhaps this fear of competition (from a rising lower class) . . . were serious hindrances blocking the progress of rural Haiti.[35]

Specifically, Holly finds three main weaknesses in the program of agricultural education: lack of vision, lack of perseverance and consistency, and a bureaucratic spirit. Because of lack of vision, nothing is done about the peasants' "ugly cottages":

> These thatched huts are altogether unsatisfactory, artistically and hygienically. . . . What has been said of the peasant's dwellings applies to every aspect of his material, social, moral, and intellectual life. The Haitian peasants must be endowed with most of the amenities of civilization.[36]

Lack of perseverance and consistency is manifested "in a rush to tackle new problems and undertake new activities, whereas the problems at hand remain unsolved. Furthermore, activities are hastily performed without any idea of duration or of yielding permanent and increasing results." The bureaucratic spirit has been displayed in a lack of interest

> in actual results as they affect the everyday life and the well-being of the people. Apparently the only important thing was to accumulate report after report and to put on paper an account of the numerous activities. . . . The activities reported did take place; only their execution was carried on in such a superficial and hasty way that they were doomed beforehand to failure. . . . They lack what in economics is called statistic and quality control, a control which is extremely important for the very life and efficiency of any business, firm, or other institution.[37]

In calling the availability of agricultural credit a secondary problem (see p. 161), our intention is by no means to downgrade its importance. Without access to such credit, Haiti's agricultural economy could never achieve its full potential; and unless one aims at the maximum possible development, one risks an unsatisfactory outcome and exposing oneself to the charge of lack of vision.

The report of the 1948 U.N. mission to Haiti had the following to say about the absence of agricultural credit facilities in Haiti:

> There is no public provision for rural credit in Haiti. To purchase land, equipment, or animals, to finance his crop, to repair his tools, or to do anything requiring more than the few gourdes the peasant manages to save from the sale of a small portion of his produce, he must go to private money-lenders, who frequently demand outrageous rates of interest. The money-lender is usually also a purchaser of peasant produce, notably coffee, and not uncommonly maintains a permanent lien upon the peasant purchaser through successive loans against forthcoming crops. In this way the purchaser, or *spéculateur*, strengthens his assurance of having a supply of produce at prices convenient to himself. The *spéculateur*, as an influential member of the community having a vested interest in things as they are, is a potent factor against change, especially since he is also active in politics.
> . . . The wholesalers and exporters, and middlemen of means, have access to credit from banks under strictly conventional commercial terms. There is no agricultural bank, nor do the existing banks provide agricultural credit as such to producers.[38]

Actually, there were in 1948 only two banks in Haiti, the BNRH and a branch of the Royal Bank of Canada. Both were strictly commercial banks, although the state-owned BNRH also issued the country's supply of gourde notes and performed certain services for the government. There had been agitation for an agricultural bank more than a century earlier, and a law creating such a bank was actually promulgated in 1862 but was not put into effect.

In 1951 the Magloire government prepared a draft law which would have created a new department in the BNRH for the purpose of granting agricultural credit. At the government's request, I, then fiscal and monetary adviser to Haiti under the auspices of the United Nations, cooperated with the BNRH in revising the government draft. The outcome was the law of September 12, 1951, which created the Institut Haitien de Crédit Agricole et Industriel (IHCAI), jointly owned by the government and the BNRH (see p. 76). IHCAI could make loans of short-, medium-, and long-term maturity, up to 15 years. Loan proceeds were to be paid out only as the operations progressed for which the loan had been granted. IHCAI made available its free advice to each borrower and reserved the right to inspect his property and operations. In order to stimulate the creation of agricultural and other cooperatives in Haiti, preferential interest rates were offered on loans to cooperatives. IHCAI was also authorized to build and operate silos, warehouses, laboratories, and implement pools for joint use by borrowers.

By the end of its third fiscal year, IHCAI had made loans and investments totaling $2.1 million in favor of more than 50 categories of agricultural and industrial production, located in all five of the country's departments. Meanwhile, with the assistance of a United Nations adviser on cooperatives, enactment of a law to encourage and regulate cooperatives through a National Cooperative Council was brought about, and IHCAI itself organized four pilot cooperatives for the production and sale of vegetables and poultry, and for the operations of shoemakers and coffee processors. By October 1955 the National Cooperative Council had approved the creation of 48 credit cooperatives and 10 cooperatives of other types.[39] The cooperative movement has been actively promoted also by SCIPA and by both the Magloire and Duvalier administrations. Under the latter the Cooperative Council was replaced by a Cooperative Service, according to whose data there were 279 cooperatives with 28,326 members in 1968, with total resources of 1,461,700 gourdes.

As already mentioned (p. 96), in 1961 the Duvalier-created Fonds Spécial d'Investissement was merged into IHCAI, the authorized capital of which was raised to $10 million and the name changed to Institut de Développement Agricole et Industriel (IDAI). A loan of $3.5 million was received from the Inter-American Development Bank to make possible the financing of the southern sugar mill and certain other agricultural and industrial projects. The name of the Technical Committee was changed to Financial Committee, and a number of other minor changes of organization and administration were made.

In 1967 an IDB report stated that the most successful effort to develop the agricultural sector in Haiti had been that of IDAI, which in 1966 was carrying out a program affecting nearly 8,000 farmers.[39] One of the most important projects has involved large-scale rehabilitation of cotton farms. Beginning in 1962, the institute initiated measures to promote cotton-growing by the introduction of new plant varieties and better cultivation methods. Complementing these measures, the institute has helped establish household cotton industries and train operators for 40 looms. Beginning in 1963, an IDAI subsidiary opened agricultural processing and storage facilities in five communities.[40]

In 1962, with the financial and technical help of AID, an Agricultural Credit Bureau was established as a subdivision of the Ministry of Agriculture to grant supervised agricultural credit to very small farmers—those too small and too lacking in creditworthiness to qualify even for IDAI financing. The bureau's initial capital was about $1 million. The Agricultural Credit Bureau has apparently confined its activities to the Artibonite Valley and the Département du Nord. By 1966 it had made short- and medium-term loans to more than 1,500 small farmers. Of the short-term loans, which averaged only $131 apiece, 39 per cent was for coffee production, 17 per cent for cattle-raising, 16 per cent for peas, 10 per cent for potatoes, and the rest for a variety of crops. Of the medium-term loans, averaging $280 each, 71 per cent was for the financing of irrigation works and 29 per cent for assistance to produce growers. During a 1968 seminar on methods of obtaining reimbursement, it was disclosed that the bureau was faced with serious difficulties caused by alleged bad faith on the part of some borrowers.[41]

A survey of Haiti's agricultural system would be incomplete without mention of marketing problems. These are of several kinds.

To begin with, since each peasant family takes its own tiny

output to market, there is much waste of time and energy, compared with modern systems under which the goods of many producers are assembled in sizable lots at or near the point of origin and from there transported to market. Next, for most products there is no grading or standardizing; the good and the bad, the big and the small, are all jumbled together, involving waste for the buyers and lower prices for the producers. Packaging, with the benefits it bestows in the way of easier transport and storage, protection from damage and dirt, etc., is practically unknown. Nor is there ordinarily any peasant processing which could increase revenue and prevent the enforced "dumping" of perishable commodities at the height of the season. There are obvious disadvantages in the system of transport on the heads of women or backs of donkeys: slowness, waste by damage, etc. Storage is either primitive (hanging ears of corn from tree branches, for instance) or not practiced at all in the absence of facilities.[42] The distributive system—if it may be called a system—is one of fragmentation. Each peasant woman trudges many miles to a market or wanders up and down city streets, often with one or two children, selling a few pennies' worth here and a few there. "Why," asks Holly, "should we not have more active and efficient grocery stores to relieve the farmers from the unproductive task of distributing their products themselves?[43]

Finally, such helps to selling as advertising, store display, and standard units of measurement have not been invoked. As to measurement units, Holly states:

> All kinds of measures and weights are used; in fact, almost any object can serve as a unit—stone, brick, a piece of wood, real weights—but falsified through injury—baskets, tins, and bottles. . . .
> The types of scales used also vary a great deal. . . . In the hands of the unscrupulous middlemen, those numerous weights, measures, and scales are so many implements of torture to exploit the ignorance of the peasants.[44]

Summing up, despite the rich variety of climates and soils, Haiti's agricultural problems are numerous and acute, as they have been ever since independence was achieved. What, then, is the most promising line of attack to make possible a solution of these problems? One can conceive of four possible strategies:

1. Continuing the present system of individual initiative and peasant production but seeking to introduce modern methods of farming and marketing;
2. Active state intervention in the form of government buying and selling of most crops;
3. Switching from the present system of peasant production to one of large estates managed by foreign or domestic technicians conversant with modern methods;
4. A combination of two or more of the above strategies.

The first of these four lines of attack would be an amplification and intensification of policies that have been followed up to the present time. Its success would depend on whether it proved possible to draw the peasants out of their present state of ignorance. Is this an impossible job? As Leyburn, Holly, and other writers have pointed out, the chief obstacle has been the attitude of most (but by no means all) of the élite, who fear the enlightenment and economic ascent of the masses, lest it mean the loss or impairment of their own privileged position. This, in my opinion, is not an insurmountable barrier; indeed, it is a barrier that has been gradually growing less formidable since World War II. A renewed effort to reform the peasant system may well succeed if it is vigorous and persistent. However, any measurable success would require years or decades.

The second alternative—state buying and selling—may well sound like the easiest way to modernize Haiti's agricultural system, since the state could then lay down the law to the producers and force the adoption of modern methods. It is not as simple as it sounds, however. Forcing new methods on people who have the education and understanding to carry out more or less complicated orders is one thing; forcing the totally ignorant to do so is quite another. It could mean stationing an inspector on every peasant plot! Moreover, in view of the wide scope of corruption in past Haitian governments, it would hardly do to open up such a rich new source of corruption as a state agricultural monopoly.

The third strategy—one of large estates for which the peasants would work as employees—has been suggested by Paul Moral, whose opinion is based on many years of close observation. Moral urges that efforts at agricultural promotion be restricted to only a few products—those for which Haiti's soil and climate are best fitted, although these products happen to be the ones requiring the more difficult techniques. These commodities, in his opinion, are (in order of importance) bananas, sugar, and cacao. He would have the government concentrate all its attention on working out plantation systems for these priority items, at least until they "bear fruit" and development can be said to be well on its way. Opening demonstration farms, handing out seedlings, organizing cooperatives, and fighting illiteracy, he feels, have proved completely ineffective and hopeless as means of reforming peasant methods. As for providing schools for all the peasant children, the cost alone, he says, would make it prohibitive. Prompt attention should, however, be given to the construction of good roads, the lifeblood of the economy. And, he adds, the rural areas should be integrated into the country administratively instead of being abandoned to the "corporalism" of section chiefs.[45]

I feel that the second strategy mentioned above would be a fatal mistake and that neither the first nor the third alternative by itself offers a complete and sure solution. I would therefore recommend a combination of the first and third methods of attack: a system of big plantations for bananas, sugar, and cacao could, if managed by adequately financed technicians, bring the quick results which are so badly needed and would allow time for the various programs of enlightenment and improvement of the peasantry to take hold and show results in the production and quality of the numerous other commodities. This assumes that the élite can be won over to sincere cooperation with such aims. I am confident that it can be. Surely the élite has absorbed by now the great lesson of the past: in a divided, two-class Haiti there is no future for anyone, but there is every reason to believe that both classes could enjoy unprecedented prosperity in a united Haiti making full use of its ample resources and talents.

# 🔲🔲🔲 13
# Animal Husbandry
# And Forestry

The nature and scope of Haiti's animal resources and the use made of them were neatly summed up by the U.N. study mission in 1948:

> Livestock is reared without much method by the peasants. Cattle and goats are entirely grass-fed on pasture, usually on tether, and swine are largely left to forage for themselves, as are also poultry. They are sold whenever necessity demands or opportunity offers, and find their way to the slaughter houses and markets of the towns and cities. The quality of livestock is poor, and there is great loss from lack of thriftiness and from infestation with parasites. A dairy industry exists only near the cities. Goat milk is not used by the peasants. Donkeys and small horses are reared for transport. There is no veterinary service and there are no breeding stations, except at a special project of recent development in the Central Plateau.[1]

As the mission's report suggests, animals are kept by peasant families principally as a sort of reserve from which, through sale, emergency and seasonal gaps in their income may be filled. In this way animals perform one of the functions of money—a store of value—much as they did among peoples of the ancient world.

Even though the peasants themselves do not consume great quantities of meat and dairy products, this system falls far short of supplying Haiti's needs, with the result that imports of meat and dairy products have for many years been a burdensome item in the balance of trade.

Improvement of a nation's livestock breeds is possible by three methods: (1) introduction of new breeds from other countries; (2) crossbreeding of native and foreign types; and (3) careful selection of the best native types. The first method was tried in Haiti without success. Imported Jersey, Holstein, and Duroc-Jersey cattle, says Holly, "deteriorated rapidly in our climate, with our scanty and inferior food, and our peasants' un-skilled labor." Holly believes that prerequisites for success by this method would be education of the peasants and the improve-ment of grasslands, meadows, etc.[2]

The second method—crossbreeding—was also the subject of experimentation in Haiti, with somewhat better success. But suc-cess on a really important scale will require proper nutrition and living conditions for the imported animals, execution of the plan on a countryside basis, and statistical control of cost and results.[3]

The third method—selection from local types—has given good results in advanced countries, but it works slowly and must be carried on carefully and consistently. Since care and consistency have not been hallmarks of the Haitian peasant, I confess to some doubt whether this is the best method for Haiti, but Holly states that "if well and consistently applied, [it] can also lead to excel-lent results in Haiti." He recommends, therefore, the most ex-tensive possible adoption of the second and third methods.[4]

Haitian cattle are not raised specifically as a source of either meat or dairy products, nor yet exclusively as draft animals. They are expected to serve all three, or at least two, of these purposes. As Holly describes their treatment:

> Cattle are used indiscriminately for all purposes, and bred at random. Usually, the peasants' cattle work on the sugar-cane plantations, where they are harnessed to carts and to mills. The males are often castrated by the most violent and primitive meth-ods and quite often die after the operation from tetanus or other infections. The cows that give milk do not generally yield more than half a liter a day, even at the highest producing weeks of the lactation period. . . . In the savannas of the Plateau Cen-tral . . . the cows are almost never milked. All their production is simply wasted or simply goes to the calves. The ultimate destination of all cattle in Haiti, apart from those which die from contagious diseases, is the slaughterhouse. . . .[5]

Having in mind the pecularities of the Haitian rural economy, Holly believes that the authorities should aim chiefly at developing a dual-purpose type, for milk and beef, although in some areas a work-and-beef type may be preferable. Unfortunately,

> the peasant is entirely ignorant of the most elementary principles of nutrition, and as he is badly fed and housed, so are his animals. They thrive by chance and in spite of all unfavorable events. They live almost entirely on grasses. . . . But the meadows and pastures are always of very poor quality—never ploughed and never fertilized—and produce poor grades of grasses. On the sugar-cane plantations, the leaves of the plants are used as food. During the dry season, the animals suffer very much and many die from starvation in the savannas.[6]

Evidently the first requirement in any cattle-development program is to teach the peasants how to provide their cattle with a year-round ration containing the essential ingredients. Some allegedly successful experiments in this direction have been carried out at Damiens, but apparently the message has not gotten across to the peasants. In any event the peasants must learn not only about good nutrition for their cattle,

> but also all the essentials of general management, such as the right age and period of breeding a heifer, the care of a cow in gestation and of the young calves, the hygiene and sanitation of the stables, the period of weaning, the manner of milking, the prevention and cure of diseases, the management of the bull, and much more.[7]

For lack of hygiene and sanitation, Haitian cattle are decimated by various diseases, anthrax undoubtedly being the most dreadful. However, vaccination against anthrax has been carried out in some areas, and at Damiens there are free weekly clinics at which animals from neighboring communities are treated for disease.

The 1948 U.N. mission recommended that livestock-development projects be set up in appropriate areas, beginning with the Central Plateau, where plant agriculture was precluded by a sharp dry season and a lack of irrigation possibilities:

> The improved pasture management practices which have been initiated by the government in this area should be greatly extended on State lands and education of the inhabitants to improve

their management of livestock should be carried out by specially-trained extension agents having the livestock station at Papaye, near Hinche, as their base.[8]

The mission also recommended a survey of land ownership and use in the area, a settlement of titles, and offers of state land to the local inhabitants under leasehold tenure to ensure appropriate use of the land. Areas susceptible to erosion should be protected by planting trees, shrubs, or erosion-controlling grasses. Water for sustaining livestock in the dry season would be ensured by impounding rainwater or water from wells with windmill pumps. Trench silos should be made and filled with fodder from sorghums, Uba cane, or other fodder plants, and the inhabitants should participate in this work in order to learn the new techniques. They should also be taught to make hay from the area's Madame Michel grass. Once the project was well launched, a pilot dairy center should be established and used as a training center. The results of this Central Plateau experience would be the basis for setting up similar projects in other parts of Haiti.

The U.N. recommendations may have been influential in causing the Magloire administration to include in its Five-Year Plan a program of livestock improvement and an experimental dairy at Papaye. Later, similar projects were set up at Déclay (northeastern Haiti) and near Cayes. Several livestock experts were supplied by FAO to advise on the execution of these projects. At Papaye efforts were made to produce a milk-and-meat breed that would be well adapted to local conditions, to multiply the varieties of high-yield fodder resistant to dryness, and to develop the region's dairy resources. A good new type of butter, called "clarified butter," was developed. At the station near Cayes, improved types of fodder were introduced, and local cattle-raisers were supplied with pedigreed stud animals. The Damiens farm concentrated on improving cattle breeds in the Cul-de-Sac and Léogane plains and on producing pasteurized milk, for which Port-au-Prince supplied a ready market. Meanwhile a number of technicians of the Department of Agriculture were sent abroad on FAO fellowships in order to improve their knowledge of techniques. It was recognized, however, that the great problem was how to transfer the results of these efforts to the understanding and practices of the peasants.

The situation regarding pigs in Haiti is similar to that regarding cattle. Haitian pigs are ill treated and ill fed, being made to forage for themselves. They are small and infested with worms or disease. They are of no particular breed, since mating takes place in a haphazard way. No systematic efforts have been made to improve them. Such efforts, when made, should consist in cross-breeding with foreign strains or in careful selection.[9]

Horses, once fairly common in Haiti, are now rarely to be seen. Horse-drawn vehicles have been replaced by motorcars and trucks. Saddle horses are still used in hilly rural areas, and a few peasants have pack horses. The development of draft and harness types would be desirable to permit introduction of the plow, not now in use, and for improved transportation of farm products.[10]

Donkeys are the most popular work animal in Haiti, outnumbering cattle probably six to one. Nearly every peasant family has a donkey, mainly for carrying farm products to market and transporting charcoal, grasses, water, etc. Their food requirements are small for the services they render. Some families have a mule, which can serve as a saddle animal as well as for transport.[11]

Goats are also numerous in Haiti. Goat meat is widely eaten but the consumption of goat milk is very limited. Goatskins are exported on a substantial scale, the technique of preparation of the skins requiring no great skill. Haitian goats receive little or no feeding and may be seen nibbling on just about anything green they come across. Holly recommends the importation of Angora types for crossbreeding, with a view to producing a breed which, in addition to supplying good meat, would provide long hair for the manufacture of carpets, tent ropes, shawls, wigs, and coarse garments.[12]

There are few sheep in Haiti, probably because they are much less hardy than goats and are not well adapted to semiarid or mountainous country. Some mutton is consumed, but there is no wool production, nor does wool growing appear to be a promising item for Haiti.[13]

Poultry-raising, on the other hand, could become important

in the Haitian economy. Although no accurate count is available, there are millions of chickens, and small numbers of turkeys, ducks, geese, and guinea hens. Every peasant family has some hens—usually less than a dozen—which wander about during the day in search of food and sleep at night in the trees. They are small, and their flesh is tough. Experimental imports of Rhode Island Reds, White Leghorns, and Plymouth Rocks from the United States

> led to the conclusion that foreign races, unless given special care, quickly deteriorate under our conditions and, consequently the improvement of our poultry should be chiefly carried on by cross-breeding and by selection from our native hens. These two methods should be applied not only to the egg-production types, but also to the two others (table and dual-purpose) which can also be advantageously bred in Haiti.[14]

In 1953, IHCAI organized and financed a poultry cooperative of nine peasant families for the scientific feeding of imported chicks and the joint slaughter, freeze storage, and sale of the mature, tender fowl on both local and foreign markets. A ready market was found in Haiti's then booming hotel industry, and the success of this cooperative induced other producers to engage in the same activity.

Haiti's shortcomings with respect to farm animals are much the same as in plant production: (1) No active and intelligent participation has been required of the peasants. (2) There has been no stimulation of a desire for excellent animals or for pride in them. (3) There has been no constant supervision, nor adequate advice. (4) There has been no plan of improvement through selection from native species.[15]

As a result of its deficient animal husbandry, Haiti has long been a net importer of meat and dairy products. Despite some improvement since the mid-fifties, well over $1 million worth of such products continues to be imported annually. On the other hand, there has been a small amount of meat exports by a company (the Haitian American Meat and Provision Company) to which a concession was granted in the late fifties to build and operate a meat-packing plant at Port-au-Prince. IDAI is putting up a meat-packing plant and dairy at Cayes, where the U.N. Special Fund has sponsored a project of livestock improvement. The Cayes plant is expected to engage in beef exports to Puerto Rico and the United States.

At the time of Columbus's landing, most of the area now known as Haiti is believed to have been densely forested. Its diversity of climate had produced stands of many different types of trees, and many new species were introduced in the course of colonization. Among the most common types have been mahogany, Haitian oak (*Catalpa longissima*), logwood, satinwood, pine, cedar, manchineel, rosewood, ironwood, fustic, lignum vitae, coconut and other palms, and an amazing variety of fruit trees.[16]

Today only a fraction of the original forests remains, mainly in the higher mountain areas of the southern part of the country. Deforestation had already begun in colonial times. The most authoritative description of Saint-Domingue as it existed toward the end of the colonial period stated that,

> in general, the French Part is warmer and more exposed to dry spells, which one sees becoming both more frequent and longer since, because of an avidity which places no value on the future, and which is frequently mistaken as to the value of the present time, people have felled the trees which covered those high points, which brought them fruitful rains, and which retained abundant moisture and a humidity the useful influence of which was prolonged by the forests.[17]

Apart from erosion caused by the deliberate deforestation referred to by Moreau de St.-Méry, there was also erosion caused by the colonialists' custom of planting coffee bushes in the open, without shade.[18]

Since 1804 deforestation has continued at an increasingly rapid pace, for a variety of reasons. During much of the time it was the custom of many peasants to shift from one area to another as the soil became depleted, each successive move resulting in the clearing of more forest land. Around each *caille* (native hut) and its immediate vegetation, a widening circle of land was cleared in order to meet the continued needs for firewood and construction material. In addition, the forests supplied the cities' needs for charcoal, distilleries, lime kilns, artisanry, etc. During the better part of a century, moreover, Haiti exported large quantities of mahogany, logwood, and lignum vitae. Altogether, the Haitian Institute of Statistics has estimated, something like 315 million cubic feet of wood was thus taken *annually* from the country's forests, without replacement.[19]

The consequent erosion is probably the gravest of all the problems facing Haiti's agriculture. In 1958 the Grand Conseil Technique (see p. 89) estimated that of the 5,115,000 acres of mountain land, 2,640,000 acres was eroded and unproductive, 1,235,000 acres was covered with forests, 990,000 acres was arable, and 250,000 acres was submarginal. It then commented:

> Because of the absence of plant cover, the rain waters sweep over the surface of the land. The rivers have become torrential, that is, the volume of water they carry in the dry season is too low in relation to the volume of water in the rainy season: the Artibonite, for instance, has a minimum flow of 17 cubic meters per second, but in the rainy season, its flow is about 50 times greater. . . .[20]

During the wet season, of course, this means heavy damage from floods:

> As a result of the transport of large quantities of rocks, gravel, sand, and arable soil torn from the mountainsides, these materials are deposited here and there and cause a rise in the river beds.
>
> At the slightest obstacle, or the slightest fissure of the banks, the massive water, handicapped or aided in its tumultuous course, forces a passage for itself toward the plains and causes not only important material damage but also the death of many people. Sometimes these rivers abandon their bed for good and dig a new one, thus plowing through great stretches of arable land, while sterilizing other equally important areas with an excessive deposit of sand and gravel.
>
> Apart from this displacement of the arable layer of soil, and apart from these floods, there are the periods of great dryness. The hot winds do not encounter, as they pass, any forested zone to cool them off, and thus in due course they give to the regions they traverse that arid aspect that we know so well.[21]

The 1948 U.N. mission made a number of recommendations

for combating erosion. These recommendations place ahead of everything else a comprehensive study of the tenure and use of land in the various regions, on the basis of which projects could be drawn up for the maintenance and regulation of the water supply, the protection of the soil from loss and depletion, and the avoidance of destruction by floods and the costly formation of marshes and swamps. These aims, said the mission, can be achieved only by restoration, protection, and careful management of the forests, especially on sloping lands.

The U.N. study recommended widening of the activities of SHADA in the pine forest of the Massif de la Selle (the south-eastern mountain range) to permit research on the growth habits and requirements of Haitian pine; that selected students from the Agricultural School at Damiens be assigned to aid in such re-search; and that one or more of them be given further training in forestry at a forestry center in the Caribbean area. Moreover, the mission recommended that high priority be given to the estab-lishment of coffee exclusively on the higher mountain slopes, where the quality is best. When a suitable area was found to be state property, its inhabitants should be permitted to remain only on condition of their strict observance of regulations made for the use of the land. Such use could include limited production of fuel wood, charcoal, etc., but the principal use would be coffee production. Some of the inhabitants could be trained to act as forest wardens. Land on lower slopes could be devoted to a similar mixture of forestry and cacao cultivation.

Mountain slopes suited neither to coffee nor to cacao could, in the opinion of the 1948 mission, become afforestation projects, but with permission to a limited number of persons to engage in carefully controlled grazing and cropping and a restricted output of fuel wood and charcoal. Certain areas could be planted to divi-divi to produce a tanning agent, or to benzolive to provide edible oil. Moderate plantings of cinchona bark might also be tried. Areas capable of spontaneous forest growth should in some cases be separated and protected from grazing, woodcutting, burning, or cropping.[22]

In the early fifties the FAO supplied Haiti with a forestry

expert who recommended a twofold approach: large-scale reforestation and the use of substitute fuels in place of wood. The first U.N. Resident Representative, A. J. Wakefield—an agricultural expert—urged that the erosion problem be fought also by teaching the peasants to build terraces on sloping land, to use contour plowing, etc.

There is little evidence that these various recommendations led to any comprehensive action by the Haitian authorities. However, the ODVA did undertake (in 1955) the planting of olive trees in a section of the Artibonite Valley with a view to protecting the vital watershed of the Artibonite River. In the absence of reforestation of the watershed slopes, the costly new dam at Peligre would soon be silted up. In 1956 the Department of Soil Conservation and Forestry claimed to have established tree nurseries at ten points (mainly in the south) as a preliminary to reforestation. Also in 1956, it was announced that 300,000 mahogany trees of a new type (Venezuelan) would be planted in the northwest.

Paul Moral argues that regardless of present legislation which prohibits the chopping down of forest trees, both the peasants and the city dwellers will continue to get supplies of wood from the forests because they have no choice. The peasants must have firewood and lumber for construction, and the towns have no other source of charcoal, nor of fuel for lime-burning, distilling, industry, and transportation. This seems to be an overstatement. Several other possibilities for peasant home-fires are known to exist. One is a low-cost clay stove, which could be made by any peasant and which burns such fuels as palm fronds, sticks, grass, and leaves, and can be located in the home, if desired, with a chimney to carry away the smoke. This "smokeless" stove, said to be popular in India, was demonstrated to peasants in the Marbial Valley in the early fifties by a U.N. expert, and it aroused great enthusiasm. A second possibility is the use of a cheap kerosene stove already being made by a Haitian metal manufacturer in conjunction with one of the foreign oil companies established in Haiti. Kerosene, known as the poor man's fuel, is widely consumed in some other underdeveloped countries. Still another possible substitute fuel for peasant use is lignite, of which Haiti has an unexploited deposit (see p. 201). Other possibilities that have been suggested are methane gas developed from garbage and sewage slime, and charcoal made from the *bayahonde* (mesquite) tree, which grows very fast and is well adapted to Haiti.

The industrial consumption of wood for fuel could probably be terminated by a legal prohibition, which would oblige industrial consumers to turn to the use of fuel oil; this has been done with respect to the essential-oil industry (see p. 155). While a general prohibition of this sort would burden Haiti's balance of payments, the vital importance of preventing further destruction of the forests may be worth the sacrifice.

Haiti no longer enjoys its former profitable export trade in precious woods, since there are few stands of these varieties left in Haiti. Mahogany trees are now so scarce that even the artisans who make souvenirs have difficulty in obtaining their raw material. Mahogany is no longer exported at all, and logwood and lignum vitae exports have dwindled to insignificant proportions.

It should, on the other hand, be possible and profitable to expand greatly the growing of coconut and oil palms. The U.N. 1948 mission estimated that between 7,500 and 15,000 acres (1.5 million trees) were then planted to coconut palms in the coastal areas. Oil palms exist on a lesser scale. Haiti has a shortage of the edible and industrial oils which these two species could supply. They could best be grown on large plantations. If they were planted on family plots, the peasants would have to be instructed in methods of controlling pests and diseases, of preparing the product for marketing, and of extracting the oil and by-products for their own use. All parts of the coconut tree are useful, for food, fuel, or housing. The milk of the coconut provides a cool drink, and its meat can be shredded for cakes and candy, or dried to make copra, the source of coconut oil. The fiber of the coconut palm can be used for cordage, mats, brushes, and other household articles. The oil of the palm-oil tree, besides its nutritive value, can be used for home or community production of soap.[23]

# □□□ 14
# Health and Housing

Haiti entered its period of independence without such health institutions as hospitals, clinics, and dispensaries, without a Ministry of Health, and practically without doctors. In the early years the government relied on justices of the peace and on police commissioners to see that a proper degree of sanitation prevailed. By 1863 there were five hospitals in the country, with a total of 300 beds. Municipal water-supply systems were not installed in most of the cities until around the turn of the century. A medical congress in 1913 called for measures against the spread of infectious diseases, for food controls, and for inspection of markets and slaughterhouses.[1]

At the beginning of the American occupation (1915), there were ten hospitals (each with its dispensary) providing 880 beds, and four provincial dispensaries. It will be recalled (see p. 38) that under the treaty governing the occupation, Haiti agreed "to undertake and execute such measures as . . . may be necessary for the sanitation and public improvement of the republic, under the supervision and direction of an engineer or engineers, to be appointed by the President of Haiti upon nomination by the President of the United States. . . . " This treaty provision was quickly implemented as follows:

> Sanitation, started by naval medical men immediately after the intervention and continued and expanded by marines and gendarmes, was placed on an efficient legal and administrative basis by the Public Health Service organized under the treaty. Sanitary and quarantine regulations were published, free clinics established, hospitals improved and new ones opened, and the training of native nurses was begun. Streets were kept clean, incinerators built and garbage was burned; sewers were opened, sanitary toilets built and drainage was installed; mosquito control was begun, water systems were repaired and markets cleaned.[2]

The occupying authorities found that a large percentage of the people were suffering from yaws, malaria, hookworm, and other diseases which accounted for their low energy and thus were a limiting factor in national economic progress. They decided to enlist the help of American civilian doctors to supplement the efforts of the naval staff. The Rockefeller Foundation made a medical survey of Haiti in 1924-25, and in 1926 it provided funds for the equipment of the medical school and for postgraduate fellowships for study in the United States and other advanced countries. A U.S. health official studied Haiti's quarantine situation and helped draft a new quarantine law.[3]

By 1929, Haiti had 12 modern hospitals with accommodations for over 10,000 patients, in addition to which there were 3 military hospitals and one other civilian hospital. Most striking was the increase in the number of clinics, of which by 1929 there were 147. In the fiscal year 1929 these clinics gave 1,341,596 consultations and treatments. A health center for infant-welfare work was established at Port-au-Prince in 1929. All this was fine, writes Millspaugh, but it was only part of the achievements of the public-health service:

> This service is to be credited also with the examination and vaccination of school children, the draining and filling of swamps, quinine distribution, control of water supplies, chlorination of the water supply of Port-au-Prince, street cleaning, garbage and trash collection, inoculation of dogs for rabies, improvement of markets and slaughter houses, construction of public and private latrines, and in general a complete sanitation campaign.[4]

According to another source, the American occupiers also reorganized the medical school and started a training school for nurses.[5]

While the occupation authorities felt that these activities had been beneficial in many ways, they gradually came to realize that more than a generation would be needed to produce lasting results and that poverty and ignorance were enormous stumbling blocks to full success. Haiti's greatest health problem in 1929 was that of

> overcoming the woeful ignorance, superstition and apathy with

regards to the real meaning and value of health. Because it was not until 1924 that any serious attempt was made to provide rural clinics, the country districts, in which . . . yaws, malaria, intestinal parasites and malnutrition persist, continue to be a serious handicap to the physician [*sic*] and economic health of the nation. . . . But the splendid advances to date will not be permanent . . . without the strong supporting movement of education. . . .[6]

The Rockefeller Foundation had found in 1924 that 67 per cent of the 4,439 persons in a sample survey showed malarial parasites in the blood, while 78 per cent of another sample of 2,564 people were infected with yaws. The Haitian government thereupon undertook a costly program to combat yaws by injections of arsenicals. By 1931 nearly 2.7 million injections had been given—practically enough to cover the whole population.[7]

Transfer of the Public Health Department to Haitian hands in 1931 brought no significant changes. The number of admissions to the hospitals increased by 70 per cent during the first seven post-occupation years. In 1942 a U.S. Sanitary Mission in Haiti inaugurated a rural health program in the course of which (1943–46) 780,954 cases of yaws were treated.[8]

The U.N. study mission of 1948 noted that Haiti had virtually no statistics of diseases and that the causes of death were established only in hospital cases, which in 1944 had made up only 14 per cent of all recorded deaths. Of the hospital deaths, no less than 46 per cent were attributed to tuberculosis. The mission found that the ratio of hospital physicians to the number of beds was relatively high at the General Hospital in Port-au-Prince (1:16) and at the hospitals located in other cities (1:21). Of the 292 physicians in service at the end of 1948, no fewer than 150 resided in Port-au-Prince and suburban Pétionville, 99 were located in other cities, 17 were studying abroad, and a mere 26 were left to take care of the medical needs of well over 2.5 million people living in the smaller towns and the rural areas, where Haiti's principal health problems existed.[9] As in the case of teachers, rural life, because of its remoteness and lack of cultural advantages, holds few attractions for Haiti's medical profession.

To begin with, according to the U.N. mission, the medical

officers in the Public Health Department were for the most part trained in hospital service only and therefore took a greater interest in hospital service than in rural health problems. Each of the 11 health districts was supervised by an *administrateur,* who was usually a surgeon with no public-health training in the field. Medical work in the rural districts was greatly handicapped by inadequate means of transport, by absence of any allowance for travel expense, and by the very low pay, which made it necessary for each doctor to carry on a private practice. The medical supervision of rural clinics and dispensaries was "manifestly deficient."[10]

Perhaps mindful of the U.N. mission's findings, the Haitian government created in fiscal 1952 a Bureau of Rural Medicine for the purpose of "bringing, through resident doctors, enlightened care to the mountain population, to the pupils in the schools and school-farms, and spreading essential notions of hygiene."[11] By this time, however, the distribution of the nation's medical personnel had become even more lopsided. According to a table made public by the Institute of Statistics, 153 of the 241 medical doctors were practicing in the Port-au-Prince district, while the number in other health districts ranged between 3 and 21; out of 94 dentists, 69 were located in the Port-au-Prince district, while those in other districts varied between 1 and 6; out of 223 nurses, 163 were in the Port-au-Prince district, as against 4 to 21 in other districts. In all but the Port-au-Prince district, the number of medical doctors per 100,000 inhabitants was between 3 and 5; there was only 1 dentist per 100,000 inhabitants (except in the Cayes district, where there were 2); and there were only between 1 and 4 nurses.

According to the same source, out of a total of 2,168 hospital beds available in fiscal 1954, 1,001 were in the Port-au-Prince district, while in other districts the number ranged only between 55 and 242. The number of hospital beds per 100,000 inhabitants was 201 in the Port-au-Prince district, as against a range of 32 to 81 in the other districts. In a country where by far the major health problem is in the countryside, these figures should be reversed if the problem is ever to be solved.

An underlying factor in the Haitian people's health problem

is the almost constant undernourishment which prevails, particularly in the rural districts. A sample survey made by the Statistical Institute in 1951 indicated that the daily calory intake of workers in the cities was about 2,450, and that of the rural inhabitants only 1,491. Fifteen years later the national calory intake was found to be between 1,600 and 2,100, with an average of 1,850, while the consumption of proteins was estimated at 40 grams per person per day.[12] No less than 78.4 per cent of all deaths were said to be due to diarrhetic affections and malnutrition. In announcing these figures, the government also announced the creation of CONALMA (Comité National de Lutte contre la Malnutrition) to work out a five-year plan (as part of the national economic and social plan) for combating malnutrition. CONALMA is financed with the help of UNESCO, FAO, UNICEF, and the Interamerican Childhood Institute.[13]

Another cause of poor health in Haiti is the inadequacy and poor quality of housing, both rural and urban. A U.S. government housing expert in 1948 described housing conditions in the following terms:

> The family has limited resources with which to rent a home, let alone buy a house. Consequently, it has been the tradition . . . for most Haitians of low income to build their own homes. The typical house consists of a single room, usually with less than 100 square feet, bare dirt floor, wood frame construction, woven clay mixed with grass . . . and a thatched roof. The homes have no sanitary facilities or running water. The cooking is done on the ground outside, over a metal brazier and charcoal fire. A handmade bed, chair, chest, counter and metal eating utensils are all one usually finds inside. The more fortunate families have a community privy nearby. The land is frequently rented from a larger land owner. Thousands upon thousands of Haitian families in urban as well as rural areas live in this fashion. . . .[14]

The above description applies, of course, only to the poorer classes, but they make up probably more than 90 per cent of the total population.

The 1950 census revealed that 54 per cent of all dwellings in Port-au-Prince were single-room units, 20 per cent were two-room affairs, and 11 per cent had only three rooms. In the slum area of Port-au-Prince, 76 per cent of the dwellings were of one room only, while 23 per cent had two rooms. Although some 20 towns had municipal water systems, very few houses in towns other than Port-au-Prince had running water. Even in Port-au-Prince only 42 per cent of the houses had running water; occupants of all other dwellings had to fetch their water from public fountains. In the rural areas practically none of the houses had running water. Only 76 per cent of the houses in Port-au-Prince had privies, and only 4 per cent of them had hydraulic or hygienic closets. In the rural areas it was the rare home that had its own latrine. Only 27 per cent of the homes in Port-au-Prince had electricity. Rural homes had none.

The peasants of Haiti never put on shoes except when they go into the city, where the wearing of shoes is compulsory. Under these conditions hookworm, which is transmitted by way of the skin, is widely prevalent. The Rockefeller Foundation found that 47 per cent of 6,652 persons examined were infected with this disease.

As already indicated (Chapter 7), there was a burst of activity under the Magloire administration in building and staffing rural clinics, dispensaries, and health centers. Much of this activity was carried on with the help of U.S. financing and advice through SCISP, the joint agency for public-health improvement.

Initial attacks on the housing problem were made by the Vincent and Estimé governments. The former built a series of low-priced workers' dwellings; the latter cleared away part of the infamous bay-front (La Saline) slum area to make way for the Bicentennial Exposition. The Magloire government constructed a number of workers' "cities." The first of these was a "garden city" of 206 brick and cement dwellings of one, two and three bedrooms, with living room, dining room, kitchen, and washroom. Located on the northern fringe of Port-au-Prince, this development included two schools, a general store, and a police station. Occupants of these houses were to obtain title after making modest monthly payments over a 20-year period. A second, adjacent development, built two years later, contained 348 dwelling units—both individual homes and apartments. These were two- or three-room units, with hall, living room, kitchen, and wash-room. The new "city" included parking space, a church, a consumers' cooperative, two schools, and a kindergarten. Later a much smaller and more modest group of dwellings was erected by the Magloire government in replacement of part of the La Saline slum area. A group of 22 modern four- and five-room houses was constructed in the town of Gonaives, and a group of three-room dwellings replaced the homes destroyed by an earthquake in the town of Anse-à-Veau.

The government of Dr. Duvalier carried out one large housing project (the Cité Simone Duvalier), consisting of about 1,000 units as of 1964, and a smaller project (Saint Martin). A National Housing Bureau (ONL) was created in 1966 to determine housing needs and priorities, to promote urban and rural home construction, and to administer the two Duvalier projects. The ONL goal of an average of 5,000 new units a year is pitifully low compared with the country's estimated shortage of 392,000 units (as of 1965).

The outstanding stages in the fight to raise the national standard of health have been the anti-yaws and anti-malaria campaigns.

Yaws is an ugly, highly contagious, pus-secreting disease which slowly eats away the victim's flesh, and even his glands and bones, and which causes horrible suffering. As already mentioned (see p. 184), the Haitian government, and later the American Sanitary Bureau, carried out massive injections of arsenicals for the cure of yaws in the thirties and forties. In 1947 a survey of Haiti's yaws problem made by two noted doctors—Rein and Kitchen—resulted in the Haitian government's launching an experimental campaign based on injections of penicillin, then a relatively new drug. The experience proved so successful that it led to the signing of contracts in 1950 with WHO and UNICEF for a jointly financed, full-fledged campaign (called SERPIAN) to eradicate yaws in Haiti. The Pan American Sanitary Bureau also cooperated in this program, through SCISP. At first one-day clinics were established at certain points, to which the peasants from the surrounding area came for injections. The clinics would then move on to other points. The 1950 census revealed, however, that by this method at least 30 per cent of the infected persons were being overlooked. A house-to-house campaign was then undertaken, and the medical officers moved up and down the mountain trails by horse or donkey to make their injections.

At the end of the two-year contracts, the results of the anti-yaws campaign were so impressive that the Haitian government and the foreign organizations involved readily agreed on a two-year renewal, again financed jointly. By the end of 1953 the incidence of yaws had been reduced to 1 per cent or less of the population—a truly spectacular achievement. Nevertheless, a second renewal of the contracts was deemed necessary in order to permit sufficient follow-up to prevent a recrudescence of the disease. Toward the end of 1955, SERPIAN was finally disbanded, leaving it to the regular health facilities to uncover any rare remaining cases of yaws.

Between 1942 and 1946, malaria-control drainage projects were carried out by the Rockefeller Foundation in two areas on the southern peninsula—Petit Goave and Aquin. The parasite rate was brought down from 86 per cent to 20 per cent at Petit Goave and from 50.5 per cent to 8 per cent at Aquin. However, upon visiting these areas in 1948, a U.N. mission expert found that maintenance of the Petit Goave drainage system had been badly neglected and that some needed repairs had not been made at Aquin.

A 1947 report on a malaria survey of Haiti showed that malaria was prevalent in many parts of the country and that spleen and parasite rates were as high as, or higher than, anywhere else in the Western Hemisphere.[15]

Further drainage projects were carried out jointly by the American Sanitary Mission and the Haitian government at six of the coastal towns. The U.N. mission of 1948 suggested that following a comprehensive survey, a DDT larviciding program would be highly desirable.

In 1955 preparations began for a joint anti-malaria campaign on a nationwide scale by the Haitian government, UNICEF, and WHO, with SCISP, SCIPA, and the ODVA all promising cooperation. Instead of the expensive dredging process, the method adopted was to spray homes in infected areas with DDT or Dieldrin. The political and economic chaos of 1956 apparently caused the temporary abandonment of this plan. In February 1961 a formal contract was finally signed, under which the U.S. government supplied $740,000 of financing, while WHO, UNICEF, and the Pan American Sanitary Bureau provided the technical staff, equipment, and supplies for the campaign. A staff consisting of about 450 persons was to visit malarial areas by jeep, horseback, or donkey, or on foot, and spray every home. Spraying was to be repeated semiannally over a three-year period. The anti-malaria campaign has, in fact, continued longer than contemplated and is not expected to end before 1972. The U.S. government is still contributing the major part of the financing for this program.

The principal other diseases which have caused considerable suffering and mortality in Haiti are syphilis, tetanus, deficiency edema, amoebic and bacillary dysentery, enteritis, granular conjunctivitis, and (sporadically) smallpox and typhoid fever.

A program of health improvement and environmental sanitation was recently prepared by the Haitian government to cover a five-year period beginning October 1, 1969. The program includes

> medical services, preventive services, public health education and sanitation services. . . . Specific goals include the immunization of 70 per cent of children up to 15 years of age against tuberculosis and 70 per cent of pregnant women against tetanus, follow-up of a malaria eradication program and consolidation of a yaws eradication program, popularization of the fundamental principles of public health, extension of the prenatal hygiene program, provision of water to rural areas and communities with over 2,000 inhabitants and improvement of water supply service in Port-au-Prince and Petionville.[16]

This is clearly an ambitious program, the successful financing of which must remain problematical in the absence of a substantial improvement of the economy. However, the U.N. is giving some technical and financial assistance, and the IDB is providing additional financing to supplement its earlier loan for water-supply projects (see pp. 103-04).

Since 1963 much attention has been paid to the problem of improved water supply. Three agencies have been set up: the Water Service of the Republic of Haiti (SHRH), created in 1963; the Autonomous Metropolitan Water Board (CAMEP), set up in 1964 to plan and provide water services to Port-au-Prince and Petionville; and the Rural Water Supply Cooperative (COALEP), organized in 1968 (as part of SHRH) to service the rural areas.[17]

After several unsuccessful attempts dating from 1938, Haiti set up in 1949 (and revamped in 1951) a system of social security covering the medical, drug, and surgical cost of work accidents, illness, and maternity. The Institut d'Assurances Sociales d'Haiti (IDASH) operated its own 40-bed orthopedic center. A National Office of Old Age Insurance was created in 1965 and was later made a part of IDASH, whose other functions are now entrusted to a section called the Office d'Assurances d'Accidents de Travail, Maladie et Maternité (OFATMA). Actually, however, only one of OFATMA's functions (accident insurance) has yet become operative.[18]

In 1954 a new wing was added to the general hospital in Port-au-Prince, and during the following year the capacity of the anti-tuberculosis sanatorium was doubled (to 200 beds). In 1956 a new 87-room hospital, privately financed by a group of doctors, was opened at Canapé Vert, a residential section of Port-au-Prince. Also in 1956, the 50-bed Albert Schweitzer Hospital opened its doors at Deschapelles for the treatment of the Artibonite Valley's peasant population. This very modern $2-million institution was erected (on land donated by the government) by a wealthy American couple—Dr. and Mrs. Larimer Mellon—who had been inspired by the accomplishments of Dr. Schweitzer in Africa and who gave up their ranching activities in Arizona in order to dedicate their lives to the medical care of a section of Haiti's population. The hospital makes no charge other than the cost of medicine and of laboratory and X-ray services. These can be paid for in kind with local produce—or not at all if the patient has no means.

In 1968, Haiti had 302 medical doctors as against the 241 reported in 1952; 415 nurses as against 223 in 1952; and 88 dentists as against 94 in 1952. The number of doctors per 100,000 inhabitants was 6.7; the corresponding figures for nurses and dentists were 9.2 and 2.0, respectively. The country had 3,329 hospital beds, as against the 2,168 available in 1954.[19] The general mortality rate (16.9 per 1,000 inhabitants) and the infant mortality rate (146.5 per 1,000 live births) in 1969 were still the highest in Latin America, despite some drop from earlier levels.[20]

While tremendous problems of health improvement remain, much has been accomplished—more, it would seem, than in any other field of development, with the possible exception of tourism. One should bear in mind, however, that a reduction of mortality means that more mouths must be fed and that productive employment must be found for more persons. Improvement of health conditions is of course desirable for its own sake, but it must be accompanied by improvement of the nation's economic potential.

# ▣▣▣ 15
# Fisheries

In view of its central location in the Caribbean Sea and its relatively long coastline, Haiti might logically be expected to engage actively in maritime fishing and fish-processing. Such, however, is not the case. Moreover, the considerable internal water resources of the republic might lead one to suppose that fresh-water fishing constituted a valuable resource. But the facts, at least until recently, have been otherwise.

Apparently no comprehensive survey of Haitian fishery resources was undertaken until 1942, when two inquiries were launched, one by the Haitian Department of Agriculture and the other by experts of the U.S. Fish and Wildlife Service (Department of the Interior). There had, however, been a number of partial studies in earlier years, and the species of fish present in Haitian waters, both salt and fresh, were fairly well known.[1]

The U.N. mission of 1948, which included an FAO fisheries expert, estimated that 4,000 Haitians were then engaged in marine fisheries, but that only 500 of them spent all their time at fishing. There were practically no full-time fishermen engaged in inland fishing. The equipment used was badly constructed and maintained, and often equipment designed for one kind of fishing was used for a different and unsuitable purpose. There were no power-boats. Larger boats ranged in size from one ton to three tons and were locally made from hardwood. Because of the shape of the hull and the rig of the sails, they were not well adapted for fishing.[2]

No fisheries statistics exist in Haiti. The U.N. mission made the following very rough estimate of the annual catch of various types:

|  | *Pounds* |
|---|---|
| Marine fish | 4,000,000 |
| Marine turtles | 250,000 |
| Other marine products | 75,000 |
| Fresh-water turtles, shrimp, etc. | 50,000 |
| Fresh-water fisheries | 250,000 |
| Total | 4,625,000 |

Haiti's fish output showed an unusually large percentage of shallow-bottom and estuarine forms and a correspondingly small percentage of deep-bottom and oceanic forms. The mission was of the opinion that this was due not to any unique deficiency in deep-water species but rather to inefficient exploitation, since the deep-water forms are harder to catch.

There was, the U.N. mission found, no lack of demand for fresh fish, and in fact the catch was sold at retail immediately upon docking. Thus only the consumers at or near landing spots were usually successful in obtaining a supply. If the supply were to be augmented substantially, it would become necessary to organize facilities for handling and marketing, including some form of preservation and transportation. Since Haiti produces salt, salting would offer advantages over ice or mechanical refrigeration (expensive under Haitian conditions) or canning. Preservation by smoking might also be feasible. For first-class restaurants and hotels, however, refrigeration would be necessary. Canning would not be feasible unless and until a sufficiently large and steady supply of fish was assured.[3]

Although Haitian marine fishing was well below its potential, the U.N. mission felt that it was not likely ever to be a large-scale activity. The type of sea bottom in the area was such that heavy trawling would not be feasible, and the only resource that could support a modern fishery would be open-water migratory fish. Schools of such fish had been seen on the northern and southern coasts of Haiti and in the Windward Passage, but almost nothing was known of the size, regularity of appearance, and behavior of these schools. Haiti would do better to concentrate on improving and expanding its local fishery, for which a modest experimental project would be in order. The difficulties in the way of such a program lay less in methods than in the temperament and tradition of Haitian fishermen. Few of them had real love of the sea, and lack of seamanship was a serious handicap. They showed little initiative toward improvements in methods and equipment and were slow to adopt improvements whose advantages were demonstrably proven. Hence "no endeavour to expand the local marine fisheries is likely to succeed without the support of determined educational efforts." Nevertheless, the mission suggested the desirability of a combined program by Haiti and other West Indian countries (Cuba, Jamaica, Puerto Rico, the Bahamas), to obtain accurate information on the movements and characteristics of the schools of fish plying between and around the islands. The data thus obtained would make it possible to determine the fishing potentialities for each of the countries concerned.[4]

The U.N. mission's report points out that the main problem in the matter of fisheries is the human element—the ignorance and backwardness of those who would have to carry out the necessary improvements and planning. Viewed narrowly, the mission's comment in this respect is certainly correct. Yet if one could assume simultaneous improvements in the basic causes of rural backwardness (poverty, disease, and malnutrition), the job of instilling modern methods and a forward-looking psychology should prove less formidable than the mission's report implies.

In 1955 the Haitian government obtained from FAO the services of a marine-fishery expert to carry out the experimental project in local fishing suggested by the 1948 mission. A Cuban tuna-fishing launch with a skeleton Cuban crew was hired, and a certain amount of modern fishing gear and equipment was imported for use in demonstrating scientific methods. The crew of the launch was filled out with Haitian apprentices. A Bureau of Fisheries was established by the government, and under its supervision exploratory fishing was carried out. Plentiful concentrations of tuna were found off Môle St. Nicholas (where Columbus had made his first landing) and in the coastal waters of the southern peninsula, with ready access to good harbors and bait fish. Môle St. Nicholas, with its excellent deep-water harbor and arid climate suitable for salting and drying, was chosen for commercial trials. These trials were pronounced successful, as an average of half a ton of fish per day was landed. A simple drying station was built ashore, and local women were taught to clean, salt and dry the fish. The product was then transported to Port-au-Prince and sold at competitive prices. Calculations were made showing how prospective marine-fishing companies could operate profitably in Haiti.[5]

In 1958 the Haitian government granted a concession to one of the largest Japanese fishing enterprises, the Taiyo Fishing Company, whose activities included tuna and salmon fishing in the Pacific, whaling in the Antarctic, and a variety of operations in Asia and South America. This company was in need of a base for new tuna operations in the equatorial Atlantic, and Haiti could serve as such a base, from which frozen tuna could be marketed in the United States. Under the concession, the Taiyo company received a monopoly of high-sea fishing rights and the right to maintain a separate fleet for the purpose of organizing Haitian coastal fishing, for both local consumption and export. It could also engage in fish-processing. Haitian fishermen were not to be deprived of their rights, and the Japanese company agreed to buy their product, if of acceptable quality, at prices agreed upon with the government. The company would also supply local fishermen with modern types of fishing gear on installment terms and would train them in its use. Unfortunately, for undisclosed reasons, this promising contract between the Haitian government and the Taiyo Fishing Company was never carried into practical effect.

In contrast to its doubts and hesitations with respect to marine fisheries, the U.N. mission of 1948 found that Haiti had favorable prospects for the development of inland fish culture. A rough calculation, it said, indicated that Haiti's "typical" fish requirements, expressed in terms of fresh fish, were something like 40.5 million pounds, of which roughly 4.5 million pounds were being obtained from the local catch. Thus a net deficit of about 36 million pounds should normally be made up either from imports or from expansion of the local catch. Perhaps as much as, but certainly not more than, 6 million pounds of this could be derived from expansion of the local catch. By applying the right methods, it should be "easy" to obtain from fish farming an additional 4 million pounds. However, the right methods, as described in the mission report, can hardly be defined as of easy application in a country like Haiti:

> Fish culture can be roughly regarded as divided into a number of degrees of specialization such as: (1) stocking of desirable species of fish in natural waters; (2) some control of predators and undesirable species; (3) adjustment or modification of natural waters to make them more suitable for the desirable species; (4) construction of artificial ponds or transformation of natural waters into essentially artificial waters; (5) fertilization of artificial waters; (6) supplementary feeding of the fish. As one passes up the grade of specialization, the expense and labour involved and the degree of technical skill required increase rapidly; at the same time the yield increases.[6]

That the procedures thus outlined would in fact entail considerable effort and persistence was recognized further on in the mission's report, when it warned that "the Government must not enter into this undertaking lightly or without full realization of the difficulties involved and the long and careful work required for ultimate success. Failing this, the result would be a waste of money, time and effort to no worthwhile purpose."[7]

It was recommended that a fish-culture expert be obtained for a period of years to make a detailed survey, lay out pilot operations and train local men in the basic principles of fish culture. Some of the obviously suitable spots for fish culture were thought to be the lower Artibonite Valley (particularly in conjunction with the rice culture planned for that region), the saline plain on either side of the mouth of the Artibonite River, the shallow-water area near Miragoane (southern peninsula), and the two large bodies of water in the Cul-de-Sac Valley (Etang Saumâtre and Trou Caiman).

Following these recommendations, the Haitian government in 1950 obtained the services of an FAO expert in fish farming (Dr. S. Y. Lin, a Chinese national). After an initial survey Dr. Lin was authorized to proceed with the construction of specimen fish ponds and was given a Haitian assistant. Within a year eight demonstration and nursery ponds were built in the outskirts of Port-au-Prince and stocked with two exotic species: the common carp from the United States and *Tilapia mossambica* from Jamaica. Several Haitian citizens expressed a desire to build ponds on their own farm lands, and in due course this wish was granted. Dr. Lin's Haitian assistant was awarded a fellowship to study fish farming in Indonesia, and a new assistant was appointed. Upon Dr. Lin's departure after three years in Haiti, another fish-culture expert was obtained through FAO (Simon Tal, from Israel) to continue this project for a further year. Upon completion of the Artibonite dam, the new artificial lake there was stocked with fish, as were the rice fields in the Artibonite Valley.

Few statistics on the present production of the fish-culture projects in Haiti are available, but apparently considerable progress has been made. It was reported in 1964 that a 15-pond experimental fish farm at Damiens had bred 1,300,000 young fish (900,000 carp and 400,000 *tilapia*), of which 1,170,000 survived and were used for restocking of ponds and rivers.[8] According to a later report, 6,000 ponds had been built, of which 4,000 were in the Cul-de-Sac Valley.[9] The continuity and persistence so far shown in following up this program augur well for its eventual success and help buttress the argument that the economic stagnation of Haiti is not a foreordained state of affairs but one which will yield to intelligent and sustained action.

Apart from fisheries, a maritime source of potential wealth is seaweed, of which several varieties abound along Haiti's shores. Rich in iodine, bromine, potassium salts, nitrogen, hydrocarbons, and minerals, seaweed can be used for the manufacture of jellies, creams, sauces, soups, cattle cakes, agar-agar, etc. A by-product, tripoli, serves for the polishing and cleaning of metals and the manufacture of dynamite.[10] It does not appear that the possible uses of seaweed have ever been considered by either the Haitian government or any of the numerous technicians who have studied the Haitian development problem.

# □□□ 16
# Industry

The industrial potential of Haiti cannot be rated very high, for a number of reasons. There is, first of all, only a small domestic market of some 4.8 million persons, and the buying power of 90 per cent of the population is about as low as it could be. In the second place, Haiti does not possess adequate fuel and power resources for any sizable industrial development. There is neither coal nor petroleum, and water power (only now being developed) will probably be barely sufficient to provide adequate electricity for homes and shops. Haiti is also deficient in most of the raw materials—timber, metals, minerals, etc.—which are needed for manufacturing industry. There is a deficiency of manual skills, as well as of technological and administrative skills. Finally, the dearth of native capital is an almost prohibitive barrier to domestic private initiative in setting up industries of any size.

It is, in any event, debatable whether Haiti would stand to benefit from industrialization on a substantial scale. Would the time and effort and resources devoted to industrialization pay off more handsomely than the same expenditure of time and effort and resources in raising the productivity of agriculture? There can be no doubt that tremendous benefits could be derived from the second course of action, in view of the extremely low productivity of Haitian agriculture in its present state.

One must recognize, however, that a moderate and cautious degree of industrialization is both advantageous and necessary for Haiti. By reducing the country's excessive dependence on a few products—coffee, sugar, sisal, bauxite—it would help to stabilize the national income and the balance of payments. This would be particularly true because industrial products are traditionally more stable in both price and output than farm products. Industrialization would be a means of creating jobs and thus absorbing part of Haiti's enormous "concealed" unemployment and expanding the national income. It could also result in a substantial improvement of the balance of payments by stimulating the domestic production of certain commodities (textiles, soap, fats and oils, beverages, cigarettes, footwear, etc.) which have been imported in large amounts, as well as the processing for export of imported materials, thus taking advantage of Haiti's low labor costs. New industries might be able to put to good use Haiti's existing surplus production of certain commodities, such as sisal, coconuts, and a variety of fruits. Should one add as a further advantage the higher degree of self-sufficiency that industrialization would bring? During World War II, Haiti, like most of Latin America, did suffer from the fact that imports from Europe and the United States were shut off or reduced by the inability of those areas to supply all needs, coupled with the activities of Nazi submarines. Self-sufficiency at that time would have been a blessing. It may seriously be doubted, however, whether a similar situation can ever arise again.

At the present time, practically the only fuel available for Haitian industries is wood, burned either directly or in the form of charcoal, although a few industries are using fuel oil or gas oil, and the HASCO sugar mill burns sugar-cane bagasse.

According to the data compiled by the Grand Conseil Technique in 1958, the total output of installed electric energy in

Haiti at that time was about 20,000 kilowatt-hours, of which 13,000 kilowatts was generated by private plants and 7,000 kilowatts by the electric-light company (Compagnie d'Eclairage Electrique), which is owned by American interests. There is at present practically no hydroelectric power, but various plans have been drawn for harnessing the Artibonite dam, and a contract for the project was recently signed (see p. 202). This will supply an additional 31,400 kilowatts. By building power facilities at Saut Mathurin (near Cayes) in the southern peninsula, a further 2,300 kilowatts could be obtained. Given the acute shortage of electric power that has existed already for many years and which has necessitated daily blackouts in Port-au-Prince, these prospective power additions will be rather quickly absorbed.

A possible additional source of power could be a series of windmills, to which small electric generators would be attached. The fairly steady breeze in most parts of Haiti would make feasible such a program, which was among the recommendations made by the 1948 United Nations mission, as well as by a U.N. wind-power technician who made a special survey of the problem in 1954 at the request of the Magloire government. In 1955 the same technician, accompanied by another specialist, returned to Haiti and installed ten experimental wind-power stations at carefully selected locations, mainly coastal or hilltop sites where wind velocities are steadiest and highest. It was arranged that the wind measurements recorded at these stations would be forwarded to experts in England for study and determination of the best locations. A windmill was also built by the students of the J. B. Damier Vocational School for use in pumping water, and the students announced that they would set up a factory to build more. According to the U.N. wind-power technicians, the potentialities of the wind as a source of energy were enormous and had scarcely been tapped anywhere. Windmills could be used for irrigation as well as for electric energy. There are, however, two obstacles to the use of wind power: first, the irregularity of the winds; and second, though the total potential energy is large, it is so thinly distributed that it must be concentrated before it can be used. Also, a special staff must be trained to ensure proper functioning and maintenance of the wind-power stations.

Since the fall of the Magloire government, nothing further has been heard of the wind-power project, suggesting that, as has so often happened, there has been no follow-through.

The 1948 U.N. mission also recommended that a thorough geological-mineral survey be made of Haiti's lignite deposits with a view to their use for the generation of electric power and for other purposes. There are two known deposits of lignite. One is at Maissade, in central Haiti; the other is at Camp Perrin, near Cayes.

In 1951 an estimate of the cost of a detailed lignite survey was obtained from consulting engineers, but the estimate was considered to be beyond Haiti's budgetary means. In 1952 a U.N. mining expert visited the Maissade lignite deposit, took samples from its outcroppings and reached the following conclusions: (1) The government should proceed urgently with the proposed hydroelectric plant at Peligre in the Artibonite, since such a plant could supply cheaper power than a thermoelectric plant using lignite. (2) The Maissade deposit of lignite should be kept in reserve for the production of electric power after demand caught up with the Artibonite plant's maximum output. (3) Lignite samples should be sent to the U.S. Bureau of Mines for thorough tests to determine whether the Maissade lignite was suited for the making of briquettes for use as domestic fuel. (4) Long-term needs for domestic fuel could best be provided by reforestation. (5) Pending reforestation and the possible availability of lignite briquettes, a tenfold expansion of the use of kerosene for domestic fuel should be resorted to as a means of preventing further waste of forest resources.[1]

As for the Camp Perrin lignite deposit, the above-mentioned American consulting engineers and the U.N. mining expert agreed that it had no commercial value, partly because of its low grade and partly because of its distance from the greater part of the country.

In 1955 the government granted a 25-year concession to a

private company, SEDREN (Société d'Exploitation et de Développement Economique et Naturel d'Haiti), to exploit the Maissade lignite deposit and any other minerals found there. SEDREN is a subsidiary of a Canadian company, Consolidated Halliwell Limited, but its president is a prominent Haitian businessman. According to press accounts, SEDREN became interested in the Maissade lignite after laboratory tests at Pittsburgh showed that it was of sufficiently high quality to justify exploitation. The company said it would spend over $2.5 million on facilities to make briquettes for use as fuel.[2] However, SEDREN has not yet begun to exploit the Maissade deposit, probably because it has had its hands full with a copper-mining concession in another part of Haiti (see pp. 203-04).

Shortly before it was overthrown, the Magloire government had been on the verge of contracting with the Westinghouse Electric Corporation for construction of the proposed Artibonite hydroelectric plant. In 1959 the Duvalier government was reported to have "approved" a contract with the Island Gas and Electric Company of New York for the installation of a hydroelectric plant at Peligre at a cost of $12 million, for the supply of power to all of the northern and western parts of Haiti (except the southern peninsula).[3] This contract never became operative, however. Up to the present time, the government has not been able to get foreign financing for the Peligre project. In a speech at the beginning of 1966, the President stated that the Peligre hydroelectric plan was "the object of all our preoccupation" and would be carried out as a priority item in 1966.[4] This evidently proved impossible. In September 1967, expounding the reasons why more development had not taken place during his first ten years in office, President Duvalier announced a decade or more of austerity to enable his government to finance the Artibonite power plant and other projects "which international institutions should have financed."[5]

Finally, a $4,850,000 contract was signed with an Italian group for the supply and installation of generators, transmission lines, and substations which would increase Haiti's installed capacity by 31,400 kilowatts. It was hoped that the project would be completed by the end of 1970, but early in 1971 the plant was not yet in operation. The additional power will be available to Port-au-Prince and to certain other parts of the country. The project is being financed over a period of 7½ years through a variety of resources: bonds issued to the National Old Age Insurance Bureau; special industrial taxes; deductions from government employees' salaries; a tax of two gourdes per bag of coffee exported (up to 250,000 bags); an increase in postage rates; and 20 per cent of the duties collected on certain luxury imports.

The most important mining activity in Haiti is that of the Reynolds Metals Company, a subsidiary of which mines bauxite in the Miragoane area of the southern peninsula, under a 60-year concession dating from 1944. Exploitation of this area was not begun until 1953. Several years were required for the purchase of land and for construction of a road, a workers' housing development, an electric-power plant, a ten-bed hospital, a drying plant, and a wharf accommodating vessels of up to 36,000 tons. In 1957 ore shipments were begun to the Reynolds aluminum plant at Corpus Christi, Texas. The annual output since 1962 has fluctuated between 414,000 and 582,000 tons (of 2,000 pounds).[6] Bauxite shipments in 1968, at $4.3 million, had the second highest value among Haiti's exports.

SEDREN, in addition to its concession to exploit the Maissade lignite deposit, received (also in 1955) a 25-year concession for the mining of copper in the Terre-Neuve area of the northern peninsula, not far from Gonaives. Various groups had tried since 1897 to exploit these copper deposits but had been handicapped by lack of funds, outdated methods, the low price of copper, and Haiti's political chaos. SEDREN reported in 1956 that the average grade of ore was 2.6 per cent and that it expected to mill at least 1,500 tons a day. Tunnels were bored through the mountain, and an access road, a small power plant, workers' housing facilities, a cafeteria, and a dispensary were built as preliminary parts of the project. An artificial deep-water harbor was prepared for the shipment to Canada of what was expected to be 45 per cent concentrate. The first shipments were made after the company's concentration plant was completed in 1960. Production rose rapidly until 1963, when the copper content of export concentrates amounted to 5,900 metric tons. Thereafter shipments gradually declined. In 1968, SEDREN's facilities suffered heavy damage from landslides, causing a further drop in production and exports. From almost 6 per cent of total exports in 1967, copper fell to slightly more than 3 per cent in the first half of 1969.

In 1954 a 30-year concession was awarded to a Haitian group to exploit manganese deposits in the areas of Jacmel (on the south coast) and Jéremie (on the north coast of the southern peninsula). The group was reported to have made a sample shipment and to have signed a contract with the U.S. Steel Corporation under which the latter would buy all the ore mined. However, the validity of the concession was conditional on the start of actual operations within a year, and, for undisclosed reasons, this was not done.

Other minerals known to exist in Haiti, according to Jacques Butterlin, a French geologist residing there, include iron, marble, and small quantities of gold and gypsum. Butterlin urged in 1955 that a state geological bureau be set up to encourage and supervise private mining companies, to prepare a detailed geological map for each project, to conduct soundings and analyses, and to serve as a center of records and documentation. This has not been done.

Both the Magloire and Duvalier governments have actively sought the creation of new industries in Haiti. Indeed, this policy has been pursued with excessive eagerness and haste. Insufficient time and care has been devoted to studying the desirability of each new industrial proposal, usually coming from a foreign individual or group. As a result many of the foreign promoters of new Haitian enterprises have abandoned their projects, usually even before these became operative. In a few instances such projects have been little more than frauds or dreams of fly-by-night or get-rich-quick adventurers. As the U.N. mission warned in 1948, "To achieve a properly balanced economic development unified planning and continuous guidance and over-all supervision by a central agency are required." The U.N. mission thought that such an agency might be a combined Ministry of Trade and

National Economy, supplemented by a Technical Research and Information Center. During the Magloire administration a Bureau de Contrôle Industriel was set up which passed on proposals for new industries, but there does not appear to have been any thorough advance checking of the experience, business reputation, and financial means of foreigners who offered to establish new industries in Haiti. Such checking should always precede the granting of government concessions, licenses, and tax exemptions. It can easily be done, not only through the foreign correspondents of Haitian banks but also through the Port-au-Prince embassies of the respective countries (or through the Haitian embassies abroad). One of the greatest helps that the U.S. embassy in Port-au-Prince could give the Haitian government (whether or not it were requested to do so) would be to check the background of all American citizens who seek industrial or other concessions from the Haitian government and make sure that suspicious characters are unmasked before they do harm to the development effort or the national finances.

In several instances the Haitian government was reported to have made possible the setting up of new enterprises by contributing to their capital. One such instance was SAFICO (S.A. de Filature et Corderie d'Haiti), which was created in 1950 for the manufacture of sisal bags and rope; another was HABANEX (see p. 82), organized in 1952 for the resurrection of the banana-export trade; still another was a tomato-canning factory at Cap-Haitien. While SAFICO has survived and appears to have had considerable success, HABANEX went bankrupt within three years. In general, it is preferable that the government not use its limited funds as a means of inducing the formation of new enterprises, which should be based exclusively on economic considerations as evaluated by competent technicians and businessmen. If a proposed new industry can be shown by a careful feasibility study to be a profitable undertaking, it should normally be possible to interest private risk capital in launching it. If thorough analysis discloses a lack of profitability, the injection of government funds is unlikely to make the enterprise viable.

By the creation of IHCAI in 1951, the Magloire government

filled an important gap in the provision of short-term credit for the working-capital requirements of both industry and agriculture, as well as of medium- and long-term credit for plant and equipment expenditures. Under its statute and bylaws, IHCAI could make such loans only after investigation by a committee of technicians and subject to constant supervision of the borrowers and their properties. This continues to be true of the institute since its reorganization in 1961 under the name of Institut de Développement Agricole et Industriel (IDAI).

Another progressive and necessary step was taken when the Magloire government cooperated with ILO technicians in the training of Haitian apprentices and workers in a variety of manual skills useful in industry. This policy continued under the Duvalier government. In addition, the government of West Germany agreed in 1966 to set up in Haiti a vocational school for 180 students with a three-year course of study and training in soldering, sheet-metal work, carpentry, forge work, plumbing, tinsmithing, saw-milling, and electromechanical work. This school prepares not only workers but also teachers for the other vocational schools. Its equipment and staff are supplied by Germany.[7]

A further step forward for Haiti might now be the provision of management training. Few young Haitians have enough knowledge of accounting, business law, finance, and business methods generally to enable them to set up and manage an enterprise successfully.

IDAI appears now to be playing something like the role which the U.N. mission of 1948 had envisaged for a "combined Ministry of Trade and National Economy, supplemented by a Technical Research and Information Center" (see p. 204). In addition to its establishment of a number of household cotton industries, of a workshop for training cotton operatives, of agricultural and storage centers, and of a spinning mill in Gonaives, IDAI is setting up an agricultural-implements factory, a slaughterhouse (at Cayes), and a cottonseed-oil refinery (at Gonaives), and it is organizing, with United Nations help, a coastwise shipping fleet. It is to be hoped that IDAI will dispose of these undertakings to private investors as soon as their feasibility is demonstrated, rather than tieing up its limited capital and energies in the owner-ship and management of numerous enterprises.

One reason why there was practically no industrialization in Haiti until after World War II was that since 1926 the customs tariff had been on a strictly revenue basis, in almost complete dis-regard of any possible benefits for potential local industries. As the 1948 U.N. mission pointed out, since import duties on manu-factured articles were often lower than the duties on the raw-material components, it would hardly have made sense to manu-facture the articles in Haiti with imported materials. In 1949 the Estimé government enacted a law granting certain tax exemp-tions to new industries (see p. 70). Its provisions were somewhat further liberalized by a law voted in 1955 and by a 1959 decree.

The 1959 decree provided for the exemption of raw materials, machinery, and supplies from import duties; for the exemption of manufactured products from export duties; and for their exemp-tion from income and license taxes, during a period varying from 5 to 10 years, according to the size of the enterprise. Enterprises representing an investment of $20,000 or less were entitled to a 5-year exemption; those representing an investment of more than $2 million received a 10-year exemption. Agricultural as well as industrial firms are eligible for these exemptions, which are not confined to new enterprises or new types of products. Eligibility is, however, subject to determination by a Consultative Commission composed of representatives of the ministers of com-merce and industry, finance, agriculture, public works, transport and communications, and labor and social welfare.

According to a radio address by an official of the Ministry of National Economy in September 1954, the following industries were operating at that time in Port-au-Prince and its environs:

| No. of Factories | Type of Industry |
|---|---|
| 5 | Underwear, polo shirts, etc. |
| 1 | Auto license plates |
| 1 | Aluminum plates and dishes |
| 1 | Foundry |
| 1 | Batteries |
| 1 | Carbon gas |
| 1 | Shoelaces |

| | |
|---|---|
| 1 | Indigo |
| 3 | Nails |
| 1 | Paper straws or tubes |
| 1 | Felt and straw hats |
| 1 | Pharmaceutical products |
| 1 | Cement |
| 1 | Cardboard boxes |
| 1 | Sisal bags and cord |
| 1 | Floor and shoe wax |
| 1 | Cotton and silk hose |
| 1 | Plastic buttons, combs, belts, toothbrushes |
| 2 | Plastic bags, wallets, garment bags, etc. |
| 1 | Aluminum, steel and glass shutters[8] |

From September 1954 to February 1956 some 20 new industries were granted tax exemptions under the 1949 law; the most important of these were:

A manufacturer of glass, chinaware and crockery
2 galvanized-iron factories
A manufacturer of bicycles, tricycles and velocipedes
3 factories making Venetian blinds and aluminum and glass windows
A motion-picture industry
A modern chocolate factory
A bottle-cap factory
A rubber-footwear manufacturer[9]

With the collapse of the Magloire government, the rate of formation of new industries slackened. Among the more important new ventures since 1956 have been the following:

A sugar mill in the Artibonite Valley
A fertilizer plant
A coffee factory
A manufacturer of agglomerates of waste products
A tomato-paste factory
A telecommunications industry[10]

In addition, operations were begun by the Haitian Meat and Supply Company (see p. 91) and by the above-mentioned enterprises promoted by IDAI. Finally, a number of labor-intensive processing or assembling plants have been set up in recent years for the re-exportation of imported products to the United States.

# 🔲🔲🔲 17
# Transportation And Communications

The citizens of an advanced country like the United States who have not experienced the serious inconveniences of travel or trade in a roadless area probably do not give the matter of transportation a great deal of thought and tend to take modern highways for granted. A knowledgeable Haitian writer has expressed himself on the subject of transport and communications as follows:

> Roads are an aid to production and facilitate exchanges by ensuring the access of merchandise to the points of consumption. They are indispensable to transport and to the sale of commodities. They encourage people to go into the interior and it is thanks to this that the elements of civilization gradually filter into the countryside, making the men of the soil more sociable, polishing their manners, refining their tastes.
>
> The lack of good means of communication throughout the Republic has been the most serious obstacle to the progress of public instruction in the countryside and to the spread of religion among the rural population. It has been an even greater impediment for this country's economic development.[1]

The road system which had existed in Saint-Domingue gradually disintegrated after independence was achieved. By the time of the American occupation of Haiti, probably not more than 210 miles of roads were passable, even in dry weather. Bridges were few and dangerous. Transportation was generally over trails or bridle paths.[2] There were only three "operational" automobiles in Haiti, and motor trucking was unknown. It took two or three weeks to cover by horse or muleback the 174 miles of coastal road from Port-au-Prince to Cap-Haitien.[3]

By the end of 1929 more than 1,000 miles of motor roads had been built or rebuilt, and a substantial amount of work had been done on the improvement of trails. Motorcars then numbered about 3,000, and there were numerous motorbus lines.[4]

As of 1948, Haiti had about 1,700 miles of roads, of which 465 miles were "national" roads connecting the principal towns: Port-au-Prince to Cap-Haitien via St. Marc and Gonaives, 174 miles; Port-au-Prince to Cap-Haitien via Mirebalais and Hinche, 122 miles; Port-au-Prince to Cayes, 122 miles. Only the first of these roads was negotiable at all times, and none of them was paved. The remaining 1,235 miles of roads, called "departmental" roads, linked the smaller towns with one another or with the national roads. There were some 50 miles of asphalted roads, mainly in the suburban area of Port-au-Prince. There were still only 3,015 motor vehicles in all Haiti.[5]

Haiti has three short railway lines (two of them narrow-gauge) totaling some 160 miles. A 90-mile line runs from Port-au-Prince via St. Marc to Verrettes and Désarmes on the Artibonite River. Shorter lines run south and east of Port-au-Prince and south of Cap-Haitien. The railways are used principally for sugar-cane and sisal transport. Passenger service exists only between Port-au-Prince and St. Marc.

Both the mountainous nature and the unusual configuration of Haiti have added to the difficulties of road and rail transport. These same characteristics, combined with the abundance of good harbors, have encouraged the growth of coastwise shipping. A glance at the map will show, for instance, that the distance from Jérémie to Gonaives by water is less than half the distance between the two cities over bad roads and extremely rugged mountain terrain. Thus long-haul traffic tends to use the goodly number of sailing vessels that ply between the numerous ports.[6]

The United Nations mission of 1948 recommended that the construction of new roads be subordinated to the proper maintenance of existing roads, to the provision of adequate drainage, to protection against erosion and landslides, and to the building of durable bridges. Road construction or reconstruction should then be confined to the key routes, namely:

Port-au-Prince–Cap-Haitien
Port-au-Prince–Port-de-Paix

Port-au-Prince—Cayes—Jérémie—Anse d'Hainault
Port-au-Prince—Fond Parisien—Savane Zombie—Saltrou
Port-au-Prince—Jacmel
Petite Rivière de l'Artibonite—Mirebalais
Môle St. Nicholas—Ouanaminthe

Feeder roads to this main network, the mission suggested, should be constructed at first only to give access to areas of particular economic importance or areas where comprehensive development projects are undertaken. Resistant local material might be used together with or in place of asphalt and cement. Expert advice should be sought on the advantages and disadvantages of different types of material, drawing on the experience of countries with similar climate, topography, and soil. The mission thought that mechanizing most of this work would be more economical than the use of low-productivity labor, that "road construction and repair should not be based on a 'make-work' philosophy," and that it was important to formulate a countrywide plan of road transport and communications to prevent "fragmentation induced by local political pressure groups." This plan should be part and parcel of the overall plan of economic development recommended elsewhere in the mission's report. Community participation and responsibility in the upkeep and building of feeder roads should be encouraged as one of the means of strengthening rural community life.

As for coastwise shipping, the 1948 mission urged the establishment of an organized coastal small-boat transportation service, to be privately owned, which would provide frequent sailings at fixed dates and unified tariff rates. This might enable foreign freighters, instead of calling at several Haitian ports, to unload at a single port, thus saving time and expense and making lower freight rates possible.

These recommendations of the U.N. mission did not find as much favor as might have been expected. There is no evidence that the Magloire administration had a countrywide road plan— certainly not as part and parcel of a general development plan— and no attention was at first paid to the warning that the highest priority should be reserved for the maintenance and protection of existing roads. No attempt appears to have been made to use resistant local materials in lieu of dollar-costly asphalt and cement, and a suggestion that a U.N. expert be invited to advise on this problem was turned down. Instead of seeking long-term financing of the road program through one of several possible channels, the government at first entered into short- and medium-term contracts with foreign engineering firms under which burdensome installment payments had to be made as the work proceeded.

Long-term road financing was not contemplated until 1953, when the projected road to Cayes was included in the program for which two American banks had tentatively agreed to float a $24-million bond issue. As explained below (p. 252), this bond issue was never carried out. Meanwhile Haiti had become a member of the International Bank, so the Route du Sud (Port-au-Prince–Cayes road) was submitted to that bank as one of several projects for which a long-term loan would be welcome. After sending several missions to study the needs and possibilities of the Haitian economy, the International Bank decided in May 1956 to make an initial loan of $2.6 million, not for the Route du Sud but for the establishment of a repair and maintenance service for the rehabilitation of a number of secondary roads under the guidance of an Italian engineering firm specializing in such work. The total cost of this repair and maintenance program was estimated at $4 million, the IBRD loan being intended to cover only the foreign-exchange expenditure involved.

In November 1962 the IDA (International Development Association—an IBRD subsidiary) extended to Haiti a 50-year non-interest-bearing credit of $350,000 to supplement the IBRD loan and stated:

> The effect of better maintenance of the road network has been to stimulate agricultural output, particularly in central and northern Haiti, and locally produced crops are beginning to replace imported foods. . . . The credit will cover the foreign exchange costs of completing work now under way and of continuing road maintenance and rehabilitation at the present level of operations for approximately one year.[7]

As of June 30, 1969, $739,000 of the IBRD loan and all of the IDA credit was still outstanding.

Beginning in 1955, a number of Haiti's rural roads were reconditioned with the assistance of funds donated by ICA (the predecessor of AID), and in 1962 the U.S. Development Loan Fund was reported ready to lend $3.4 million for construction of the Route du Sud. But, as already mentioned, all U.S. assistance except for the anti-malaria program was terminated shortly thereafter.

Unable since 1962 to obtain financing from abroad for the Port-au-Prince–Cayes road, the Duvalier government announced that it would gradually carry out the project with its own resources, thanks to its austerity program. A start was made by paving the first few miles out of Port-au-Prince.

Commercial aviation began in 1929 with the granting of a concession to Pan American Airways. During fiscal 1943 the Haitian Army organized a domestic air service between the principal towns. In the early fifties this military network was converted into a civilian service known as COHATA (Compagnie Haitienne de Transports Aériens). The COHATA flights are particularly useful for travel to points such as Jacmel and Jérémie, to which travel by road is inordinately long and tiring, as well as dangerous. For example, the flight from Port-au-Prince to Jacmel is made comfortably in fifteen or twenty minutes, as against a full-day journey over a twisting and bumpy mountain road with nearly a hundred river crossings, not to mention several stretches where the river itself serves as road. At the present time Haiti is served internationally by Air France, American Airlines, Caribair, Dominicana de Aviacón, Dutch Antillean Airlines, and Pan American World Airways.

The United Nations recommendations regarding coastwise shipping were not put into practice, presumably because the Magloire government was committed to a policy of *de*centralization. As a candidate for the presidency, Magloire had pledged "to restore the autonomy of the provinces," and one of his first steps under the Plan Quinquennal was the renovation and improvement of the port of Cap-Haitien. In fiscal 1949, 79 per cent of all imports, measured by volume, was unloaded at Port-au-Prince; only 5.6 per cent was unloaded at Cap-Haitien. Of the total tonnage of exports, 36.4 per cent was shipped from Port-au-Prince, while 13 per cent was loaded at Fort Liberté, the northeastern port which was next in importance because of sisal shipments. The 1948–49 report of the BNRH set forth the decentralization problem as follows:

> The crisis of maritime transport occasioned by the war had resulted in an excessive concentration of import trade at Port-au-Prince. Several of the provincial firms had even found it advantageous to move their head office to the capital. In 1942-43 Port-au-Prince received no less than 93.74 per cent of total imports. It is therefore satisfactory to note that the movement toward decentralization of merchandise receipts is becoming stronger, to the benefit in particular of Cape Haitian, Cayes, Fort-Liberté, and even Jacmel.[8]

The U.N. pointed out that for some $300,000 it should be possible to procure a half dozen or so diesel-engine barges of 300-ton capacity, suitable as replacements for the sailing vessels now used and capable of transporting annually four or five times the tonnage now handled between the various ports of Haiti. This suggestion, too, has had no sequel. However, IDAI is now endeavoring to organize a coastwise shipping service.

For a number of years after World War II, Port-au-Prince was a regular port of call for the passenger vessels of the Panama Line shuttling between New York and the Canal. When this service ceased a few years ago, the Grace Line's cruise ships began calling at Port-au-Prince during their weekly trips to the Caribbean and the west coast of South America. Early in 1970 steamers of the Netherlands Caribbean Line scheduled calls at Cap-Haitien. A fortnightly service between New York and Port-au-Prince by boats of the Royal Netherlands Line was recently discontinued.

None of the rivers of Haiti can be used for transport. Since bridges are few and far between,[9] rivers are usually forded at selected shallow points during dry seasons. During rainy seasons the crossing of rivers becomes hazardous or impossible.

Oxcarts are in use only in a few sugar-cane areas. In order to encourage their more general use, as well as familiarity with the advantages of the wheel in other ways, the U.N. during the fifties supplied Haiti with the services of an expert wheelwright.

By the end of World War II the telephone system which had been installed during the American occupation had practically stopped functioning. As of September 1953 there were 3,071 telephone subscribers, of whom 2,620 were in Port-au-Prince and the suburb of Pétionville.[10] In 1954 the Magloire administration contracted with the General Electric Company of England for the installation of an entirely new telephone and telegraph system at a cost of $3.2 million. This project, however, could not be carried to completion, first because of the extensive damage done by the 1954 hurricane to the work in progress, and second because of the collapse of the Magloire government and the ensuing chaos. In 1961 there were still only 3,519 telephone subscribers, of whom 2,912 were in Port-au-Prince and Pétionville.[11]

Shortly after taking office, the Duvalier government signed a contract authorizing the Société Haitienne de Télécommunications S.A. to "exploit and open to public correspondence" international and local interurban radio channels and granting the company certain tax exemptions. This apparently was not intended to displace RCA Communications and All-America Cables, which had for many years been handling international wireless and cable communications in Haiti.

# ◻◻◻ 18
# Tourism

In its 327-page report the U.N. study mission of 1948 devoted only a page and a half to tourism as a factor in Haiti's development. This was in contrast to the 61 pages devoted to agricultural development and rural welfare. Yet in the decade which followed, it was the tourist industry which showed by far the greatest expansion of all the sources of Haiti's national income. The subsequent political and social turmoil resulted, however, in a relapse, and any important revival of the tourist industry must probably await a period of assured tranquillity.

The scant attention devoted to tourism by the U.N. mission by no means signified disbelief in its potential benefits to Haiti. Indeed, the mission pointed out:

> With its magnificent scenery, unique historical landmarks, and striking customs, Haiti has the natural requisites for the development of tourism with favourable effects on employment and income, on the scope of markets for indigenous craft work, and on the balance of payments.[1]

On the other hand, the mission felt that concentration on the development of tourism should not be allowed to lessen attention to the more vital development requirements in the fields of production and transport, education, and health. Accordingly, the mission set forth no detailed recommendations for the encouragement of tourism and merely suggested that the "point of gravitation" in this field might with advantage be shifted to the private sector (hotels, travel agencies, shipping lines, etc.), which should organize itself to serve the tourist effectively.

Actually, there is no dichotomy between the tourist industry and the rest of the Haitian economy. The tourist industry can hardly realize its full potential in the absence of a satisfactory development of production and transport, education, and health. Tourists must be fed and transported, a full understanding of their needs for comfort and enjoyment presupposes a good degree of education, and poor health conditions are a deterrent to tourists.[2]

The first step taken by any Haitian government to stimulate tourism appears to have been the law of August 28, 1947, which stated as one of its considerations that

> it is desirable, for the purpose of furthering tourism in Haiti, within the limits compatible with the fiscal interests and the public safety, to repeal the restrictions on the entry, sojourn and departure of foreigners in Haiti. . . .[3]

This law spelled out the requirements and formalities relating to the movement of both foreigners and Haitians into and out of the ports and airports of the country. It provided for a special type of visa for visits to Haiti of up to three months, and for exemption from the visa requirement and other formalities in the case of Americans and Canadians visiting Haiti for a period not exceeding 30 days.

The second step in the direction of developing a tourist industry was taken when the Estimé government enacted the law of June 22, 1948, granting exemption from the income tax, and from customs duties on the construction materials, equipment, and furnishings, of hotels conforming to modern comfort requirements as detailed in the law.[4]

The organization in 1949 of a Bicentennial Exposition celebrating the 200th anniversary of the founding of Port-au-Prince had as one of its purposes the attraction of additional tourists. Part of the shabby slum area on the waterfront was leveled and replaced by modern and attractive Exposition buildings located in parklike surroundings. Many of these structures now serve as Haitian government offices, foreign embassies, cultural and recreation centers, restaurants, and shops. Without these modern improvements, tourists would have found Port-au-Prince much less attractive and interesting.

In 1953 the above-mentioned exemption of American and Canadian tourists from the visa and other formalities was extended to the citizens of all other countries entering into agreements with the Haitian government to that effect.[5]

As World War II came to an end the number of tourists visiting Haiti annually was in the neighborhood of 4,000. By fiscal 1947 the number had risen to around 7,000. Moderate increases in the next two years were followed by a substantial jump in fiscal 1950, no doubt attributable to the Bicentennial Exposition, to almost 14,000. In the fiscal years 1951 and 1952 the number of tourists rose to 16,851 and 20,149, respectively.[6] At this point the Resident Representative of the United Nations, impressed by the country's unique touristic attractiveness, offered to arrange for an expert in hotel administration to come to Haiti and teach at a hotel school to be opened by the government. The offer was accepted, and since then a succession of European hotel experts have helped train employees for the country's hotels. The hotel school turned out to be one of the most successful and popular forms of U.N. technical aid to Haiti, and it is still in operation.

A number of other measures were taken to promote tourism. Between 1951 and 1955, IHCAI extended loans totaling approximately $1 million to hotel enterprises in Port-au-Prince and Cap-Haitien, thus making possible a 140 per cent expansion of the number of rooms to accommodate the rapidly growing tourist influx. The institute also provided some financing of local travel agencies. A shelter and information booth was built at the dock where tenders landed and re-embarked passengers from visiting cruise ships, and four new tenders were put into service. Taxi fares were regulated, and chauffeur-guides were trained and licensed. Customs duties on some items purchased by tourists (watches, jewelry, cameras, etc.) were reduced to 5 per cent, while certain items were made duty-free. Government subsidies were paid to the Centre d'Art, where Haitian artists' "primitive" paintings aroused tourist admiration, and to the Foyer des Arts Plastiques, where both paintings and ceramic art were displayed and sold. Modern beach facilities were built on an island in the bay of Port-au-Prince. An intensive propaganda and advertising campaign was carried on in the United States, where three tourist information offices (in New York, Chicago, and Miami) were opened.[7]

Thanks in large part to these efforts (and in some measure, no doubt, to the increasing popularity of foreign travel among U.S. citizens), the number of tourists rose to 34,439 in fiscal 1953, to 46,755 in 1954, to 55,007 in 1955, and to 67,703 in 1956.[8] Precise data on tourist expenditures in Haiti during these years are not available, but average daily expenditure per tourist has been conservatively estimated at $30 or more and the average stay at roughly three days. For fiscal 1956 this gives total tourist receipts of more than $6 million. In addition, several tens of thousands of U.S. sailors from the Guantánamo base visited Haiti in 1956, as they had been doing for years; the number of dollars spent by them is not known. At any rate, next to coffee, tourism had become Haiti's largest dollar-earning product.

After the collapse of the Magloire government in December 1956, tourist receipts continued to grow, despite some initial wavering. By 1960 the number of tourists arriving in Haiti had reached 85,833, of whom, however, 60,929 were passengers on cruise liners and only 24,904 arrived by air.[9] Cruise passengers ordinarily remain less than 24 hours, while plane passengers ordinarily spend several days, if not a week or more, in Haiti. In 1960 the number of tourists staying one day or less was 63,419; 5,913 were recorded as remaining two days; 5,565 were three-day visitors; and the remaining 10,936 spent from four to eight days or more.[10] Thus the average duration of stay for all visitors was less than two days. If the average daily expenditure was (as in 1956) around $30, total receipts from tourism in 1960 was probably just under $9 million.

After 1960, as reports of shooting and violence in Haiti seeped through the tourist world, cruise boats and tourists tended to shy away from Haiti. Contributing to the tourist decline was the fact that Haiti did not yet have an airport which could handle jet planes, and propeller planes were rapidly disappearing from international flight schedules. The total number of planes arriving and departing at the Port-au-Prince airport fell from 2,865 in 1958 to 1,515 in 1961.[11] By 1964 the number of tourists had dropped to a mere 19,400, who were estimated to have spent in Haiti only about $900,000. The three following years showed a small increase in tourist receipts but a further drop in the number of tourists, according to figures published in the U.N. *Statistical Yearbook* for 1968 (p. 459):

|  | No. of tourists (000's) | Estimated tourist receipts (millions of dollars) |
|---|---|---|
| 1965 | 20.6 | 0.9 |
| 1966 | 12.4 | 1.0 |
| 1967 | 15.0 | 1.5 |

Some of the hotels in Haiti were shut down as a result of the tourist slump. Since the new jet airport was opened in 1965, a moderate improvement in air tourist traffic has been reported, permitting the reopening of some of the hotels.

The efforts which Haiti has put forth to stimulate tourism have been, on the whole, well conceived and successful. The present lull in tourist activity is believed to be temporary. There can be no question about the country's attractiveness from the touristic point of view. However, past efforts must be supplemented by the organization of tourist travel opportunities in other parts of Haiti than Port-au-Prince. There is no good natural beach at Port-au-Prince, but lovely beaches lie deserted on the northern and southern coasts. Some of Haiti's unique features have so far been practically unavailable to the tourist—for example, the Pine Forest in the southeastern mountains, the new artificial lake at Peligre, and the extraordinarily impressive ruins of Christophe's palace (Sans Souci) and mountain fortress (the Citadelle) near Cap-Haitien. The last-mentioned structure is by itself worth a trip to Haiti. At the present time, however, because of poor road conditions between Port-au-Prince and Cap-Haitien and the absence of even a jeep road up the mountain on which the Citadelle is perched, only a small fraction of those who visit Haiti have the time, stamina, and courage to make this excursion. In 1960, for example, only 5,443 persons visited the Citadelle, and of these only 2,916 were foreigners (as against the 85,833 tourists who came to Haiti during that year).[12] By opening all of Haiti to the foreign visitor, who is now confined to Port-au-Prince and its environs, it should be possible to increase greatly not only the number of tourists but also the average duration of their stay. Action along this line will probably entail the construction of a few comfortable motels.

Another possibility that Haiti's tourist planners seem to have overlooked is to build up a large summer traffic of teachers and students by offering special courses at the university in the French language and French literature (including the works of Haitian writers). Most tourists now come in the winter months. Many teachers and students who might otherwise go to France for summer courses would no doubt welcome the opportunity to attend such courses in Haiti, in view of the lower cost.

Still another possible source of tourist increase is the Negro population of the United States, who have not been made sufficiently aware of Haiti's attractions and, in particular, of the common bond of African ancestry between themselves and Haitians. In view of the present intense concern among American Negro students about racial and African studies, Haiti should be of special interest to them. Indeed, the suggested courses in French language and literature might well be supplemented by a few courses in African history and culture. Profound studies in these fields have been made by a number of Haitians, some of whom would no doubt be willing to give lectures or conduct seminars.

The stay of tourists in Haiti would be rendered more agreeable and interesting if they were supplied with maps of Port-au-Prince and of the country, as well as a weekly guide to current entertainment and attractions. They should not be exclusively dependent on the information (or misinformation) supplied to them by chaffeurs, hotel employees, etc.

Finally, a system of autocar tours of Port-au-Prince and environs should be organized. Tourists with only a few days or hours to spend in Haiti do not have time to ferret out the interesting sights by themselves and may not be able to afford taxi hire for the purpose. There should be at least one daytime autocar sightseeing tour and one "Port-au-Prince by Night" tour, starting always at a time and place fixed in advance. Daytime tours should include not only the principal buildings, monuments, museums, cultural centers, etc., but also visits to a sugar refinery, a rum distillery, and a mahogany workshop.

Haiti definitely has a future in tourism, once political calm is assured and the government follows the right policies to attract tourists. In 1957, Haiti's next-door neighbor, Cuba, received 269,000 tourists, who spent $43 million. In 1969 more than a million tourists visited Puerto Rico and spent there an estimated $228 million, while more than 2 million tourists spent some $600 million in Mexico. It is unlikely that Haiti can ever equal the Mexican or the Puerto Rican record, but there is surely no reason why it cannot equal or surpass the pre-Castro Cuban record.

# Foreign Trade

A country's foreign trade is a reflection of its domestic economy. It exports that part of its production that is not needed for home consumption, and it imports whatever it needs (or wants) but cannot produce economically or at all at home. Since Haiti's domestic production is so low, its exports also are necessarily low. Because it needs (or wants) so much that is not produced in Haiti, its imports tend to be as high as it can afford to pay for. Any increase in exports tends to be quickly offset by a corresponding rise in imports.

There is thus a fairly close balancing of Haiti's exports and imports, and in the absence of abnormal circumstances there is ordinarily an alternation of relatively small annual surpluses of exports or imports. This does not mean, however, that the level of either exports or imports remains steady. Rather wide year-to-year swings take place in the annual value of exports, which is affected even in "normal" times by the fluctuating size of harvests and by changes in world prices, while of course such momentous events as war, worldwide depression, and hurricanes entail severe distortions of the usual pattern.

Fortunately, there is one feature of Haiti's trade which helps to prevent or mitigate excessive fluctuations, namely, the variety in its exportable commodities. Haiti is not entirely a one-crop economy. When the coffee crop is short (as it tends to be every other year), there is at least a chance that one or more of the other export items may show an improvement in price or quantity. Nevertheless, there is still too great reliance on coffee, which produces anywhere from one-third to three-fourths (or even more) of aggregate export proceeds in a given year.

Since World War II, total annual exports have ranged in value between $24.8 million (fiscal 1946) and $55.5 million (fiscal

1954). The low figure corresponded to approximately $8 per capita of the population, the high figure to $15 per capita. These pitifully low amounts underline the scantiness of the country's output and the urgent need of economic development.

An outstanding characteristic of Haiti's foreign trade is the lack of balance in the value of exchanges with individual countries, despite the fairly even balance in trade with *all* countries. Thus Haiti regularly imports much more from the United States than it sells to us, while it exports much more to France and Europe generally than it buys. So long as currencies are freely convertible, these imbalances present no particular problem, but in the thirties and forties, when blocked currencies and exchange controls were the rule, it was impossible for Haiti to maintain its traditional pattern of trade, as will be shown below.

Partly because the élite has been reluctant to engage in business, and partly because the rest of the population lacks the necessary training, the foreign trade of Haiti is largely in the hands of foreigners. A survey made in 1954 by a former Minister of Commerce showed that foreigners made up the following percentages of those engaged in the activities listed:

| | | |
|---|---|---|
| Sugar exports | | 100% |
| Imports of gasoline, textiles, soap | | 75% |
| Exports of coffee, sisal | over | 50% |
| Fish imports | | 50%[1] |

Exports of bauxite and copper (which had not yet begun in 1954) are now made by an American and a Canadian company, respectively. Most insurance companies operating in Haiti are foreign, as are all steamship lines. Of the 971 foreigners who were licensed to do business in Haiti in fiscal 1952, 260 were U.S. citizens, 154 were French, 96 were British, 82 were Italian, 66 were Syrian, 37 were Dominican, 35 were Lebanese, and the remainder were distributed among 18 other nationalities.[2]

In the last year before the revolution, the value of Saint-Domingue's exports is estimated to have been $50 million in terms of modern money.[3] One hundred and sixty-four years later, in Haiti's best postwar year (fiscal 1954), total exports had a value of only $55.5 million, despite a 750 per cent population increase. Since 1954, annual exports have averaged only $35 million. A long-time student of Haitian affairs has pointed out that Haiti's total foreign commerce on the eve of the revolution was approximately equal in value to that of the United States.[4] Today it is only a small fraction of 1 per cent of U.S. trade (though the comparison is unfair to the extent that the U.S. has in the meantime expanded geographically). There could hardly be a more revealing and disturbing demonstration of Haiti's failure to advance economically since political freedom was achieved. The whole battle for economic and social freedom—freedom from poverty, ignorance, hunger, and disease—remains to be won.

The principal export in colonial times was sugar, with coffee ranking next. Other products (cotton, indigo, cacao, lignum vitae, mahogany, logwood) were shipped in much smaller amounts. With independence, sugar exports suffered a rapid decline, and coffee became the leading export. The sugar mills had been destroyed, and the former slaves found it easier to pick coffee from the bushes growing wild than to attempt reconstruction of the sugar mills. Dessalines feared the contacts with white foreigners which foreign trade involved. His policy was one of isolation and self-sufficiency. As a protection against foreign invasion or influence, he even planned to withdraw the native population to the interior and then to destroy the seaports. He allowed foreign vessels to enter only designated ports and to sell their cargos only to designated buyers, all of them Haitians. This system led to much corruption and discontent.[5]

Christophe had an entirely different policy. He proclaimed certain free ports where all foreign flags would be welcome, and put in his Constitution a guarantee of the security of the persons and property of foreign merchants. However, his great admiration for the British and his annoyance at the failure of the United States to recognize his kingdom led him to discriminate in favor of the United Kingdom.[6]

Pétion put forth great efforts to encourage trade with both the United States and the United Kingdom. Boyer continued more or less the same policy of encouraging foreign commerce, but with little success. The élite was uninterested, and the masses were too ignorant to engage in such activities. Thus the task of carrying on trade with the outside world fell to foreigners resident in Haiti, who have never really relinquished it.

Leyburn found that there were ten major obstacles to the growth of Haiti's commerce between 1806 and 1915: (1) the exclusion of foreign investment and enterprise; (2) overmilitarization; (3) poor methods of agriculture; (4) inefficient marketing and the absence of banking and exchange facilities; (5) a temperamental tariff policy, subject to abrupt changes, and inefficient customs procedures; (6) the assumption of an undue burden in the form of a "liberation" loan for the benefit of France; (7) currency debasement and instability; (8) dependence upon a single crop; (9) political instability; and (10) indifference of the élite to economic pursuits.[7] This is a depressingly long list of defects, of which only a few would have sufficed to prevent progress. Even more serious, most of the listed defects are to this day still holding back the economy. Items 6 and 7 above are no longer deterrent factors, and there has been some improvement in items 4, 8, and 10. Otherwise, Leyburn's list is still valid.

In modern times coffee has consistently ranked first among Haiti's exports, but there are evidences of its gradual decline as a result of the emergence of other exports, such as sisal, bauxite, bananas, essential oils, and handicraft articles. On the other hand, not all of these newer export items have had a steady growth, and one of them (bananas) has for the moment almost vanished from the trade returns. During the 25 years preceding World War II, cotton ranked as the second most valuable export, making up usually well over 10 per cent of the aggregate value of exports. The loss of European markets, combined with the ravages of the boll weevil, the greater ease of production of some other items, and the emergence of a domestic textile industry which could consume much of the domestic cotton, combined to restrict cotton exports after the war. From 7.6 per cent of the aggregate value of exports in fiscal 1946, cotton shipments gradually declined to 1.2 per cent in 1954. Since then they have become negligible. However, the program inaugurated a few years ago for the stimulation of cotton production may make possible a revival of cotton exports.

During World War II sugar became Haiti's second most valuable export, reaching in fiscal 1943 no less than 26.8 per cent of the value of all exports. Immediately after the war, however, bananas took second rank, with 17.6 per cent of the total in fiscal 1946 and 19.5 per cent in fiscal 1947. As the mistaken policies of the Estimé government with respect to bananas led to the demise of the trade in that fruit, sisal moved into the second rank of export commodities. Sisal shipments made up 26.3 per cent of total exports in fiscal 1948, 30 per cent in fiscal 1949, slightly over 24 per cent in the two following years, and 19.5 per cent in fiscal 1952. Thereafter world sisal prices slumped, causing the value of Haiti's sisal exports to fall to 12.6 per cent of total exports in fiscal 1953 and 8.9 per cent in fiscal 1954. Following a temporary resurgence between then and fiscal 1959 (when sisal again made up over 18 per cent of total exports), sisal shipments have declined substantially. By 1968 they made up only 5.4 per cent of the value of total exports and were in only the fourth rank, after coffee, bauxite, and sugar. Bauxite shipments, which began in 1957, have shown a fairly steady year-to-year increase, and by 1968 they had risen to second rank, with 11.2 per cent of the total value of exports. They retained second rank in 1969, with a value of about $6.2 million.

After the overthrow of Napoleon the French government, while not yet willing to grant formal recognition of Haiti's independence, opened negotiations for a renewal of trade. Once re-established, trade between the two countries gradually increased until France was again the principal market for Haiti's exports. In fiscal 1925, 63.5 per cent of all Haitian exports went to France, as against 12 per cent to the United States, 3.6 per cent to Belgium, 2.9 per cent to the United Kingdom, and 2.7 per cent to Germany. Until 1936 more than two-thirds of Haiti's coffee exports went to the coffee importers of Le Havre. In 1936, as a result of a disagreement about the terms of repayment of the French loan of 1910 (see p. 33), France denounced its trade agreement with Haiti and refused to take more coffee. Meanwhile, under a U.S.-Haitian trade agreement signed in March 1935, the United States became Haiti's principal customer. With the outbreak of World War II, the U.S. share in Haiti's exports became temporarily overwhelming (72.9 per cent in the five years ended with fiscal 1946). After the war, however, the U.S. share gradually declined, amounting in fiscal 1966 to only 38.6 per cent. In the same year Haiti's second largest customer was Belgium, which took 11.9 per cent of the total exports, followed by Italy with 11.1 per cent, France with 9.1 per cent, and the Netherlands with 7.2 per cent.

Haiti's import statistics reveal a surprisingly large percentage of imports of consumer goods that appear suitable for domestic production. During the first nine years following the war (fiscal 1946 to fiscal 1954 inclusive), for instance, such consumer items came to roughly one-half of the total cost of imports. Foodstuffs made up about 20 per cent of total imports; cotton textiles and other cotton manufactures, 20.6 per cent; soap, 3.8 per cent; tobacco products, 1.7 per cent; and shoes, 1.5 per cent. Other items in Haiti's imports during the same period were iron and steel products, 6.0 per cent of total imports; petroleum products, 4.3 per cent; textiles other than cotton, 3.5 per cent; chemical and pharmaceutical products, 2.4 per cent; household utensils, 2.4 per cent; agricultural instruments, 2.3 per cent; passenger automobiles, 2.3 per cent; trucks, 2.1 per cent; and cement, 1.6 per cent.

The United States has been Haiti's principal supplier since the early years of independence. In the first year after World War II, Haiti made 86 per cent of its purchases in the United States. The next most important suppliers were Canada with a mere 2.1 per cent, and Curaçao with 2.0 per cent. By fiscal 1954, however, the U.S. share in Haiti's imports had dropped to 63.2 per cent, Canada's share had risen to 8.1 per cent, the United Kingdom was third with 4.4 per cent, and Germany was fourth with 3.6 per cent. France was only in seventh place with 2.4 per cent. By 1966 the U.S. share in Haiti's total imports had dropped still further to 49 per cent, Canada continued to hold second rank, and Germany had displaced the United Kingdom in the third rank.

It is clear from Haiti's trade statistics that there is ample opportunity for improvement on both the export and the import sides. In particular, the balance of trade could be substantially bettered by taking whatever steps are necessary to bring about domestic production of some of the consumer goods now purchased abroad. Importing flour, meat, fish, edible oils, soap, etc., in large quantities does not make sense for a country which has the natural and human resources to produce all these things at home and which, moreover, cannot afford to pay for them in dollars.

# ▫▫▫ 20
# Money and Banking

Haiti's 1964 Constitution contains (Article 146) the following provision with respect to currency:

> The gourde shall be the monetary unit.
> The law shall fix the fineness and weight of the gourde and of any fractional money that the state is empowered to issue as legal tender throughout the territory of the republic.
> The National Bank of the Republic of Haiti, whose charter shall be determined by law, shall be accorded the exclusive privilege of issuing paper currency representing the gourde.
> No paper currency or coins may be issued except in accordance with a law determining the amount and the use thereof.
> In no case may the said figure be exceeded.
> The state shall direct the monetary policy in such a way as to create and maintain the conditions most favorable to the development of the national economy.

The above language is almost identical with that used in the currency clause of the 1950 and 1957 constitutions, except that the final paragraph above did not appear in the earlier versions.

The word "gourde" had its origin in colonial times as a short name for the *piastre-gourde* or *peso-gordo* (heavy peso), one of the several foreign coins then in circulation. The *peso-gordo,* minted in the Spanish colonies, had a higher silver content and a higher value than the peso minted in Spain, which also circulated in Haiti.[1]

Upon achieving independence, Haiti found itself with a scarcity of circulating money. France and England had drained off most of the supply of *piastres-gourdes,* and colonists fleeing the colonial revolution had carried away substantial quantities. In the north Christophe put some fractional coins into circulation, while in the south Pétion had the centers cut out of the piaster coins and declared the centers to be fractional coins, without any diminution in value of the piasters. In 1813 these fractional coins were withdrawn from circulation and replaced by a small issue (300,000 gourdes) of government notes. In 1817 silver coins bearing Pétion's likeness were minted.[2]

In order to lighten the crushing burden of the liberation payments to France, to which Boyer had agreed in 1825, an 1826 law authorized creation of a government bank (Banque d'Haiti) which would issue notes in exchange for the metallic money in circulation, but (probably for lack of initial capital) the bank was not established. Later in the same year the government issued its own notes, in denominations of 1, 2, and 5 gourdes. These notes carried no promise of redemption, although they were partially covered by a reserve of silver piasters. By 1841, 3.5 million gourdes of the notes were outstanding and had retained roughly one-third of their original value in terms of gold, despite large-scale counterfeiting. In 1838 a government proposal for a state bank of issue led to no legislative action, and the following year efforts to create a privately owned bank of issue failed to achieve the amount of subscriptions needed.[3]

Beginning in 1843, Haiti went through a period of political chaos and civil war which was a primary cause, not only of economic impoverishment but also of inflation and depreciation of the paper currency. From a value of one-quarter of a U.S. dollar in 1843, the gourde gradually fell to one-thirtieth of a dollar in 1867. By the end of 1869 the dollar was quoted at 4,000 gourdes or more (some say 5,000). Under a currency reform instituted in

1870 by President Nissage Saget, new gourde notes were issued at a 1:10 ratio in exchange for the old notes (except the 1- and 2-gourde denominations). Two years later the new notes in turn were withdrawn and replaced by silver coins at a ratio of 1 metallic gourde (equivalent to one U.S. dollar) for 300 paper gourdes. At the end of Nissage Saget's administration in 1874, however, inflationary forces were again predominant.[4]

In 1874 a concession was granted to an American citizen to set up a National Bank of Haiti with a one-third participation by the government, but the recipient of this concession was unable to put up his share of the capital, and the Haitian public, invited to fill the gap, failed to do so. In 1880 a 50-year concession was awarded to the Société Générale de Crédit Industriel et Commercial of Paris to establish the Banque Nationale d'Haiti as a bank of issue and commerce. The bank was organized as a French company with its head office technically in Paris and its Board of Directors in Port-au-Prince. It was appointed fiscal agent of the government and was given a monopoly of note issue. The government agreed not to issue any money itself other than coins. The gourde was legally defined as having a gold content of 1.612 grams nine-tenths fine (the approximate equivalent of the pre-1933 U.S. dollar). Unfortunately, the law specified that the bank's notes were to be in denominations (10, 20, 100, and 200 gourdes) that were much too large for the diminutive transactions of most Haitians. Even when the law was amended to provide for notes of 1, 2, and 5 gourdes, there was no demand for the new currency. A ten-month insurrection that began in 1883 placed such a financial burden on the government that in addition to borrowing from the bank, it broke its promise not to issue paper currency of its own. Having done so, the government found that the easiest way out of its difficulties was to expand its note issue. As the paper currency grew and political disturbances flared, the value of the gourde in the foreign-exchange market sank. The bank joined the community of foreign speculators in the exchange market. A series of scandals developed around disclosures of corruption among both government and bank officials in the handling of government transactions. In 1905 the government rescinded its appointment of the bank as its fiscal agent, and in 1910, as the government negotiated with a foreign group to set up a new bank in Haiti, the Banque Nationale d'Haiti went into liquidation.[5]

The new bank, called the Banque Nationale de la République d'Haiti (BNRH), was created under a 1910 contract between the Haitian government and an international banking consortium headed by the Banque de l'Union Parisienne; other banks in the consortium were the Berliner Handelsgesellschaft; Ladenburg, Thalmann and Company; and Hallgarten and Company. A simultaneous contract between the same parties provided for the flotation abroad of a 5 per cent 50-year loan of 65 million francs. Of the proceeds, 10 million francs was to be used for a monetary reform and the rest for redemption of the internal debt and for current Treasury needs. The net proceeds, after the bankers' profit and the market discount on the bonds, were 47 million francs. The concession granted to the BNRH was almost identical with that which the BNH had held. The authorized capital was 20 million francs, of which one-fourth was paid up. The bank undertook to make "statutory advances" to the state up to $600,000.[6]

Before signing the above-mentioned contracts, the Haitian government had received similar proposals from the National City Bank of New York but rejected them because of a requirement that control of the Haitian customs be given to the bank which the National City Bank would set up. The government thereupon received an amazing memorandum from the U.S. State Department pointing out alleged defects in the Banque de l'Union Parisienne proposals, violently criticizing the planned contracts and warning that the U.S. government would not permit those contracts to operate to the detriment of American citizens or interests. The Haitian government ignored the American memorandum, but following its approval of the contracts, the Banque de l'Union Parisienne consortium agreed to let the National City Bank have a share in both the loan and the BNRH. In the end the majority share (75 per cent) was French, the American share 20 per cent, and the German share 5 per cent. After the American occupation of Haiti, the French and German shares were gradually eliminated and the BNRH became a full-fledged subsidiary of the National City Bank of New York.[7]

Difficulties were not long in developing between the new bank and the government. At first they centered on the best way of carrying out the monetary reform called for by the 1910 loan contract. The bank put forth its own plan of monetary reform, under which all government fiduciary money would be withdrawn from circulation and the bank would issue in exchange its own notes redeemable in gold or dollars at the rate of 5 gourdes per dollar and for this purpose would take over the 10 million francs of monetary reserve. The government insisted on the so-called Lespinasse plan, under which its existing issues would be withdrawn only gradually and partially in exchange for gold or dollars, at an average rate of 3.5 gourdes to the dollar. Actually, neither of these plans was carried out, and under a new government a compromise plan (the Bonamy law) was voted under which the government's paper issues were to be retired against gold and silver coins at a 5-to-1 gourde-dollar ratio, without invoking the bank's note-issue powers. About 2.5 million gourdes of the government notes had been retired under this plan, when its further application was halted by still another new government. A fresh dispute between government and bank then arose as a result of insurrections which were causing lowered customs collections, leading the bank to stop its contractual budgetary payments to the government. The United States was now openly backing the bank in its altercations with the government. When the bank, in December 1914, loaded aboard a U.S. warship $500,000 of gold forming part of the monetary-reform fund, the breaking point was reached. The government rescinded the bank's appointment as fiscal agent, entrusted collection of its revenues to a group of businessmen, issued 8 million gourdes of its own paper currency and announced that it would set up a new bank. Immediately thereafter (March 1915) another revolutionary government took over under the ill-fated Guillaume Sam, to last only until U.S. marines arrived in July.[8]

We have already noted (Ch. 5) the steps taken by the occupying authorities to straighten out and strengthen Haiti's finances, and the monetary reform which was carried out in 1919 (pp. 56-57).

In 1934, when the American occupation ended, the assignments of the General Receiver and Financial Adviser were also terminated, but the U.S. and Haitian governments agreed on the appointment of an American Fiscal Representative to ensure execution of the terms on which the 1922 dollar loan had been issued. The Fiscal Representative was given active direction of the customs and the supervision and control of the Administration Générale des Contributions, which had been set up in 1924 under the management of the General Receiver. The restrictions on the Haitian government's freedom to contract new indebtedness and modify its tax system were maintained. The government was further enjoined from liquidating certain investments without the assent of the Fiscal Representative. Ownership of the BNRH was transferred to the Haitian government. Two members of the six-man board of directors were to be chosen from lists submitted by the Foreign Bondholders' Protective Council (New York) and by the Fiscal Agent of the Series A 1922 bonds, i.e., the National City Bank.[9]

Upon abolition of the office of Fiscal Representative in 1941, a Fiscal Department was created in the BNRH to carry on roughly the same duties. The Finance Minister was made honorary president of the board, half of whose voting members were to be Americans (one with the title of co-president). The board was made responsible for preparing estimates and fixing limits for the government's annual budgets, and for setting aside monthly from the government revenues the amounts required for the 1922 loan service. As related in Chapter 6 (pp. 67), the final step in Haiti's financial liberation was taken in 1947 with the redemption of the 1922 loan out of the proceeds of a new internal loan. At that time the bank's directors were reduced in number to five, all of them Haitians appointed by the President of the Republic.[10]

By 1950 memories of the harsh control exercised by the American financial advisers during the occupation had dimmed sufficiently to make it possible for the government to consider the desirability of seeking the help of a foreign technician for its financial problems. The Estimé government flirted with the idea of offering the presidency of the BNRH to a Swiss banker. When he became President, Magloire rejected this idea as an infringement of Haiti's sovereignty and instead asked the United Nations to supply a fiscal and monetary adviser. In this capacity I proceeded to Haiti in April 1951 and served, under the U.N. aegis, as adviser to the Haitian government and the BNRH during most of the period ended October 1956.[11]

There is a world of difference between an adviser imposed by the U.S. government and one made available by the United Nations in response to the applicant country's request. For one thing, those who accept assignments under the U.N. technical-assistance program must take an oath obligating them to serve only the interests of the United Nations and (by implication) of the country to which they are assigned. They are international civil servants, not representatives of the country of their own nationality. Second, under the U.N. regulations and the bilateral agreements signed by the United Nations with the developing countries, U.N. advisers must never try to impose their own views; they offer advice, as persuasively as they can, which the assisted government is free to take or to leave. This approach has definite advantages over that used by the American financial advisers in Haiti during the occupation. On the other hand, it also has the great weakness that the advice can be ignored with impunity; indeed, there is a temptation on the part of the developing country's ministers and officials to go ahead on their own without seeking the adviser's opinion whenever they have reason to believe that that opinion may be unfavorable to whatever they are planning to do.

At the start of my mission in Haiti, I was informed by President Magloire that the government would like to find ways and means by which the BNRH could give help to its program of economic development. The President complained that the bank was financing only the most routine commercial transactions and should be doing a great deal more, particularly in the direction of helping to finance industry and agriculture. He stated that the Finance Ministry had drafted a plan for the creation of an agricultural credit department in the BNRH and that he would welcome comments on this draft. With an improved banking system, the President felt, Haiti would be able to take better advantage of the country's good credit standing abroad. During the same interview the President and his Finance Minister (François Georges) commented that under a revised money and banking system, the Haitian gourde should become a gold currency untied from the dollar, which would no longer be legal tender in Haiti. They had been impressed by the success of a similar monetary reform in the Dominican Republic.

It was true that the BNRH financed only routine commercial transactions, primarily those related to exports and imports. The same was true of the only other bank then existing in Haiti, which was a branch of the Royal Bank of Canada. The risks of agricultural loans had always been deemed too great to warrant that type of credit, in the peculiar conditions of Haiti. Industrial credit, too, entailed more risk than did the financing of international trade through standardized procedures. Nevertheless, there seemed to be possibilities of some gradual broadening of credit by means of improvements in the banking and monetary system.

At my suggestion it was decided to set up a new institution, jointly owned by the government and the BNRH, for both agricultural and industrial credit, in lieu of a department within the BNRH for agricultural credit only. A project worked out by the Finance Ministry, the BNRH, and me was voted into law in September 1951, and in February 1952, IHCAI (Institut Haitien de Credit Agricole et Industriel) began operations with an authorized capital of $2 million, of which one-half was paid up (see pp. 76).

I also urged that Haiti apply for membership in the IMF and the IBRD, two institutions of great potential value to a country in Haiti's circumstances. It is indeed fortunate that Haiti decided in 1951 to do so. When Haiti's dollar reserves began to shrink as a result of the decline in exports which followed the 1954 hurricane, I was able to recommend that the BNRH apply to the IMF for a standby credit. Although that recommendation was not immediately heeded, two years later, when the collapse of the

Magloire government led to political and economic chaos, the BNRH was glad to be able to fall back on the IMF, which not only granted a standstill credit but also sent a representative to Haiti to help with advice. President Duvalier repeatedly rendered warm tribute to the aid received by Haiti from the IMF. As of June 1971, Haiti still had net drawings of $5.0 million from the IMF; the amount had been as high as $11.4 million at the end of 1967.

Haiti had no central bank in 1951. The BNRH had a note-issue monopoly, but its notes were only a part, possibly only half, of the total means of payment circulating in the country. Nobody knew what amounts of dollar notes and coins were in circulation. The BNRH was legally responsible for the convertibility of its notes into dollars, but only upon presentation at its windows in Port-au-Prince. Until Haiti became a member of IMF, neither the BNRH nor the Haitian government had any responsibility for the external value of the gourde in international transactions. The bank's very strong gold and dollar reserve was, in fact, not easily available for defense of the currency abroad. It was largely frozen as a purely nominal backing for the gourde notes. Theoretically these were supposed to be covered one-third in gold and dollars and two-thirds in short-term commercial paper (except for a small amount of government securities). But short-term commercial paper was virtually nonexistent in Haiti, so the gap in the note cover had to be filled with dollars. The result was that only a small part of the bank's dollar holdings could be termed "free" dollars, utilizable for the defense of the currency internationally. The rest was frozen as note cover and thus unavailable for use in an emergency.[12]

The National Bank was not a "lender of last resort" to other banks; in fact, it looked upon the only other bank in Haiti as an unwelcome competitor. Neither the BNRH nor anyone else was charged with supervising banking policies, operations, and interest rates generally. The system of two legal-tender currencies per-mitted the public to discriminate whenever any question might arise as to the soundness or value of one or the other. If for any reason a depreciation of the gourde came to be feared, there could be a heavy demand on the bank to pay out dollar notes, not only in exchange for gourde notes but also for all its demand liabilities (although there was no legal cover requirement against deposits).

The physical circulation of dollars was an expensive luxury for a country as poor as Haiti. The dollars would obviously be much more useful if held in the monetary reserve of the BNRH, where they not only could be the basis of a larger gourde-note circulation but could at the same time strengthen Haiti's ability to borrow abroad for economic development and could help fill occasional gaps in the balance of international payments. In Haiti dollar notes were playing a role similar to that played by gold coins before World War I in Europe and before 1933 in the United States. The main difference was that in Haiti dollars made up a much larger percentage of the money supply than gold coins had in other countries.

There was no savings bank in Haiti. Both the BNRH and the Royal Bank of Canada accepted savings deposits, but the former credited interest on them only at rates ranging from ¼ of 1 per cent to 1½ per cent, while the Royal Bank of Canada paid no interest at all on savings accounts. This was hardly an encouragement to savers in a country where the usual interest charge on bank loans was 12 per cent and where private lenders charged much higher rates. Moreover, the opening of new banks in Haiti was discouraged by an impossibly high capital requirement of $1 million.

My recommendation to the Haitian authorities on reform of the money and banking system was that an autonomous Monetary Department be set up within the BNRH, to act as a central bank until such time as a full-fledged central bank was needed. The Monetary Department, whose director would preside over both that department's board and the board of the Commercial Department, would have its own balance sheet and would be responsible for the creation and maintenance of the monetary and banking conditions most conducive to economic stability, to the steady growth of the national output, and to the full utilization of the national resources. It would be responsible for maintaining at all times stability of the domestic value of the gourde, stability of the dollar-exchange rate at the existing 5-to-1 level, free convertibility of the gourde in gold or dollars, and the solvency and liquidity of the banking system generally. It would have the power to rediscount for and make advances to other banks, to engage in open-market operations, to buy and sell gold and foreign exchange, to fix and regulate reserve requirements for the other banks, and to do the various other things which central banks are usually empowered to do in carrying out their regulatory mission. The Monetary Department would be prohibited from making loans to the government or its agencies, but the Commercial Department would be authorized to make short-term advances to the government up to 10 per cent of the average government revenues of the preceding three years.

The recommendations also called for creation within the BNRH of an autonomous Savings Department charged with an intensive campaign for the stimulation of savings through attractive interest rates, publicity, the organization of deposit and withdrawal facilities through schools and post offices, and the offer of a variety of types of deposit, including the "capitalization" accounts with a lottery feature.

Under the plan the dollar would cease to be legal tender in Haiti, except for the transactions of tourists.

In order to encourage the opening of new banks in Haiti, it was recommended that the minimum paid-up capital for new banks be lowered from $1 million to $100,000, but that all private banks be required to maintain certain minimum liquid reserves.

Although this plan of monetary and banking reform had been formulated at the request of the President of the Republic and in close cooperation with the managers of the BNRH, and despite repeated reaffirmation of the government's intention to carry it out, the only items that were enacted were the ones lowering the minimum capital for new banks and prescribing minimum reserves. Thanks to their enactment, Haiti acquired several additional banks: in 1955 the Banque Populaire Haitiano-Colombienne (a subsidiary of the Banco Popular de Colombia), in 1959 the Haitian Industrial Mortgage Bank, and in 1961 the Banque

Commerciale d'Haiti. Also, the BNRH raised the interest rate on savings accounts to a uniform 2 per cent and began to solicit such accounts actively. No doubt these actions were at least partly responsible for the substantial rise in the bank's time and savings deposits, from 12.7 million gourdes at the end of 1951 to 27.1 million at the end of 1956. In 1957 (the year of political chaos) these deposits receded to 23.4 million gourdes, and they continued to fall thereafter until the end of 1966, when they stood at only 10.8 million. By the middle of 1969 they had recovered to 20.1 million.

In 1955 the authorized capital of the BNRH was raised from 5 million to 25 million gourdes, and the paid-up capital to 10 million gourdes.

Haiti became a charter member of the two new subsidiaries of the International Bank (the International Finance Corporation and the International Development Association) in 1955 and 1960, respectively, and of the Inter-American Development Bank in 1959.

During the political and economic chaos of 1957, Haiti's dollar receipts from export trade and tourism fell drastically, but the country successfully avoided such measures as exchange control and devaluation, thanks to (1) the generous aid given by the IMF, and (2) the decision of the BNRH to play, in part, the role of a central bank by arranging with the government to enact higher reserve requirements for the private banks, thereby forcing a curtailment of credit and consequently of the normal demand for dollars, but at the same time offering its rediscount facilities to the other banks. This was a small but important step in the direction of monetary control and management, and it appears to have been adequate for the purposes of the immediate emergency. For longer-term purposes, however, it will be essential to separate the purely commercial from the monetary functions of the BNRH, either by setting up an autonomous Monetary Department as described above or by creating a separate central bank. Central and commercial banking cannot properly be placed under a single management, in view of the serious conflicts between their respective purposes and principles.

# □:□:□ 21
# Public Finance

Toussaint, Dessalines, and Christophe had the same system of state finance: they applied a "territorial tax" of one-fourth of all native produce, payable in kind. Christophe, in addition, levied a tax on the titles of nobility which he bestowed. Whereas Dessalines's administration of the government revenues was carefree and marked by corruption in subordinates, Christophe devoted careful attention to the state finances, requiring a report each morning from his principal officials. As a result, when Christophe died, he left in his Treasury a nest egg equivalent to several million dollars, which Boyer inherited. Pétion and Boyer, instead of taxing domestic production, derived state revenues from export and import duties.[1] This practice has continued ever since, although in modern times a slowly increasing share of government revenue is being derived from internal sources.

We have already described (Ch. 5) the state of Haitian public finances at the beginning of the U.S. occupation, as well as the principal measures taken by the occupying authorities to restore order and soundness to those finances.

As the reader may recall, a measure of American control over Haiti's finances continued until 1947, at first (until 1941) through a Fiscal Representative, thereafter through the Fiscal Department of the BNRH. During these years large amounts of Haiti's foreign indebtedness were paid off. The public debt declined from 177.2 million gourdes at the end of fiscal 1918 to 50.0 million at the end of fiscal 1947. Five years later it had fallen to 28.3 million.

Customs receipts rose from 15.4 million gourdes in fiscal 1915 to 45.1 million in fiscal 1928; then, after fluctuating at lower levels during the depression and war years, they reached 52.4 million in fiscal 1947. Receipts from internal taxation, which in fiscal 1915 had been inconsequential (0.4 million gourdes), rose to 6.0 million gourdes in fiscal 1929 and to no less than 11.9 million in fiscal 1947. Customs duties in fiscal 1915 had made up 96.1 per cent of total government revenue (55.1 per cent from import duties, 41 per cent from export duties). In fiscal 1947 they still made up 83 per cent of the total revenue, but duties on exports made up only 23.9 per cent of the total revenue. This, of course, reflected the Americans' sharp criticism of the excessive reliance on regressive taxation.

As of 1951, when I went to Haiti to advise on monetary and fiscal matters, the fiscal function was a responsibility partly of the Finance Ministry and partly of the BNRH. Customs duties were collected by the Fiscal Department of the BNRH, while internal revenue was collected by the Administration Générale des Contributions. The Fiscal Department also verified the internal-revenue accounts and preaudited all government expenditures. The Finance Minister had to submit the draft government budget to the cabinet each January and to the legislature during the early days of its regular session, i.e., in April. The fiscal year, as in the past, ran from October 1 to September 30.

The budget up to that time had been little more than an enumeration of the salaries of government employees and of the supplies purchased by government departments for routine operations. To the extent that there might be expenditures of a capital nature, no attempt was made to distinguish these from the routine costs of government. A serious flaw was the exclusion from the budget of about fifty "non-fiscal" accounts, some of which were trust accounts or the accounts of the state's commercial enterprises, while others represented the earmarking of special taxes, the proceeds of which were required by law to be used for a designated purpose. Other drawbacks were the long interval (nine months) which elapsed between the presentation of the budget and the beginning of the fiscal year, and the absence of any provision for revised budget estimates. Many items which were overlooked or underestimated in January thus led, after the start of the budget year, to votes of "extraordinary credits," over and above the budgeted amounts. In 1949-50, for example, extraordinary credits amounted to more than 30 per cent of the budget total.

Both the customs tariff and the internal taxes had a single aim: revenue with which to cover the costs of government. There was little or no thought of using either system for the protection of local producers against foreign competition, or of influencing the national economy in one direction or another.[2] Duties and taxes were in general regressive and inflexible. The 1926 tariff had by 1951 become outmoded and in need of general revision. Many taxes were of the nuisance variety; in fiscal 1951 there were more than 40 internal-revenue taxes which brought in less than $20,000 each.

Haiti had both personal and corporate income taxes, with rates ranging (on both types) from 5 per cent on incomes of less than $3,000 to 30 per cent on incomes in excess of $40,000. However, only a handful of persons (mainly salaried employees) were paying the personal income tax, and the government was making no effort to enlarge the roll of income taxpayers by checking it against other official records. Various arbitrary features of the corporate income tax created serious inequities. There was neither a general property tax nor a capital-gains tax, and inheritance and gift taxes were inordinately low as well as inequitable.

These and a number of other defects of the fiscal system were pointed out by me to the Haitian authorities, and at times concrete suggestions were made on how they might be remedied. Although many expressions of goodwill and good intentions were received, not much ensued in the way of action. A committee was set up to study revision of the customs tariff, but it had not completed its work when the Magloire administration came to an end. A new type of budget nomenclature and presentation was considered, along lines approved by the Fiscal Division of the United Nations, but it too was still in process when the 1956 collapse occurred. Tax-collection methods were improved, and the number of income taxpayers was raised from less than 3,000 to more than 7,000. An Inspectorat Général des Finances was set up in 1953 as a sort of budget bureau, which was expected to achieve a more scientific system of budget estimates, of recording and controlling government commitments, and preventing unauthorized or improper expenditures. However, this new agency was placed in the hands of inexperienced personnel and was made a part of the Finance Ministry instead of the more prestigious and powerful office of the President of the Republic. Import duties on luxuries and semi-luxuries were slightly increased, and the tax on radio sets was raised. The individual and business income taxes were revamped and broadened to close various gaps. To combat a severe decline in overall revenues which occurred in fiscal 1953, caused by a fall in the price of sisal and a small coffee crop, a temporary additional tax on coffee exports was proposed by the Finance Minister. I pointed out that the incidence of such a tax would fall on the already overburdened peasant producers of coffee, but the tax was nevertheless voted (see p. 78).

There were frequent complaints by the Haitian authorities about the absence of a capital market in Haiti and the unwillingness of well-to-do citizens to buy government bonds or any type of local securities. This unwillingness did not appear to be due to any lack of confidence in the currency, which was freely convertible and (at that time) strongly backed by dollars and gold. It reflected rather the existence of more profitable fields for local investment, such as mortgages and real estate. Mortgages were attractive, in part, because of their high rates in the absence of a mortgage or savings bank. Real estate was attractive because of the very low property and inheritance taxes and the absence of capital-gains taxation. As one means of competing more effectively with these types of investment, I suggested the issuance of a strictly limited amount of very short-term, tax-exempt Treasury notes (6 and 9 months) at attractive interest rates (say up to 5 per cent). The government thereupon obtained legislative authorization to issue such notes in a maximum amount of 12 million gourdes, secured by the proceeds of the temporary coffee tax, and carrying certain privileges with respect to the payment of customs and income taxes. If these notes were sold gradually to domestic investors and paid off punctually at maturity, they could be followed later by a slightly larger issue, or an issue with a slightly longer maturity, and in due course the public might begin to look upon such government securities as a reliable and profitable domestic investment. However, instead of being gradually offered to the public, the notes were (to my surprise) promptly disposed of in a single block to two American banks. A wealthy Haitian later complained to me that he had not been given an opportunity to make such an attractive investment.

When the first mission of the International Bank came to Haiti, I urged the managers of the BNRH and IHCAI to seek an arrangement with the International Bank under which IHCAI could sell to that institution some of the negotiable bonds it was authorized to issue, say up to $2-$3 million. This would have enlarged very substantially IHCAI's own lending potential. The IBRD had entered into similar arrangements with development banks in other countries. For unaccountable reasons the BNRH management failed to pursue this idea. However, many years later —in 1961—IHCAI (reorganized as the Institut de Développement Agricole et Industriel, or IDAI) applied for and received a credit of $3.5 million from the Inter-American Development Bank (IDB) to supplement its own resources.

A constant source of concern to the monetary and fiscal adviser during the Magloire administration was the government's practice of signing public-works agreements with foreign engineering firms under which the cost of the improvements was made payable in installments over a very brief period of months or years. I discovered in 1953 that several contractual obligations of this sort were not being shown in the statement of the public debt. Agreements of this kind usually entail a higher cost for the public works involved than under public bidding and long-term financing from an international institution. Moreover, the short-term nature of the payments constitutes a threat to the liquidity of the public Treasury. Often new agreements were entered into without the knowledge of the monetary and fiscal adviser, whose first news of the contract would be through the official gazette or the newspapers. The members of International Bank missions were rightly critical of such "suppliers' credits," and they urged the abandonment of the practice, but to no avail. So long as the price of coffee remained high and the tourist tide kept rolling in, and so long as there were no untoward events, Haiti had no insuperable difficulty in meeting its short-term obligations under these contracts, but even so, it was occasionally found necessary to negotiate some rearrangement of maturities.

The months of August, September, and October 1954 were a fateful turning point for Haiti. In August the high world price of coffee suffered an abrupt decline. In September the government undertook the issuance of two loans totaling $16 million in a way which, as I stressed at the time, was contrary to sound financing principles. And in October, Haiti suffered the devastating Hurricane Hazel, which was to cause a sharp decline in exports, imports, and government revenues, as well as a severe disequilibrium of the country's balance of payments.

The two September loans were a $13-million "internal" loan and a $3-million sale of Treasury notes to an American bank. The $13-million internal loan was issued for two purposes: (1) in order to convert the $3 million still outstanding of the 1947 internal loan and spread its amortization over a longer period; (2) in order to provide $10 million of financing for new economic-development projects. Of the latter amount, it was proposed to sell $5 million to the BNRH and to use the remainder as collateral for a $3-million loan to be obtained from American banks. When the monetary and fiscal adviser was informed of this $13-million loan project, a bill to authorize it had already been introduced in the legislature, which was on the point of voting it. In other words, it was too late to do much more than attempt to get some last-minute minor improvements into the text. I pointed out to the Finance Minister what I had previously emphasized in the monetary-reform project and on other occasions, namely, that for the government to borrow from the national bank was a dangerous procedure which should be resorted to only in an emergency. If the government insisted on selling $5 million of bonds to the BNRH for the financing of public works, it should at least make it clear to the public that this was a one-time procedure which would not be repeated.

The *exposé des motifs* covering the loan proposal listed a

great variety of projects, including those which were originally
to have been financed by the torpedoed Utah Construction Company program (see pp. 78-80), and from this list the Finance Minister was to determine which items should be financed out of the
$10 million of new money. The monetary-fiscal adviser stressed
that the choice and priority of projects to be financed was a highly
technical and difficult task, and he suggested that provision be
made for a committee of technicians to make at least the preliminary determination in this matter. This suggestion was incor-
porated in the bill, but the final decision on priorities was left to
be made by the Finance Minister after considering the committee's recommendations. The monetary-fiscal adviser urged that
special attention be paid to whether each project would reasonably
soon yield income in gourdes *and in dollars*, whether it was generally of a productive nature, and whether its cost was reasonable
in relation to the total funds available. Some of the projects listed
quite obviously did not meet these criteria.

Notwithstanding my warning of the dangers of selling large
amounts of government securities to the National Bank, I found
upon my return to Haiti after my 1955 home leave that the whole
$3 million of the 1954 loan was in the hands of the BNRH. It
had proved impossible to obtain a loan from American banks
collateraled by bonds of the 1954 issue.

The $13-million issue of new short-term Treasury notes had
the unfortunate consequence of necessitating a prolongation of
the temporary coffee tax to which I had expressed my opposition
two years earlier.

The damage done to Haiti's economy by Hurricane Hazel in
October 1954 was so severe that a question immediately arose
whether, toward the end of the export season several months
later, the BNRH would have enough free dollars (dollars not
frozen as cover for the note issue) to tide it over the dull season
of 1955. I therefore recommended to the BNRH that for some
months it use the utmost discretion in granting credits in order
not to add unnecessarily to the drain on its dollar holdings. This
advice was apparently heeded. I further recommended that application be made to the IMF for a standby credit, which could be
drawn on at little or no cost in case of need. This recommendation

was not put in effect, and the explanation given was that the public might be frightened by any such action, which would necessarily be a matter of public record. Instead, the bank borrowed (at a needlessly high cost) $2 million from an American private bank, regarding which no public announcement was made.

The year 1955 brought two more body blows to the already shaky economy. First, there was a months-long drought in the northern and southern peninsulas, leading to much suffering from acute hunger and actual starvation. Second, on two occasions during the year it was found that the cost of the Artibonite Valley project had been grossly underestimated, making it necessary to get an increase in the Export-Import Bank's loan from $14 million to $21 million, and then to $27 million, while at the same time increasing the Haitian government's budgetary contributions to the project. The total cost ended up in the neighborhood of $40 million instead of the $18 million estimated in 1951. For a small, impoverished economy like Haiti's, this was a major catastrophe. Haiti's debt to the Export-Import Bank on account of the Artibonite project was approximately equal to all its other debts combined.

Fortunately, the ravages of Hurricane Hazel had aroused the concern of the U.S. government to the point where, for the first time, it decided to give Haiti some special assistance, over and above the routine aid which had been given for some years through the agricultural, health, and education *servicios.* After supplying food, clothing, and medicine for the hurricane victims, the United States made available an emergency grant of $750,000 for the repair of roads, small irrigation systems, etc. This was followed a few months later by an ICA grant of $4,175,000, of which $2,175,000 was to ease the financial situation with respect to the Artibonite project, while $2 million went to a variety of small irrigation, road, and agricultural projects. This was the beginning of a long series of grants and loans from U.S. government agencies, most of them made after the fall of the Magloire government.

Since 1956, despite substantial U.S. financial and technical aid (until 1963), loans from IDA and IADB, financial support and advice from IMF, and important technical assistance from the

United Nations and its specialized agencies, the public finances of Haiti have shown little if any improvement. The golden flood of tourists which featured the decade of the fifties and fell to a trickle thereafter has not returned, and the proceeds from trade have generally remained far below the levels recorded in the first half of the fifties. Under the circumstances, a policy of austerity has had to be followed, undoubtedly under the strict surveillance of the international institutions which have been giving aid.

Some of the financial measures which have been put into effect by the Duvalier government have been of a constructive type. A modern form of budget has been introduced, a budget office was created in 1962 (again attached, however, to the Finance Ministry), and a new tariff has replaced the 1926 tariff. The budget has been kept in balance for some years at levels slightly lower than the levels of the early fifties. Despite these measures, and notwithstanding the aid received from the international agencies, Haiti has been unable to pull out of the slough of despond and misery. It has therefore been necessary to renew periodically the standby credit of the IMF and to draw on that credit repeatedly. Until 1968, drawings, in fact, increased almost without interruption, as indicated by the following figures of the drawings outstanding at the end of each year:

|  | *Millions of U.S. dollars* |
|---|---|
| 1957 | 1.0 |
| 1958 | 3.5 |
| 1959 | 5.4 |
| 1963 | 8.2 |
| 1967 | 11.4 |
| June 1971 | 5.0[3] |

As the figures show, substantial net repayments have been made to the IMF since 1967, but a long road remains to be traveled.

In the absence of large-scale American aid or some sort of windfall, such as a sharp rise in the price of coffee or sugar, or a strong upsurge of tourist expenditures in Haiti, the country must go through years of painful belt-tightening before it can emerge from the economic doldrums in which it has been languishing for more than a decade.

# The Approaches
# To Planning

Probably the major difficulty encountered over the years by those who have endeavored to assist the economic development of Haiti has been the absence, at least until recently, of an overall, well-coordinated system of development planning. This difficulty was foreseen by the United Nations mission of 1948, which, in addition to outlining in its report numerous specific steps that needed to be taken on the road to development, pointed out the desirability of a general plan and of a central body to operate it. In the mission's words,

> Good plans have been laid at different times in the past and worthwhile development projects undertaken for their realization, but they would appear not to have formed part of a well-conceived general programme embracing all the different aspects of the national economic development; they have therefore lacked in co-ordination and continuity, have frequently been piecemeal in nature, have often not been consistently followed up by appropriate care for and maintenance of capital assets created, and have therefore in the long run fallen short of the desired results. This unsatisfactory state of affairs is largely explained not only by lack of adequately trained technical personnel—which, in principle, could have been remedied, at least in some degree, by more extensive use of external technical assistance—but also and above all by lack of organization for comprehensive planning and continuous supervision of the developmental endeavor.[1]

The mission went on to recommend the creation of an "independent advisory national resources and development board" of five members, appointed by the President of the Republic for five-year terms and reporting directly to the President. The members would be distinguished, non-political Haitian citizens with knowledge and experience of the country's problems. The ministers of agriculture, national economy, and finance, as well as the president of the BNRH, would be non-voting associate members, and other ministers would be entitled to attend meetings as non-voting associates when a matter of concern to their ministries was under consideration. The board could invite other officials and technicians for "hearings." It would be provided with a secretariat of technicians "to work as an independent organ in close contact with the President of the Republic" and, with the President's approval, it would be able to call upon "outside technical assistance and advice, particularly from international agencies." The board would have a Secretary-General qualified to guide the conduct of surveys and studies of development projects, to aid in the technical evaluation and choice of projects, and to supervise the secretariat. The board would make recommendations to the President of the Republic "concerning plans, programmes, and specific projects and on over-all policy with regard to economic development."

The mission recommended, furthermore, that the Secretary-General of the board be made chairman of an Interministerial Technical Coordination Committee, at the Under Secretary of State level. Through mutual information, contact, and cooperation, it was expected, such a committee would facilitate the practical coordination of development work and the checking of progress of projects in course. Finally, it was suggested that the Secretary-General also be an ex officio member of a proposed new General Board of the BNRH; the latter would include a "Special Adviser in financial and economic matters" and a number of non-governmental persons with experience in agriculture, trade, industry, banking, etc.[2]

This key recommendation of the 1948 mission did not, however, find favor with the Haitian government, despite later efforts of the U.N. Resident Representative to convince the government of its great importance to the success of the country's development efforts. One explanation given for the government's negative attitude was that the 1950 Constitution already provided for a Conseil de Gouvernement of nine members to advise the government on all laws and contracts submitted to it and that that body had the authority to call upon experts for technical advice.

Another explanation was that the President and his cabinet were the country's central planning organization and that they could not shift this responsibility to other shoulders.

The Magloire government, as already noted (pp. 74-75), announced during its early months a Five-Year Plan of economic development, entailing expenditures of $40 million for a series of development projects, to be financed partly out of the budget and partly by suppliers' credits. This was really just a list of projects without determination of priorities, without provision for follow-up by a planning agency, and apparently without precise advance determination of costs of individual projects. There has never been a public accounting of the final cost of this plan, as against the initial estimate of $40 million.

In the light of the Magloire government's attitude toward central planning, the then U.N. Resident Representative (A. J. Wakefield) decided that the best that could be done would be to work up for the government an informal plan of economic development, with the emphasis on things that could and should be done urgently in the field of agriculture. Thanks to his vast background of experience in African and Caribbean agriculture, Mr. Wakefield was able to submit an impressive series of practical recommendations. However, in the absence of machinery for following up and pushing through these recommendations, few of them appear to have been implemented.

Mr. Wakefield's successor as Resident Representative (Raoul Aglion) also submitted to the government a general plan of economic development, but in skeleton form only. His recommendations involved creation of a Bureau du Plan attached to the office of the President of the Republic and directed by a High Commissioner with ministerial rank. It would prepare a detailed development plan for approval by the President and the legislature, in which priorities, location of projects, and methods of financing would be determined. The Bureau du Plan would also be responsible for following up the proper execution of the plan. Pending the organization of the Bureau du Plan and the preparation of its plan, a temporary planning office would be set up in the Ministry of Finance and National Economy, staffed by Haitian and foreign economists, to prepare a provisional plan as quickly as possible. These recommendations, however, led to no concrete action by the government.

Upon taking office as Finance Minister in 1953, Dr. Lucien Hibbert proposed to the cabinet a different approach to planning, namely, by entering into a contract with a large foreign engineering firm of wide international experience for the execution over a six-year period of a series of major projects, and leaving the priority of projects and the amount to be spent on each during each year to the joint decision of the government and the engineering firm. The engineering firm would be obligated to submit at the beginning of each fiscal year a plan for that year, with detailed cost estimates, plans, drawings, specifications, etc. With the help of the engineers, long-term financing would be sought from American private banks. After Dr. Hibbert's proposal was agreed to by the cabinet, the Utah Construction Company was selected for the engineering, and a preliminary agreement for an issue in the American market of $24 million of 10-year public-works bonds was reached with two large Boston banks.

The projects included in this program were a new electric-light plant; a new telephone and telegraph network; an international airport; new port facilities at Port-au-Prince; a road-improvement program, to be worked out in detail; a 200-bed hospital at Port-au-Prince; a modern tourist beach; studies and estimates for various municipal water works and for an electric-power grid for the whole country. For two projects (paving of the Port-au-Prince-Cayes road, and new Port-au-Prince harbor facilities), the engineers made detailed surveys and cost estimates. But the Hibbert plan failed of final approval by the government, and a cabinet reshuffle brought in a new Finance Minister, Clément Jumelle, with quite different ideas (see pp. 79-80). Actually, neither the Hibbert nor the Jumelle approach constituted planning in any scientific sense, since the final choices and priorities had to be made from a preliminary list of projects arbitrarily determined. Moreover, neither approach involved any control over the number and cost of other projects that might be independently put forward from time to time by the executive and voted by the legislature.

The next proposal for a central planning mechanism which came under governmental consideration was that of a visiting technician from one of the international institutions. This proposal, which involved entrusting the BNRH with the general management of the preparation and execution of a national development plan, was not acceptable to the government, which had too often found the BNRH opposed to its way of thinking in financial and economic matters.

A break in the log jam finally occurred early in 1956 when the Minister of Finance and National Economy, Clément Jumelle, was won over to the idea of central planning. It was generally understood at that time that Jumelle was the choice of President Magloire to succeed him in the presidency in 1957. The creation of a central planning mechanism no doubt appeared to Jumelle to be a powerful plank for his eventual candidacy. At any rate, he requested me (who had become the government's general economic consultant under U.N. auspices) to draw up a detailed "plan of planning," under which a provisional planning body could be set up forthwith in the Ministry of National Economy. The plan which I drew up received cabinet approval, and in August 1956 the government announced the creation of a National Commission of Economic Development under the chairmanship of the Under Secretary of State of the Department of National Economy, charged with preparation of a plan to take the place of the expiring Plan Quinquennal. In addition to its chairman, the commission was composed of seven Haitian technicians chosen from the various ministries, the BNRH, and the ODVA, and of two U.N. technicians as advisers. I was invited to be one of the two advisers; the other adviser was a national-income expert.

It was expected that the commission would prepare both an interim plan of one or two years and a long-term plan of four or five years to take effect at the termination of the interim plan. In addition, the commission was to recommend what form of permanent organization should eventually succeed it in the planning and follow-up of national development projects. It was considered important that the commission and its eventual successor should have exclusive jurisdiction over *all* planning, and that any projects originating outside it be required to be submitted to it for final approval, since otherwise it would have no real control. It was my hope that this requirement would put an end to the practice of signing contracts for miscellaneous projects on the basis of short-term suppliers' credits.

There were to be seven subcommissions or "working parties," each headed by one of the commission members. The detailed work was to be done by the working parties, each of which was to be responsible for a particular economic sector (agriculture, trade and industry, transport and communications, etc.). Active cooperation was to be solicited from the United Nations, ICA (now AID), the International Bank, ECLA, and ODVA, each of which was invited to appoint a General Adviser to the commission and to permit some of its experts to serve as part-time consultants to the working parties. I suggested that the interim plan might best be restricted to a specific field, such as education or agriculture, or to a specific geographical area, such as the southern peninsula. I pointed out that since the 1954 hurricane Haiti's finances and balance of payments had been in a difficult situation and that this made it necessary to proceed cautiously in the planning of expensive projects, especially during the next year or two.

The commission had held only one or two meetings when, at the end of September, my connection with it ceased as a result of my acceptance of an urgent U.S. government assignment in Bolivia. Early in December saw the downfall of the Magloire government, and the ensuing chaos put a temporary end to the preparations for systematic economic planning. An emergency short-term plan was devised in 1957 by IHCAI (see p. 88), but the conditions for putting it into effective operation were not present.

The next phase in the evolution of planning techniques was the creation by the incoming Duvalier government of the Grand Conseil Technique des Ressources Nationales et du Développement Economique, which we have already described (p. 89). According to a statement made some years later by the Minister of Agriculture, the two-year plan of the Grand Conseil Technique "remained a study document." For one thing, the expense involved for its plan would have been far above Haiti's capacity, and the Minister cited other defects, such as the insufficiency of basic statistical information, and lack of integration with the programs of the other economic sectors.[3] According to another source, the Grand Conseil Technique was "a high-level agency which lacks the necessary technical-administrative personnel and functions only in an advisory capacity."[4]

In December 1958 the Duvalier government decided to try a different type of planning. It signed a contract with a Washington, D.C., firm of management consultants (Klein and Saks) and a New York banking firm (Lehman Brothers) under which the two American firms were to send a mission of technicians to act as economic and financial advisers to the President in the fields of public administration, fiscal problems, banking, and agricultural and industrial development. As already mentioned (p. 90), this contract was allowed to expire at the end of a year, apparently because the Haitian government was disappointed in its expectation that the mission's help would make it eligible for early financing in the New York capital market.[5]

About the middle of 1961 the government invited the Tripartite Committee of ECLA, the OAS, and the IDB to provide technical assistance in making a survey of the Haitian economy, preparing a short-term development plan and setting up a planning mechanism. An OAS-ECLA-IDB mission of 12 technicians began its work in Haiti in November 1961 and rendered its report in December 1962. As a result a National Development and Planning Council (CONADEP) was established and made directly responsible to the President of the Republic. It was charged with the coordination and direction of studies related to economic planning and with advising the President in matters of economic and social development. In August 1963, CONADEP produced a short-range plan entitled *Le Démarrage* ("The Take-off") calling for investments of 978 million gourdes ($195.6 million) over a three-year period. This plan was enacted into law, and the execution of projects not included in it was prohibited. For its financing, an Investment Budget was set up, based on several earmarked taxes (gasoline, sisal, etc.) and on internal loans.[6]

A decree of February 1964 declared that the purpose of the plan was to promote economic expansion within the framework of the free-enterprise system and to stimulate private initiative. An Advisory Council on the Private Sector was set up to advise on measures to promote increased private investments and improved utilization of raw materials and equipment, and to keep the private sector informed of the government's plans and development objectives. The Advisory Council was to consist of the Executive Secretary of the Haitian Chamber of Commerce and of representatives from manufacturing, artisanry, labor, and trade. In October 1964 another decree listed the pre-investment and feasibility studies to be carried out in fiscal 1965.[7]

However, the funds actually available for investment under the plan in fiscal 1964 and 1965 were less than 4 per cent of the planned investment.[8] The 20 million gourdes invested in fiscal 1964 and 1965 amounted to only ½ of 1 per cent of Haiti's tiny gross domestic product.[9] Three years later the IDB's Social Progress Trust Fund reported the absence of new developments with respect to CONADEP and concluded that "the current shortage of investment funds deprives planning of any practical significance."[10]

CONADEP nevertheless went ahead with the preparation of an Economic and Social Plan of Action for fiscal 1969 under which $13 million of development expenditures was projected. Of this amount, $4.5 million was to be obtained from foreign sources. By the middle of the year, however, only $2.6 million in all had actually been invested, and of this only about $150,000 was from foreign sources."[11] Of the total planned investment, 32.4 per cent was to be allocated to power, transportation, and telecommunications; 26 per cent to agriculture, industry, and commerce; and 23 per cent to public health and water supply. The extent to which these targets were actually achieved ranged from 16 per cent in the case of industry and commerce to 90 per cent in the case of power. This improved performance apparently reflected in part some strengthening of CONADEP's representation within the various government departments and the creation, as an annex to CONADEP, of the Office de Supervision du Revenu Publique (Bureau of Public Revenue Supervision).[12]

Clearly, development planning in Haiti has had as many downs as ups. Nevertheless, some net progress has been made—perhaps as much progress as might be expected in the extraordinary circumstances that have prevailed. Two things, particularly, have been lacking for success: (1) large-scale financing from outside such as probably can come only from the U.S. government; and (2) internal peace and confidence.

# ▣▣▣ 23
# Whither Haiti?

The question considered in this chapter should be of considerable concern to the United States, as well as to Latin America. Despite its diminutive size, Haiti has great strategic importance. Only 50 miles of water separate it from Communist Cuba. Should a communist government emerge with close links to Cuba and Russia or mainland China, the United States would face the possibility of finding itself cut off from what has been the main shipping route between its east coast and the Panama Canal, namely, the Windward Passage between Cuba and Haiti. The U.S. naval base at Guantánamo could suddenly become much more difficult to reach with supplies, ships, and men. Under the circumstances, it would be foolhardy to ignore what goes on in Haiti or what becomes of that country. Yet the present policy of the United States appears to be simply to look the other way and passively permit the indefinite continuance of a festering sore in the center of the Caribbean.

While the dictatorship of François Duvalier lasted, there could be no hope of satisfactory economic and social progress in Haiti, because the two basic conditions for such progress were lacking: (1) the availability of generous U.S. financing; and (2) a reconciliation between the élite and the masses of Haiti. With the death in April 1971 of Papa Doc, the possibility of real progress remains problematical, depending on the political evolution of the country. Grave doubts exist about the ability of Duvalier's son, Jean-Claude, to maintain himself in power. Should he succeed in doing so, it remains to be seen whether the above-mentioned two basic conditions for progress will be fulfilled. The second condition—reconciliation—would require a complete and convincing renunciation of the brutal methods of the past and extension of the hand of sincere friendship to the élite. It would require disbanding the Tontons Macoutes. There is no guarantee that even such actions would retrieve the situation, and there has not yet been any convincing evidence that they will be taken.

Should the régime of Jean-Claude Duvalier prove to be transitory, everything will depend on the particular way in which it comes to an end. If there should be a peaceful change of government, with a new administration clearly devoted to democratic means, the road would be open to national reconciliation and to a renewal of sizable aid from the United States. If, on the other hand, the administration of Jean-Claude were to end in chaos and bloodshed, with communist elements vying for power, one could not foreclose the possibility of another military occupation of Haiti. In that event, it is to be hoped that the United States would not act alone and thus lay itself open once more to the charge (whether true or false) of imperialism. Any such occupation, if it cannot be avoided, should be by the OAS acting as a body, or at least by a group of OAS nations. Haiti is of concern to the whole Western Hemisphere, not merely to the United States.

Should occupation be resorted to, moreover, it is all-important that the mistakes made during the 1915–34 occupation should not be repeated. Some of those mistakes are pointed out in Chapter 5. Any eventual occupation must be based firmly and clearly on helping the Haitians do for themselves the things that need to be done, and not on forcing things down their throats.[1] And finally, occupation, if it occurs, should not last one day longer than absolutely necessary to restore order and permit the resumption of constitutional government.

Over Haiti's long history, the obstacles to progress have been political, psychological, and educational, rather than economic. The country has plentiful and varied resources, and its inhabitants are basically intelligent and capable if given half a chance. Assuming generous sustained American aid, there is no fundamental reason why Haiti could not forge ahead to much higher levels of productivity and living standards. In order for this to occur, however, two very great and long-standing obstacles must be overcome: class antagonism and peasant ignorance.

By class antagonism is meant, of course, the obstinate determination of most of the élite to hold down the masses, and the bitter, confused resentment of the masses at what they vaguely sense is a form of economic exploitation. One can understand how, in an isolated Haiti with its unique history, these conditions arose. One cannot, however, condone them. Nor can one envisage Haiti as a respected member of the family of modern nations if such conditions continue. The élite must realize—and it is, I believe, beginning to realize—that it has no choice in this matter. It will have from now on the challenging task of uplifting the masses. The successful completion of this task is a precondition for the welfare not only of the masses but also of the élite itself. Like it or not, the two classes are bound together for better or for worse.

The second great hurdle that must be cleared if Haiti is to enjoy any substantial degree of development is peasant ignorance. In chapters 9 to 15 inclusive, we have seen how this has constituted the most powerful and persistent obstruction on the road to progress. What can be done to bring the Haitian peasant into the modern world? To begin with, he does not realize that there *is* such a thing as the modern world. How could he, cut off and isolated as he has been from all contact with that world? Language, religion, geography, even history, have all conspired to isolate him.

The first priority is, of course, education—for both adults and children. Adult education on a nationwide scale is an urgent necessity. For this purpose every medium of communication—radio, television, cinema, mass meetings—should be intensively invoked in an effort to make the peasant realize what the modern world is all about and why he must want to be a part of it.[2] Such concepts as "economic," "social," and "development," which have had no meaning whatsoever to the peasant, must be gotten across to him. He cannot want what he does not know exists. And he will make no effort to get what he does not want. He must be *motivated* to change his ways.

Adult education can be only in the Creole language, and the peasants must be made literate in that language. In order to promote and sustain literacy once acquired, there must be newspapers, magazines, and books in Creole. These, too, must contribute to the campaign of enlightenment about the modern world, about the meaning of and need for economic and social development.

The education of children must be conducted on a far wider scale than it has been. Instruction in the first year or two should be in Creole, thereafter in French. The extreme shortage of schools, teachers, and textbooks must be quickly overcome. Temporarily, classes can meet in churches, *houmforts*, and public buildings, or in any shady spots outdoors. The building of schools should be vastly speeded up by organizing local *coumbites* for the purpose throughout rural Haiti. The United States should contribute Peace Corps or other teachers with a knowledge of French in order to help fill provisionally the present gap in teaching staffs. It should, over a period of years, make scholarships and fellowships available to large numbers of Haitian teachers. More normal schools should be opened promptly. The United States should also make a special annual contribution to the Haitian budget for educational purposes. Life in the rural areas of Haiti must be made much more attractive for teachers (as well as for doctors, nurses, etc.) by organizing recreational, social, and artistic activities in those areas. Teachers' salaries and fringe benefits may have to be improved. While vodou should certainly not be banished, much more should be done to instruct both children and adults in the Christian religion.[3] School instruction should aim, among other things, to combat superstition and the practice of malevolent magic.

The importance of overcoming peasant superstition and ignorance has been well summarized by a Catholic priest in Haiti in the following words:

> The way for us to fight it is to go out into the countryside and teach the peasant modern methods of agriculture, so he will have a fuller stomach, teach him health so he will no longer blame his ailments on evil spirits, put electricity into his lonely *kay* so he will no longer dread the dark, and, above all, educate him. Only thus can we ever hope to convince him that the commonplace things to which he attaches such supernatural importance—the springs and waterfalls, the fields and trees and the cross-roads near his home—are really unimportant. Abstract talk of a loving God is unavailing because the Haitian peasant is incapable of thinking in the abstract. His language contains no words to guide such thought. His concern is with the here and now, and he ponders only the things he can see, feel, hear, smell and taste.[4]

One Haitian writer has expressed the opinion that many traditional beliefs of the Haitian masses are already undergoing a gradual evolution:

> Old concepts on property ownership and inheritance are disappearing under the influence of the school. Rural clinics are reducing the clientèle of the bonesetter and herb doctor. In the villages, near urban centers, it is becoming fashionable to found one's home through legitimate union. In any case, it is important to abandon violence in the matter of religion and to find ways to harmonize old institutions with the needs of present-day evolution.[5]

This may be an overstatement, but it does suggest that at least some sort of evolution has begun. The important thing now is to step up greatly the pace of evolution.

The measures recommended above are a minimum prerequisite for Haiti's emergence into the modern world. Other steps will be needed if economic and social development is to be significant and durable. Some of these steps must be taken by the Haitian government, others by the United States.

In the Haitian government category, a solution of the erosion and fuel problem must be found as soon as possible, along one or more of the lines suggested in chapter 13. A vigorous effort must be made to clear up the confusion about land titles; the difficulty of this task has been greatly exaggerated by past Haitian governments. In the absence of clear property titles, the granting of agricultural credit is seriously hampered. Improvements in government administration are long overdue and are badly needed to ensure persistence and follow-through in tasks once undertaken, as well as to reduce corruption. A tremendous waste of time and effort has resulted in the past from the almost automatic failure of incoming governments to continue programs begun by their predecessors. At least a beginning should be made at setting up a civil service system.

In the second category of supplementary measures, the United States should recognize that the Haitian government's debt on account of SHADA and the exaggerated size of its debt on account of the Artibonite Valley program are due to no fault of its own. The SHADA program was conceived by Americans for the benefit of the United States, and if it failed, it was because of a mistaken concept and poor administration by an American-controlled agency. If the Artibonite program cost $22 million more than the original estimate, it was because of mistakes made by the American engineers approved by the American lending institution, the Export-Import Bank. The United States would deserve, and undoubtedly win, the praise of all Haitians if it offered to cancel the SHADA debt and to reduce the Artibonite debt to its original dimensions. This would make it possible for Haiti to contract new loans for the financing of other needed projects, notably the Route du Sud. Finally, the United States should, through its embassy in Haiti, keep a watchful eye on all American citizens coming to Haiti for the purpose of offering public-works contracts or industrial investments, and see to it that the Haitian government is made fully aware of the dubious background or lack of resources or experience of some of these persons. Haitian governments have in the past wasted much time and effort in negotiations with foreigners (usually American) who were either wishful thinkers or deliberate frauds.

Lifting Haiti out of its rut will not be an easy task that can be accomplished by routine half-measures. The country is small, but the job that needs to be done is stupendous. It should be tackled with the energy and persistence which Americans have been wont to put into some of their greatest accomplishments. Its successful performance will be a vivid demonstration of our willingness to help a good neighbor who, because he got off to a bad start in life, has never been able to find his proper place in the world. It could even restore some of our diminished prestige in Latin America generally.

# 🔲🔲🔲 Notes

## CHAPTER 2

1. Under the Duvalier administration the number of departments was increased to nine, but the departmental borders have not yet been fixed.

## CHAPTER 3

1. He was freed by order of King Ferdinand. A few years later he was able to make a fourth and final voyage to the New World.

2. A diabolical ruse was employed to conquer the southwestern region, known as Xaragua. Anacaona, the Indian queen of that area, was informed that a Spanish delegation would pay her a visit of friendship. The Spaniards on arrival invited Anacaona and her chiefs to a festival, in the course of which the guests were suddenly seized and bound. All except Anacaona were burned alive; she was later hanged.

3. Selden Rodman, *Haiti: The Black Republic* (New York, Devin-Adair, 1954, p. 5).

4. The buccaneers of Tortuga had been using the name Saint-Domingue for the western part of the island. Actually, this was just the French translation of the name Santo Domingo which the Spaniards had come to apply to the whole island.

5. The term "Creole" was applied to all persons, whether white or black, born in the colony.

6. The surname "L' Ouverture"—meaning "the opening"—was added by Toussaint in the course of his rise to power, presumably to signify that he was providing an opening for the blacks' attainment of freedom.

7. J.-C. Dorsainvil, *Manuel d'Histoire d'Haiti* (Port-au-Prince, Procure des Frères de l'Instruction Chrétienne, 1949), p. 87.

## CHAPTER 4

1. James G. Leyburn, *The Haitian People* (New Haven, 1941) p. 41.

2. *Ibid.*, p. 42.

3. *Ibid.,* p. 46. The *liane* (a thick vine) had been substituted for the whip formerly used by the French.

4. *Ibid.,* p. 50.

5. *Ibid.*

6. "The President was putting into practice the then novel idea of Adam Smith that the more freedom an enterpriser is allowed, the more he will produce, so that by pursuing his own self-interest he unintentionally benefits the state." (*Ibid.,* p. 55.)

7. *Ibid.*

8. Dantès Bellegarde, *Histoire du Peuple Haitien* (Port-au-Prince, 1953), p. 124.

9. "Under the three previous Negro rulers, agriculture had prospered, for these men kept state lands intact and forced the population to work; under Pétion, on the contrary, prosperity steadily declined with the division of land and the removal of compulsion. To expect a body of illiterate, inexperienced ex-slaves automatically to develop such economic virtues as industry, foresight and thrift in a land which never knew any of these is not realistic, but merely quixotic." (Leyburn, *op. cit.,* p. 63.)

10. *Ibid.,* pp. 69-70.

11. Mercer Cook, *Education in Haiti* (Washington, D.C., Federal Agency, 1948), p. 14.

12. *Ibid.,* p. 15, quoted from Elie Dubois, *Deux Ans de Ministère* (Paris, 1867).

13. This experiment was largely a failure, and only a few of the American immigrants remained permanently in Haiti.

14. Dorsainvil, *op. cit.,* pp. 273-74.

15. Bellegarde, *op. cit.,* p. 224. The railway was never completed.

16. *Ibid.,* p. 241.

## CHAPTER 5

1. Arthur C. Millspaugh, *Haiti under American Control, 1915-1930* (Boston, World Peace Foundation), p. 15.

2. Joseph Chatelain, *La Banque Nationale: Son Histoire—Ses Problèmes* (Port-au-Prince, 1954).

3. Millspaugh, *op. cit.,* p. 18.

4. Alain Turnier, *Les Etats-Unis et le Marché Haitien* (Washington, D.C., 1955), p. 231.

5. The *cacos* were revolutionary fighters who were organized in groups, sometimes by professional bandits, for the purpose of overthrowing the existing régime, plundering the towns in the process and placing a new régime in office. Many of them indulged in these lawless activities only because they were rounded up in the countryside and compelled to take part. Defining a *caco* as a crafty fellow who strikes by surprise, a Haitian

writer states that for this reason the term was applied to guerilla fighters of the north during the civil wars of the late nineteenth century. They were, he says, unseizable, refused to engage in conventional combat and disrupted their enemies by their unexpected appearances. (J. B. Roumain, *Quelques Moeurs et Coutumes des Paysans Haitiens* [Port-au-Prince, 1959].)

6. James H. McCrocklin, *Garde d'Haiti, 1915-1934* (Annapolis, Md., U. S. Naval Institute, 1956), p. 24.

7. Leyburn, *op. cit.,* p. 102.

8. Bellegarde, *op. cit.,* pp. 253-94, and *La Résistance Haitienne* (Montreal, Eds. Beauchemin, 1937), *passim.* See also Georges Sylvain, *Dix Années de Lutte pour la Liberté, 1915-1925* (Port-au-Prince, Eds. Henri Deschamps), Vol. 2, pp. 163-71.

9. Millspaugh, *op. cit.,* pp. 15-16.

10. *Ibid.,* pp. 162-63.

11. *Ibid.,* pp. 163-64. Rayford W. Logan states: "In 1929-30 the Service Technique administered about 65 per cent of the educational budget. . . . American teachers in the Service Technique received salaries of $300 or $400 a month. These salaries would not have been unreasonably high if the teachers had been competent. But many of them did not have the requisite training and few of them spoke French. All of them were white and many of them, especially the director, George Fouche Freeman, were Southerners who considered Negroes inherently inferior. Teachers in the Haitian schools received as little as $15.00 a month, and they taught in dilapidated buildings, while the Service Technique built new ones of a relatively modern type." (Rayford W. Logan, *Haiti and the Dominican Republic* [New York, Oxford Univ. Press, 1968], p. 137.)

12. Bellegarde, *La Résistance* . . ., pp. 85-86.

13. *Ibid.,* p. 113.

14. McCrocklin, *op. cit.,* pp. 53-54. The citation is from *The United States and the Caribbean Area* (Boston, World Peace Foundation, 1934). Dana G. Munro was the U. S. Minister to Haiti during the early thirties (see p. 60).

15. Millspaugh, *op. cit.,* pp. 146-50.

16. McCrocklin, *op. cit.,* p. 53.

17. In a speech which he made on Aug. 18, 1920, as the Democratic candidate for the vice-presidency, Franklin D. Roosevelt (who had been Assistant Secretary of the Navy in 1918) said: "I wrote Haiti's Constitution myself, and if I do say it, I think it is a pretty good constitution" (*ibid.,* p. 74).

18. Millspaugh, *op. cit.,* p. 152.

19. *Ibid.,* p. 153.

20. The Cul-de-Sac plain extends eastward from Port-au-Prince to the Dominican border.

21. *Ibid.,* p. 154.

22. *Ibid.,* p. 156.

23. *Ibid.*

24. *Ibid.,* p. 157. The first quotation is from the Report of the American High Commissioner (1929, pp. 19-20), the second from the Report of the Financial Adviser-General Receiver (1928-29, p. 71).

25. *Ibid.,* p. 144.

26. *Ibid.,* p. 92.

27. *Ibid.,* p. 94.

28. McCrocklin, *op. cit.,* p. 42.

29. Millspaugh, *op. cit.,* pp. 17-19. According to one Haitian author, the Haitian currency (the gourde) fluctuated between 44 and 24 U.S. cents in value during the 25 years before the occupation. (Hogar Nicolas, *L'Occupation Américaine d'Haiti: La Revanche de l'Histoire* [Madrid, Industrias Graficas España].) However, a Haitian banker has written that the gourde was quoted as low as 13.4 U.S. cents in January 1915 and at only 10.5 cents at the time of the American intervention. (Chatelain, *op. cit.,* p. 122.)

30. The National City Bank itself owned 10 per cent of the bank's stock. Three other American banking firms held 10 per cent each. In addition, the Berliner Handelsgesellschaft had agreed to vote its 10 per cent of the bank's stock in conformity with the wishes of the American group. (Turnier, *op. cit.,* p. 247.)

31. Millspaugh, *op. cit.,* pp. 28-30.

32. *Ibid.,* pp. 31-32.

33. Chatelain, *op. cit.,* p. 114.

34. *Ibid.,* p. 115. The Council of State, an advisory body, was substituting for the legislature, which had been dissolved in June 1917.

35. Millspaugh, *op. cit.,* p. 120.

36. *Ibid.* Of the Series B bonds, $766,000 was not actually issued.

37. There was a rapid turnover of individuals holding these posts. Beginning in 1924, a single man held both titles.

38. Millspaugh, *op. cit.,* pp. 124-25.

39. McCrocklin, *op. cit.,* pp. 47-49.

40. Millspaugh, *op. cit.,* p. 132.

41. The Haitian fiscal year is from Oct. 1 to Sept. 30.

42. Millspaugh, *op. cit.,* p. 127.

43. *Ibid.,* p. 130.

44. O. Ernest Moore, "Monetary-Fiscal Policy and Economic Development in Haiti," *Public Finance/Finances Publiques* (Amsterdam), No. 3, 1954.

45. A detailed discussion of this dollar-gourde currency dispute is contained in Chatelain, *op. cit.,* pp. 129-38. It appears that the Haitian government's insistence upon having the dollar as well as the gourde as legal

tender was primarily due to its distrust of the National Bank and the latter's owner, the National City Bank of New York, which it did not wish to see as the sole source of currency issues in Haiti.

46. This account of the Forbes and Moton commissions and their aftermath is based on Millspaugh, *op. cit.,* pp. 177-94.

CHAPTER 6

1. This description of SHADA's activities is based on the accounts given by Bellegarde, *Histoire* . . ., pp. 309-10, 315-16, and by Turnier, *op. cit.,* pp. 300-03. According to an American account, less than ½ of 1 per cent of Haitian land was taken out of its "usual usage" by SHADA (*Foreign Commerce Weekly,* [U.S. Dept. of Commerce], Nov. 6, 1943). The truth probably lies somewhere between the Haitian and American versions. Turnier places the final loss on the cryptostegia project at $6,733,000.

2. Bellegarde, *Histoire* . . ., p. 313.

3. The U.S. and Dominican governments are said to have contributed to Lescot's downfall. The U.S. government refused a new loan requested by Lescot, causing him to denounce the U.S. publicly. American interests in Haiti are alleged to have supported the general strike, and our legation to have passed word to the Haitian army that it would sanction Lescot's ouster. (Diederich and Burt, *op. cit.,* p. 46.)

4. UNESCO, *The Haiti Pilot Project* (Paris, 1951), p. 62.

5. U.N., *Mission to Haiti* (New York, 1949), pp. 7-13.

CHAPTER 7

1. O. K. Armstrong, "When Good Neighbors Get Together," reprinted from *Nation's Business* by Institute of Inter-American Affairs, Washington, D.C.

2. Kenneth R. Iverson, "Ten Years of 'Point Four' in Action in Latin America," *Foreign Commerce Weekly,* Feb. 4, 1952.

3. The number of tourists visiting Haiti rose from 12,000 in the fiscal year 1949-50 to 67,000 in 1955-56, according to the Haitian Institute of Statistics (1949-50) and the N.Y. *Times* of Sept. 27, 1957.

4. The $7-million additional credit of 1955 had carried an interest rate of 4¼ per cent.

5. Diederich and Burt, *op. cit.,* p. 73.

6. According to a usually well-informed source, the U.S. ambassador and the papal nuncio also played a role in Magloire's decision to step down. (Diederich and Burt, *op. cit.,* p. 74.)

7. The U.N. monetary and fiscal expert calculated that in the six-year

period from Sept. 30, 1949, to Sept. 30, 1955, the Haitian government spent $75.3 million on projects classified as economic or social development. The amount invested annually increased from $6.2 million in fiscal 1950 to $18.1 million in fiscal 1955. Of the total expenditure, $53.5 million was derived from government revenues and $21.8 million from borrowing.

8. *Le Nouvelliste* (Port-au-Prince), Apr. 26, 1957, quoted by Clément Célestin in *Compilations pour l'Histoire: Les Gouvernements Provisoires, 6 Décembre 1956 au 25 Mai 1957,* Tome I, p. 291.

CHAPTER 8

1. *Journal of Commerce* (N.Y.), Sept. 27, 1957.
2. *Ibid.*
3. Diederich and Burt, *op. cit.,* pp. 103-04.
4. *Haiti Sun,* Feb. 16, 1958.
5. *Ibid.,* Nov. 9, 1958.
6. *Ibid., Le Nouvelliste,* June 7, 1958.
7. Diederich and Burt, *op. cit.,* p. 136.
8. According to a N.Y. *Times* dispatch of Jan. 21, 1959, "opposition estimates of those jailed at various times range from 300 up."
9. *Ibid.*
10. Berkeley Rice, "Haiti: Last Act of a Tragicomedy," *Harper's,* May 1963, p. 72.
11. According to the N.Y. *Times* (Apr. 30, 1961), these results were achieved only after the legislative palace had been surrounded by troops and the President had appeared in person in military dress.
12. Diederich and Burt, *op. cit.,* p. 160.
13. *Ibid.*
14. *Ibid.,* pp. 165-66.
15. IDB, press communiqué, June 7, 1961.
16. Diederich and Burt, *op. cit.,* pp. 171-74.
17. *Time* magazine of Jan. 12, 1962, mentioned a debt of $1 million which had been owed for six years to a Peoria, Ill., construction firm. Substantial arrears were due also to the American-owned electric-power plant in Port-au-Prince.
18. *Ibid.*
19. N.Y. *Times,* May 23, 1962.
20. *Wall Street Journal,* Nov. 30, 1962.
21. N.Y. *Times* (Paris ed.), Dec. 27, 1962.
22. By the end of 1962, $4.8 million of this credit had been used. (IMF, *International Financial Statistics,* Supplement to 1966/67 issues.)
23. The N.Y. *Times* on May 24 commented that an American inter-

vention for political motives would be generally condemned, but that the U.S. need not worry whether or not the OAS approved of intervention to save lives and restore order; such action, it said, would be well understood.

24. *Vision,* June 14, 1963.

25. Diederich and Burt, *op. cit.,* p. 382.

26. N.Y. *Times,* Feb. 13, 1964; Diederich and Burt, *op. cit.,* pp. 267-69.

27. N.Y. *Times,* Apr. 2, 1964.

28. *Ibid.,* Jan. 21, 1965. According to the *Times* correspondent, there were at the time about 500 political prisoners in Haiti.

29. *Newsday,* June 24, 1967; N.Y. *Times,* July 1, 1967, and Aug. 3, 1967; Col. Robert D. Heinl, Jr., in *Atlantic* magazine, Nov. 1967.

30. *Newsday,* Dec. 4, 1967.

31. N.Y. *Times,* Nov. 28, 1968.

32. IDB, press communiqué, Mar. 6, 1964.

33. N.Y. *Times,* Mar. 21, 1964.

34. IDB, press communiqué, Nov. 19, 1966.

35. Raymond Alcide Joseph, "Haiti: Ripe for the Marines?" *Nation,* Mar. 31, 1969.

36. Katherine Dunham, *Island Possessed* (Garden City, N.Y., Doubleday, 1969), pp. 167-68.

37. N.Y. *Times,* Dec. 28, 1964; Diederich and Burt, *op. cit.,* pp. 383-84.

38. Joseph, *op. cit.* It is interesting to observe that this merger was also reported in *Tass* on Mar. 31, 1969. The united party, said *Tass,* "will guide the struggle of the proletariat to . . . seize power and build socialism in the country."

CHAPTER 9

1. A leading Haitian educator and statesman has said of the Creole language: "But one could not think of elevating this patois—a colonial mixture—to the dignity of a national language. Having neither grammar nor written literature, Creole cannot be made the subject matter of methodical instruction. Unstable, subject to continual variations in its vocabulary, prounciation and syntax, it can be preserved or transmitted only through usage. A local tongue, spoken and understood by a small number of persons, it would condemn Haitians to isolation if they made it their exclusive language—isolation not only in a political and commercial sense, but also intellectual, which would prevent their entering into communication with the great minds whose immortal works have enriched the patrimony of civilized mankind. . . ." (Dantès Bellegarde, *La Nation Haitienne,* p. 344.)

2. Charles Fernand Pressoir, "Progrès des Etudes Linguistiques," *Le Nouvelliste,* Jan. 5, 1956; also, *Débats sur le Créole et le Folklore* (Port-au-Prince, Imprimerie de l'Etat, 1947), *passim.*

3. Robert Rice, "Profiles: The Thousand Silver Threads," *New Yorker,* Feb. 16, 1952; H. Ormonde McConnell, "Teaching Them to Read: The Literacy Campaign in Haiti," *International Review of Missions,* Oct. 1953, pp. 438-45.

4. McConnell, *op. cit.,* p. 443.

5. *Ibid.,* p. 444.

6. F. Morisseau Leroy, "A Propos de Diacoute," *Le Nouvelliste,* June 26, 1953.

7. U.N., *op. cit.,* p. 47.

CHAPTER 10

1. This word is spelled variously by different authors: voodoo, vodu, vaudou, vodun, etc. The spelling here used comes reasonably close to the native pronunciation (voh-doo- with the second syllable slightly nasalized). The spelling "voodoo" not only departs from the native pronunciation but also seems to have undesirable connotations growing out of its use by ignorant or unscrupulous writers in the past, as well as the tendency of some persons to associate it with the similar-sounding English term "hoodoo."

2. Leyburn, *op. cit.,* p. 116.

3. Bellegarde, *La Nation . . . ,* p. 127.

4. According to a British anthropologist, "Psychologically regarded . . . the function of religion is to restore men's confidence when it is shaken by crisis. Men do not seek crisis; they would always run away from it if they could. . . . Religion is the facing of the unknown. It is the courage in it that brings comfort.

"We must go on, however, to consider religion sociologically. A religion is the effort to face crisis, so far as that effort is organized by society in some particular way. A religion is congregational—that is to say, serves the ends of a number of persons simultaneously. It is traditional—that is to say, has served the ends of successive generations of persons. Therefore inevitably it has standardized a method. It involves a routine, a ritual. Also it involves some sort of conventional doctrine, which is, as it were, the inner side of the ritual—its lining." (R. R. Marett, *Anthropology* [London, Henry Holt], pp. 211-12.)

This definition of religion can be applied in every respect to vodou.

That vodou is a true religion was argued by the late Dr. Price-Mars, Haiti's foremost anthropologist, in the following terms: "Vodou is a religion because all its followers believe in the existence of the spiritual beings that live somewhere in the universe in intimate communion with the human beings whose activities they control. . . . Vodou is a religion because the cult devoted to its gods demands a hierarchical priestly body, a society of the faithful, of temples, of altars, of sermons, and finally a whole oral tradition . . . thanks to which the essential parts of this cult are transmitted. Vodou is a religion because through the remains of legend and the corruption of fables one can discern a theology and system of representation thanks to which, primitively, our African ancestors explained to themselves the phenomena of nature. . . ." (Dr. Jean Price-Mars, *Ainsi Parla l'Oncle* [Bibliothèque Haitienne, Imprimerie de Compiegne, 1928], p. 32.)

5. Leyburn, *op. cit.*, p. 134.

6. Louis Mars, "Phenomena of Possession," *Tomorrow,* Vol. 3, No. 1, p. 62.

7. This was admitted by no less an authority than Dr. Jean Price-Mars, who wrote, "Vodou is a very primitive religion made up in part of beliefs in the total power of spiritual beings—gods, demons, disembodied souls— and in part of beliefs in sorcery and magic. . . ." (Price-Mars, *op. cit.,* p. 37.)

8. Louis Maximilien, *Le Vaudou Haitien* (Port-au-Prince, 1945), p. 181.

9. Marcus Bach, *Strange Altars* (Indianapolis, Bobbs-Merrill, 1952), pp. 46-51.

10. One such feature is the practice of at least some *houngans* of serving as oracles on the basis of such fortuitous phenomena as the manner in which a candle burns or the way grains of corn react to roasting. According to one Haitian author, moreover, some *houngans* customarily dispense "ouangas" and charms to their followers. (J. B. Roumain, *Quelques Moeurs et Coutumes* . . . , pp. 57-58, 202-3.)

11. Maya Deren, "Religion and Magic," *Tomorrow,* Vol. 3, No. 1, pp. 37-39.

12. Leyburn, *op. cit.,* pp. 159-61.

13. *Ibid.,* pp. 162-63.

### CHAPTER 11

1. Institut Haitien de Statistique, *Bulletin Trimestriel,* Sept. 1953, pp. 87-93.

2. *Ibid.,* Nos. 41-44 (1961), p. 210.

3. *Ibid.*

4. Dr. Camille Lhérisson, in *Etincelles* (Port-au-Prince), Apr. 10, 1952. Dr. Lhérisson himself arrived at a much smaller ratio (8%), based on an attendance figure of 88,000, which appears quite erroneous.

5. Institut Haitien de Statistique, *op. cit.,* Sept. 1953, p. 91.

6. *Ibid.,* p. 92. In its Oct. 1951 *Bulletin* (p. 23) the institute pointed

out that in actual fact absenteeism was far worse than these figures indicate, due to the schools' peculiar methods of reporting enrollment and attendance.

7. Report of the Murville-Férère Commíttee on the Revision of Programs of Secondary Education, quoted in Bellegarde, *La Nation Haitienne,* p. 256.

8. Chapter V of Dr. Bellegarde's *La Résistance Haitienne* gives a detailed and revealing account of the incredibly obtuse and highhanded attitudes of the American authorities on the subject of Haiti's educational needs.

9. A former Haitian Minister of Education has written: "In the rural districts, most of the peasant families have only two meals a day. The children come to school atfer a scanty and inadequate breakfast and carry with them a piece of sugar, or fruit, or a baked sweet potato, and a piece of cassava bread for their lunch. Many of them bring nothing and pass the day without eating until they go home and have their evening meal at five or six p.m. In some schools the teachers provide lunches, especially where there are courses in home economics, but owing to the lack of funds this cannot be done more than once a week. (Maurice Dartigue, "Haiti" in *Educational Yearbook* of the International Institute of Teachers College, Columbia Univerity, N.Y., 1942, quoted by Pan American Union in *Vocational Education in Haiti,* Washington, Mar. 1952, pp. 51-52.)

10. Institut Haitien de Statistique, *Bulletin Trimestriel,* Dec. 1951, pp. 27-29.

11. Paul A. Jaume, *Education de Base et Enseignement Primaire* (Port-au-Prince, Département de l'Education Nationale, Dec. 1951), pp. 8-9.

12. UNESCO *Courier,* Vol. 1, No. 3 (Apr. 1948), p. 4, quoted by Marian Neal, "United Nations Programs in Haiti," *International Conciliation* (New York, Carnegie Endowment for International Peace), Feb. 1951, p. 103.

13. U.N., *Mission to Haiti* (New York, 1949), p. 47.

14. *Ibid.,* p. 54.

CHAPTER 12

1. Paul Moral, *L'Economie Haitienne,* p. 6.

2. *Ibid.,* p. 20.

3. *Ibid.,* pp. 53-54.

4. Marc Aurèle Holly, *Agriculture in Haiti* (New York, Vantage Press, 1955), p. 48.

5. Moral's figure of $31 million for "today's" exports is on the low side. Average annual exports during the fifties were about $41 million; since then they have tended to run somewhat lower.

6. Moral, *op. cit.*, pp. 88-89.

7. U.N., *Mission to Haiti*, pp. 95-96.

8. Banque Nationale de la République d'Haiti. Annual Reports of Fiscal Dept.

9. Moral, *op. cit.*, p. 105.

10. *Ibid.*, p. 108.

11. Holly, *op. cit.*, pp. 84-85.

12. Moral, *op. cit.*, p. 109.

13. Institut Haitien de Statistique, *op. cit.*, p. 46.

14. U.N., *op. cit.*, p. 97. A Haitian writer has suggested that the U.S. tariff rate on rum be reduced from $1.75 to $1.25, although such a reduction would be fought by Puerto Rico (whose rum enters the United States duty-free) and by American, British, and Canadian whisky producers. He concludes that the problem of marketing Haitian rum in the U.S. can be solved only by a combination of greater output, better publicity, and a lower tariff. (Turnier, *Les Etats-Unis et le Marché Haitien*, pp. 322-24.)

15. Moral, *op. cit.*, pp. 119-21; BNRH, Annual Reports of Fiscal Dept.

16. *Ibid.*, p. 122.

17. *Ibid.*, p. 121.

18. Holly, *op. cit.*, pp. 70-71.

19. Moral, *op. cit.*, p. 117.

20. Holly, *op. cit.*, p. 76.

21. Inter-American Development Bank, Annual Reports of Social Progress Trust Fund.

22. Holly, *op. cit.*, p. 65.

23. *Ibid.*, p. 66.

24. U.N., *op. cit.*, pp. 131-32.

25. *Ibid.*, pp. 136-37.

26. FAO, *Production Yearbook*, 1968, p. 74.

27. Holly, *op. cit.*, p. 114.

28. *Ibid.*, pp. 105-8.

29. U.N., *op. cit.*, p. 137.

30. Jean-Charles Magnan, *Haiti: La Perle Noire* (Montreal, 1951), p. 62.

31. Holly, *op. cit.*, pp. 210-12.

32. *Ibid.*, pp. 210-13.

33. *Ibid.*, pp. 214-16.

34. *Ibid.*, pp. 216-17.

35. *Ibid.*, pp. 217-18.

36. *Ibid.*, pp. 219-20.

37. *Ibid.*, pp. 220-21.

38. U.N., *op. cit.*, pp. 92-93.

39. *Ibid.*, p. 189.
40. *Ibid.*, p. 201.
41. Secétairerie d'Etat de la Coordination et de l'Information, *Bulletin*, Feb. 9, 1968, p. 3.
42. Holly, *op. cit.*, pp. 259-86. Early in the fifties a U.N. expert demonstrated the building of inexpensive silos, but his teachings were soon forgotten owing to the government's failure to follow through. The IDAI program is now beginning to fill this gap.
43. *Ibid.*, p. 288.
44. *Ibid.*, pp. 268-69.
45. Moral, *op. cit.*, pp. 167-82.

CHAPTER 13

1. U.N., *Mission to Haiti*, pp. 99-100.
2. Holly, *Agriculture in Haiti*, pp. 129-31.
3. *Ibid.*, pp. 133-34.
4. *Ibid.*, pp. 135-36.
5. *Ibid.*, p. 137.
6. *Ibid.*, p. 139.
7. *Ibid.*, p. 141.
8. U.N., *op. cit.*, p. 128.
9. Holly, *op. cit.*, pp. 142-46.
10. *Ibid.*, pp. 152-54.
11. *Ibid.*, pp. 154-55.
12. *Ibid.*, pp. 147-50.
13. *Ibid.*, pp. 151-52.
14. *Ibid.*, p. 157.
15. *Ibid.*, pp. 160-63.
16. Bellegarde, *La Nation Haitienne*, pp. 20-21.
17. Moreau de St.-Méry, *Description de la partie française de l'Isle Saint-Domingue*, 1797 (reprinted by Société de l'Histoire des Colonies Françaises et Librairie Larose, Paris 1958), p. 27.
18. Moral, *op. cit.*, p. 20. Paradoxically, says Moral, this practice was destructive of natural shrubbery *(végétation arbustive)*, whereas the planting of coffee in the shade protects the natural shrubbery.
19. *Ibid.*, pp. 21-23.
20. Grand Conseil Technique, *Plan Biennal de Développement Economique du ler oct. 1958 au 30 sept. 1959*, p. 54.
21. *Ibid.*, pp. 54-55.
22. U.N., *op. cit.*, pp. 132-34.
23. *Ibid.*

CHAPTER 14

1. Institut Haitien de Statistique, *Bulletin Trimestriel,* Sept. 1953, pp. 27-28.
2. Millspaugh, *Haiti under American Control,* pp. 93-94.
3. *Ibid.,* pp. 138-39.
4. *Ibid.,* p. 140.
5. McCrocklin, *Garde d'Haiti,* p. 51.
6. Kent C. Melhorn, *Health of Haiti,* 1930, quoted in Millspaugh, *op. cit.,* p. 141.
7. Leyburn, *The Haitian People,* pp. 274-75.
8. Institut Haitien de Statistique, *op. cit.,* p. 31.
9. U.N., *Mission to Haiti,* pp. 62-63.
10. *Ibid.,* pp. 64-66.
11. Institut Haitien de Statistique, *op. cit.,* p. 31.
12. Since 1966 the nutritional situation has apparently worsened, the average per capita consumption of calories being estimated at 1,728 and that of protein at 39 grams (IDB, Annual Report of Social Progress Trust Fund, 1970, p. 244).
13. Secretairerie d'Etat de la Coordination et Information, *Bulletin,* Mar. 4, 1966, pp. 1-2; Département des Affaires Etrangères, *Bulletin d'Information,* Feb. 18, 1966.
14. Philip W. Bourne, *Housing Study of the Republic of Haiti,* prepared in consultation with the Office of the Administrator, Housing and Home Finance Agency, Washington, D.C., Oct. 1948, quoted in U.N., *op. cit.,* p. 38.
15. J. Harland Paul and Athémas Bellerive, "A Malaria Reconnaissance of the Republic of Haiti," *Journal of the National Malaria Society,* Vol. 6, No. 1 (Mar. 1947), quoted in U.N., *op. cit.,* p. 68.
16. IDB, *op. cit.,* 1969, p. 361.
17. *Ibid.,* 1970, p. 244.
18. *Ibid.,* p. 247.
19. *Ibid.,* 1969, p. 360.
20. *Ibid.,* 1970, p. 243.

CHAPTER 15

1. U.N., *Mission to Haiti,* pp. 167-68.
2. *Ibid.,* pp. 145-46.
3. *Ibid.,* pp. 150-51.
4. *Ibid.,* pp. 151-54.
5. *Haiti Sun,* June 29, 1958.

6. U.N., *op. cit.*, pp. 154-56.

7. *Ibid.*, p. 158.

8. Département des Affaires Etrangères, *Bulletin d'Information,* June 30, 1964.

9. Secrétairerie d'Etat de la Coordination et de l'Information, *Bulletin,* July 28, 1967, p. 4.

10. Magnan, *Haiti: La Perle Noire.*

CHAPTER 16

1. Maurice Gratacap, *Rapport Préliminaire sur les Possibilités d'Utilisation des Lignites d'Haiti* (Port-au-Prince, 1952); *Le National,* Nov. 19, 1952.

2. *Le Nouvelliste,* Oct. 7, 1954, and Sept. 8, 1955.

3. *Haiti Sun,* Jan. 22, 1959.

4. Secretairerie d'Etat de la Coordination et de l'Information, *Bulletin,* Jan. 7, 1966, p. 4.

5. *Ibid.*, Sept. 29, 1967, pp. 1-8.

6. American Bureau of Metal Statistics, *Yearbook 1968,* p. 94.

7. Département des Affaires Etrangères, *Bulletin d'Information,* Feb. 18, 1966.

8. Report of speech by Justin Sam, Division Chief, Dept. of National Economy, *Le Nouvelliste,* Sept. 16, 1954.

9. *Haiti Journal,* Mar. 21, 1956.

10. Miscellaneous reports in the Haitian press.

CHAPTER 17

1. Bellegarde, *La Nation Haitienne,* pp. 219-20.

2. Millspaugh, *Haiti under American Control,* p. 19.

3. McCrocklin, *Garde d'Haiti,* pp. 49, 93.

4. Millspaugh, *op. cit.*, pp. 158-59. Unfortunately, the Americans resort to the *corvée* system for road construction during the early years of the occupation aroused much resentment and was an important cause of Haitian resistance to the occupation. Under the Rural Code of the Republic, inhabitants could be obliged to work on the roads in their respective local areas. For this purpose the American occupiers were supplied by the local authorities with lists of the male inhabitants. This system worked well until it was abused in two ways: (1) by the American supervisors' transfers of workers from their local districts to other areas; (2) by the Haitian local authorities' repeated exemption of inhabitants who were willing and able to pay a "tax" and putting others back on the list of draftees after they had done their share of the work. (McCrocklin, *op. cit.*, pp. 94-97.)

5. U.N., *Mission to Haiti*, pp. 201-3.

6. Bellegarde, *op. cit.*, p. 220. The U.N. mission estimated that there were in 1948 about 700 boats (of which 600 of less than 25 tons deadweight), with an aggregate capacity of 10,000-12,000 tons, almost all of them using sails *(Mission to Haiti*, pp. 207-8).

7. IDA, Annual Report, 1962-63, p. 18.

8. BNRH, Annual Report of Fiscal Dept., 1948-49, p. 6.

9. In 1953 there were only 106 bridges in all of Haiti (Institut Haitien de Statistique, *Bulletin Trimestriel*, Sept. 1953, p. 52).

10. *Ibid.*, p. 65.

11. *Ibid.*, 1961, p. 98.

## CHAPTER 18

1. U.N., *Mission to Haiti*, p. 221.

2. A foreign visitor once jokingly remarked that tourism was bound to thrive in Haiti for the simple reason that the country would fall further and further behind other countries, and tourists would therefore flock increasingly to Haiti to observe its archaic folkways. This is hardly the type of tourism that Haiti seeks or should seek.

3. Administration Générale des Contributions, *Code Fiscal*, p. 452.

4. *Ibid.*, pp. 613-16.

5. Administration Générale des Contributions, *Supplément Fiscal et Economique*, 1953, p. 61.

6. Département du Commerce, *Bulletin Mensuel* (Port-au-Prince, Nov. 1955), p. 27.

7. *Ibid.*, pp. 4-26.

8. *Ibid.*, p. 27; *West Indies and Caribbean Yearbook*, 1960.

9. Institut Haitien de Statistique, *Bulletin Trimestriel*, 1961, p. 99.

10. *Ibid.*

11. *Ibid.*, p. 19.

12. *Ibid.*, p. 207.

## CHAPTER 19

1. Jules Domond, "L'Etranger dans le Commerce National," *Le National*, Apr. 13, 1954.

2. *Ibid.*

3. Leyburn, *The Haitian People*, p. 250.

4. Rayford W. Logan, *Haiti and the Dominican Republic*, p. 86.

5. Leyburn, *op. cit.*, pp. 250-52.

6. *Ibid.*, pp. 253-54.

7. *Ibid.*, pp. 254-55.

CHAPTER 20

1. The weight of the Spanish piaster was reduced by about one-third in 1686, but the colonial piaster continued to be minted without loss of weight, causing it to be known as the *peso gordo* or *piastre gourde.* (Robert Lacombe, *Histoire Monétaire de Saint Domingue et de la Republique d'Haiti* [Paris, Eds. Larose], pp. 18-19.)

2. *Ibid.,* pp. 52-57.

3. *Ibid.,* pp. 57-64.

4. *Ibid.,* pp. 64-66.

5. Chatelain, *La Banque Nationale,* pp. 15-75.

6. *Ibid.,* pp. 79-81.

7. *Ibid.,* pp. 81-83.

8. *Ibid.,* pp. 85-106.

9. *Ibid.,* p. 197.

10. Moore, "Monetary-Fiscal Policy and Economic Development in Haiti," *Public Finance/Finances Publiques,* No. 3, 1954.

11. At the time I began this assignment, I was an officer of the Federal Reserve Bank of New York, by whom I was loaned to the United Nations for the Haitian task. In October 1952, I returned to the Federal Reserve Bank, from which I resigned in June 1953 in order to resume the Haitian assignment under the direct auspices of the U.N.

12. Moore, *op. cit.*

CHAPTER 21

1. Bellegarde, *La Nation Haitienne,* pp. 90-91; Leyburn, *The Haitian People,* pp. 317-18; Lacombe, *Histoire Monétaire . . . ,* p. 58.

2. The principal exception was the 1949 law granting certain tax exemptions to new industries.

3. IMF, *International Financial Statistics,* Supplement to 1966-67 issues, and subsequent monthly issues.

CHAPTER 22

1. U.N., *Mission to Haiti,* p. 7.

2. *Ibid.,* pp. 8-9.

3. Address by Louis Blanchet, Minister of Agriculture, in *Bulletin,* Secrétairerie d'Etat de la Coordination et de l'Information, June 9, 1967, p. 3.

4. IDB, Second Annual Report of Social Progress Trust Fund, 1962, p. 301.

5. I was a member of the Klein and Saks mission during its first three or four months.

6. IDB, Social Progress Trust Fund, Annual Reports 1961-64, chapters on Haiti.

7. *Ibid.,* 1964, p. 345.

8. *Ibid.,* 1965, p. 377.

9. *Ibid.,* 1967, pp. 184-85.

10. *Ibid.,* 1968, pp. 195-96.

11. *Ibid.,* 1969, p. 356.

12. *Ibid.,* 1970, p. 241.

CHAPTER 23

1. A distinguished Haitian who organized and vigorously led the resistance to the American occupation explained as follows the reason for that resistance: "So long as we can believe, on the basis of assurances given and oft repeated declarations, that we are dealing with friends who have come to help us combat disorder and who have no hostile intentions with respect to our territory and our independence, we will hold ourselves ready to discuss in good faith how to compensate the services rendered, even if those services have not been requested and even though this fraternal cooperation has too often assumed the character of armed aggression. But from the moment when our alleged friends, tearing off the mask, want only to be our masters, they will have to go all the way in the reality of their role. As masters, they can take everything, but they will not receive anything from us." (Georges Sylvain, in *La Patrie,* No. 2, Aug. 25, 1915, quoted in *Dix Années de Lutte . . .* , Vol. 1, p. 9.)

2. Television sets should be provided in large numbers for school and adult instruction, along the lines of what has been done by the U.S. government in Samoa and by international agencies and the French government in Niger and the Ivory Coast. In the last-mentioned country, primary schools for a million pupils are being equipped with television sets. "Where a school system is not yet developed, where buildings, equipment and the teachers are lacking, both radio and television are cheaper than the rapid establishment of conventional school instruction, and they are able to provide immediate educational services to a wider audience." *(Report on the U.N. Conference on the Application of Science and Technology for the Benefit of the Less Developed Areas, Vol. 4, Industry [New York, U.N., 1963], p. 197.)*

3. One of the later governors of Saint-Domingue was quoted as saying, "The safety of the whites demands that the Negroes be kept in profound ignorance." This sentiment, states Leyburn, "perfectly expressing the conviction of the majority of planters, not only prevented any secular education of the blacks, but actually kept many of them from instruction in

catechism, creed, or any part of the Catholic faith. If instruction is forbidden, few of the sacraments can be administered, for how can a person be confirmed, confess, do penance, if he know not even the first principles of the faith . . .?" (Leyburn, *The Haitian People,* p. 116.)

4. Hugh B. Cave, *Haiti: Highroad to Adventure* (New York, Holt, 1952), p. 216.

5. J. B. Roumain, *Quelques Moeurs et Coutumes* . . . , p. 248.